Bradford Abbas

The History of a Dorset Village

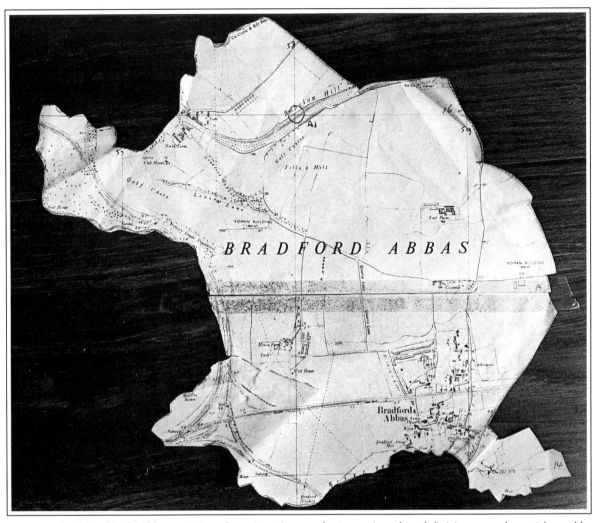

The Parish of Bradford Abbas as it is today. According to the Saxon boundary definition 933, the parish would have extended another half a mile to the east.

Bradford Abbas

The History of a Dorset Village

by ERIC GARRETT

© 1989 Eric Garrett

ISBN 1 85010 547 2

Published by:
The Oxford Illustrated Press Limited
Haynes Publishing Group, Sparkford, Nr Yeovil,
Somerset BA22 7JJ, England.

Haynes Publications Inc., 861 Lawrence Drive,
Newbury Park, California 91320, USA.

Printed in England by:
J.H. Haynes & Co Limited, Sparkford, Nr. Yeovil, Somerset.

British Library Cataloguing in Publication Data
Garrett, Eric
    Bradford Abbas: History of a Dorset village
    1. Dorset. Bradford Abbas. History
    I. Title
    942.3'31
    ISBN 0-85010-547-2

Contents

Foreword

Eric Garrett is one of the best-known faces in Bradford Abbas. He hails from a family that has resided in this village for more than four hundred years. He was born in the neighbouring hamlet of Clifton Maubank and moved to Bradford Abbas while still a young baby. As a young boy he moved to Sherborne where his father took up employment. On marrying he returned to Bradford Abbas some twenty-six years ago with his bride Sheila.

Ever since returning to the village, Eric Garrett has taken more than an active interest in many village organisations, serving as an officer of the Horticultural Society, the Historic Society, of which he is the founder member, and the Village Hall Committee to name but some. At present he is Clerk to the Parish Council, an office he has held for more than twenty years; he has also represented the village as a member of West Dorset District Council.

With his obvious desire to serve his fellow men and the very long association of his family with the village it is no surprise that he has always had a great interest in the village and its people as well as its present activities. Over the years Eric Garrett has become an authority on Bradford Abbas history; if anyone wishes to know anything about our village they are always directed to him. In 1975 Eric, by popular demand, wrote a limited edition book, *The Story of Bradford Abbas*—all the available copies were quickly sold and have been in great demand ever since. This demand has resulted in this further book *Bradford Abbas: The History of a Dorset Village* being produced.

This book has been written by the author on similar lines to his previous book and has been expanded to include additional information from considerable research.

The book is a study of the parish of Bradford Abbas from its early medieval days through the years when it was a small rural community, when people had few worries, no concern regarding rising prices as they produced most of their own food, when wood was readily available for fuel, when there was little noise except from the blacksmith's forge and horses did the work of mechanical vehicles, to the present day. The book gives us considerable information on how the village, the villagers, their church, their school and community life have developed over the years and includes a pot-pourri of interesting items and anecdotes.

At first glance the book may seem to be of purely local interest, parochial and of little general interest, but I am sure it is much more than that because it gives a vivid picture in words and photographs of a rural community that is typical of many Dorset villages—certainly up to the period between the two world wars—when population movement began to take place and truly rural self sufficiency began to disintegrate.

The last twenty-five years have seen a steady expansion of the village with people coming to reside here who are employed in industry or commerce in neighbouring towns. Fewer villagers are now employed in agriculture and cottage industries and this has resulted in the community character changing; a new picture and new format has emerged which is fortunately satisfactorily, and now happily, integrating the old with the new. It is good to see so many young and old 'newcomers' interested and determined to carry on and expand village activities and maintaining a close community spirit.

For the older generation this book provides an opportunity to travel down memory lane, to reminisce, to relive parts of their lives and hear the origins of some of the stories of the past which have been passed down through the years. For the younger generation and new members of the community it takes them back in time and mood to a time of peace, tranquillity, fellowship, community spirit and self-contentment which pervaded the Dorset rural communities in the past.

It may seem strange that a 'townie', born in the centre of one of the country's largest industrial cities and having lived over half his life in the hurly burly, hectic, noisy atmosphere of such an environment should write a foreword to a book that tells the story of a serene, quiet, peaceful way of life in a Dorset village. But having lived in such an environment, I have learnt to value, love and appreciate the village, village life and the surrounding countryside. As a 'newcomer' (I came to Dorset in 1963), I have always been interested in maintaining those village activities which have survived over the years and as such I have worked closely with Eric

Garrett and my wife and I have shared a long friendship with him and his family.

Finally may I thank Eric Garrett on behalf of the many people who will read and enjoy this story of Bradford Abbas, for all the work he has put into the research and the writing of it. I know his aim is to share his love for his village with others.

Doug F. Anthony
Chairman: Bradford Abbas Parish Council
Churchwarden: St Mary's Church, Bradford Abbas

Preface

It is now over 12 years since I started to write this book. In fact you may say I started when I completed my earlier work as I felt that there was still much to learn about the village of Bradford Abbas. It turned out I was right, as I have found stories and legends which I never knew existed and I am sure that there are many more yet to be revealed.

I hope, therefore, that all who read these pages will get as much pleasure from them as I have had in writing them and that this book will give a greater insight into the history of Bradford Abbas and help many to understand the factors and characters which have helped make it what it is today.

I am very grateful to the many people who have assisted me with the preparation of this book and for their willingness in providing me with information. I shall be for ever indebted to the following:

Mr C. J. Gillham, Mr H. Gillham, Mr W. Gale, Mr H. Garrett (my father), Mr D.F. Anthony (Chairman of Bradford Abbas Parish Council), Mr J. Cutts, Mr W. Cleal, Mrs M. Carter, Mr D. Penney (Headmaster of St Mary's School), the late Mr P Pettitt, former Rural District Councillor, Mr R. Leaney, landlord of the Rose & Crown Inn, Rev. R. J. Mentern, former Priest in Charge, St Mary's Church and Mrs F. Smith.

I would also like to thank my publisher, Mr J. Haynes, whose patience has been beyond my understanding and many others.

I must, however, say a very special thanks to my wife Sheila, who undertook the formidable task of typing these pages without complaint and without whose very special help this work could not have been completed.

Dedicated to my children
Beverley & Kevin Garrett
who grew to adulthood in this village
and to my wife, Sheila
without whose assistance this book
could not have been written.

CHAPTER I
The Beginnings

The village of Bradford Abbas lies on the north side of the Yeo valley whilst the parish itself extends to the south side of the River Yeo at the foot of Babylon Hill. In fact, the village is in the south-east corner of the area of the parish which is mainly open landscape. The northern part of the parish is mainly sandstone but the village itself stands upon oolitic limestone, which in fact covers the whole of the northern side of the Yeo valley in this area. It produces a gently undulating dip slope with fertile soil and a pervious subsoil. Thus it is admirably suited to arable farming, and oats, barley, wheat and maize as well as root crops are grown. The clay and alluvium in the lower-lying riverside areas result in dairying being predominant but in places the fields are liable to serious flooding, and this is probably the reason why the village follows the line of a culvert stream rather than running immediately alongside the bank of the River Yeo. The area has always had a basic agricultural economy and this, to a large extent, is still true today although many of the villagers work other than on the land.

When the history of the parish commenced—or at least when it became an area of human habitation—is impossible to say, but certainly there was considerable animal life in the area judging by the number of fossils that have been found and are continuing to be found.

Not so many years ago a stone axe of the Old Stone Age was discovered at Lenthay, Sherborne, whilst in 1912, two Sherborne schoolboys found, in one of the Coombe dry valleys to the north of that town, a piece of bone upon which was engraved the head and forequarters of an easily recognisable horse, also of the Old Stone Age era. It has been suggested that this latter find may not be genuine but if it were it would probably be the earliest form of human art yet found in southern England. Neither of these finds would have been any more than five miles from Bradford Abbas and as these early men were known to be great hunters and to cover considerable distances after their prey, it is not unreasonable to assume that they hunted throughout the Yeo valley, of which Bradford Abbas is a part.

Joseph Fowler, in his excellent book *Medieval Sherborne* records:

'The Yeo valley was definitely occupied by a people whose tools and weapons, for the most part of flint, litter the Sherborne fields in quantity. These men seem to have preferred the northern side of the valley rather than the south, probably for the same reasons that have always influenced man in his marked preference for the hillside overlooking the right bank of the River Yeo—because it is more open and sunny, better supplied with water and its soil adaptable to primitive cultivation.'

Professor Buckman, on his arrival at Bradford Abbas in the latter part of the nineteenth century also recorded:

'On going over the lands of my present farm I was particularly struck with the fact that in most fields were found some interesting archaic remains. Worked flints and rude pottery took me back to the Celtic inhabitants of Dorset.'

To further emphasise that there was early human habitation in the area Joseph Fowler goes on to say:

'There is a corner of a field on Silverlake Farm, "Bobs Ground", where a Bronze Age flint knapper must have sat one day shaping barbed and tangled arrow heads apparently to see how small he could make them. Three or four he left lying on the ground within a yard or two of one another, and another one nearby, he began, but after roughing out the barbs threw it aside unfinished.'

Silverlake Farm is about two miles to the east of Bradford Abbas whilst immediately to the south-west, in the parish of Clifton Maubank, a bronze rapier, reputed to be some three thousand years old, was found in a quarry a few years ago. With these finds, both on the perimeter of the parish, one can be sure that the area in which Bradford Abbas now stands was not unknown to these early people. In fact the area may have been extremely well known and the name of the village could be some indication of this. The name Bradford literally means 'Broadford', and in days when there were no such structures as bridges the crossing point of a river would have been a very important place. It is easy, even today, to cross the River Yeo on foot and in the summer it is not unusual to see children paddling in the river near Smiths (or Smear's) bridge or at the Bay, with the water barely reaching their ankles.

The Celts were certainly inhabitants of the parish and evidence has been found of their occupation in the field now known as Vicarage Oak, which is part of the mass of East Hill. These Celtic inhabitants would almost certainly been of the Durotriges tribe which dominated the county at this time and from which the county name of Dorset is derived. For how long the Durotriges were in Dorset or when they originally arrived is not known, but it is a fact that it was these Celtic people whom the Romans found here when they invaded England, and it was the Durotriges whom they conquered.

Very little is known of the Roman occupation of Dorset, and of Bradford Abbas itself virtually nothing. This is probably due to the fact that the Romans led a peaceful life throughout this area and there were never any troops posted to the county for any length of time. It seems that after their original invasion there were no local rebellions and this is borne out by the considerable number of domestic relics that have been found and also the large number of sites of Roman villas throughout the county.

There are known to be sites of at least two Roman dwellings in Bradford Abbas whilst there is also the site of another Roman villa to the south of the River Yeo but within the boundaries of Thornford parish. The sitings of these buildings are of interest in so far as it was the custom of the Romans to reside a little way from the homes of the earlier inhabitants, and if this is the case with Bradford Abbas, and there is no reason to doubt that it is not, it would mean that the village of those days would have been situated almost exactly where it is today.

When the Romans withdrew from Britain in the early years of the fifth century the Saxons wasted no time in launching an invasion. Exactly when they occupied this part of Dorset is far from clear but it is reasonable to assume that they found an existing settlement at Bradford Abbas and if so, the inhabitaants would have received no better treatment under the Saxons than they did under their departed Roman masters. However, as Bradford Abbas is situated in an area which was one of the last to be conquered by the Saxons, the treatment meted out by their new masters would have been less severe than in areas which had been conquered earlier. This is because the Saxons had by then largely been converted to Christianity and were nothing like as barbarous as the early invaders.

The delay in the Saxon conquest of Dorset was not due to any heroics on the part of the local inhabitants but due to the county being extremely well protected on the eastern side by the great Selwood forest, whilst strong earthworks like Maiden Castle and others in the south gave adequate protection from that direction. Eventually an attack was made from the north and the inhabitants of the county whom the Saxons called 'Welsh' were overcome, which means that any persons living in Bradford Abbas at that time would have been amongst the first of the county to come under the Saxon yoke.

There is only one 'Welsh' name that survives in the village today and that is 'Coombe', which derives from the original 'cwm', which means 'valley'. Coombe, it must be said, is remarkably close to the original Celtic settlement—only a few yards.

Bradford became part of the West Saxon kingdom of Wessex and ecclesiastically under the care of the Bishop of Dorchester on the Thames, but as the Saxon advance continued westwards it became necessary to create a new bishopric, with the result that in 705, King Ine made St Aldhelm a bishop, and he decided that his cathedral would be at Sherborne, where he immediately came to reside. St Aldhelm was a very devout man and considered to be one of the great scholars of his day as well as a man of considerable foresight. Upon becoming Bishop of Sherborne he adopted a policy of encouraging village settlements and, when possible, the building of churches. It is therefore most likely that the church in Bradford Abbas originated about this time. The building, of course, would have been nothing like the magnificent edifice we have today but more likely a wooden structure with a thatched roof. Of there being a Saxon settlement at Bradford Abbas there can be little doubt but surprisingly there is only one Saxon name remaining in the village today and that is the field named 'Worth'—Worth being the Saxon word for enclosure.

Like so many other villages there is really no record of Bradford Abbas during the Dark Ages until we come to the first written reference to the village in a charter of King Ethelwulf (839–58) when he gave to the church at Sherborne:

'36 hides of which 5 at Getemynster [Yetminster], the rest at Bradford, Cerdel [Cerne] and Algerstoke [Halstock].'

Again we go into a period of darkness in the history of the parish until 26th January 933 when, in one of the two Sherborne Charters issued at Chippenham, King Athelstan, a grandson of King Alfred, made a grant of 10 cassates of land to the religious community of Sherborne at a place which 'those who dwell there call Bradenford'.

In making this grant the King requested that: 'Annually on All Saints Day the Clergy in the Convent will say a mass for his soul in return for the land he is giving them for all time.'

This was an extremely interesting charter in several respects, most particularly because it included a survey of Bradford in which the boundaries were defined as follows:

1. First from the head of the East spring and the east side (of the grant)
2. Along the slow stream to the Mill Burne
3. Then along the stream to the Gifle
4. Then along the stream to Aenna's Pool
5. Then along the slow stream as far as the Old Dyke
6. Then along the Dyke to the head of the Coombe of the Pigsty
7. Then to the edge of the slope
8. Along the edge of the slope to the Dyke
9. Then along the Dyke as far as Ecgulf's tree
10. Then east to Aetta's Dean to the middle of it
11. Along the Dean to the East spring.

The Old Dyke referred to above can still be seen and lies at the eastern end of Wyke Firs and the 'Coombe of the Pigsty' is what is now known as Loscombe's Cross, which is the modern crossroads one has to pass over to go to Over Compton and Trent. The River Yeo is also recorded for the first time by its original name Gifle—a fork—whence it has passed from Yevel and Ivel to the modern Yeo.

The area of land which was granted, 10 cassates, cannot be defined in exact terms—a cassate being enough land to support one family. It has been suggested that a cassate was about equivalent to a hide, i.e. about 120 acres, but many eminent historians have disagreed about this figure. It can, however, be clearly ascertained from the charter that the boundaries of the parish in 933 were considerably different to those of today as it seems that quite a large chunk of Castleton was included.

Bradford was again confirmed to the Bishop of Sherborne in 998, and except for one short period when it was in the custody of the Bishop of Salisbury it was to remain the property of the Church at Sherborne for the next five centuries or so.

Only three years later, in 1001, it is possible that the village was ravaged by the Danes, who were still very active, for an entry in the Anglo-Saxon Chronicle for that year reads:

'The Danes invaded England, and having ravaged parts of Devon, marched from Exmouth to Peonn-Ho in Somerset where happened an action between them and the English to the disadvantage of the latter, and next day they burn't Peonn-Ho and Clistune and many other villages.'

Clistune was the old English name for Clifton (now Clifton Maubank) which adjoins the western and southern boundaries of Bradford and it seems most unlikely that Bradford would have escaped unscathed. It was probably one of the 'other villages' mentioned in the Chronicle. It is most certain that the Danes would have had to cross the river at Bradford and it would be most unusual if they had passed by without claiming some spoils of war.

In 1075 a Decree of Council in London directed that bishop's seats in out of the way country places like Sherborne should be removed to places of more importance and easier access. This, in effect, meant that the Bishop of Old Sarum (Salisbury) obtained the custody of Bradford, and it is, in fact, the Bishop of Salisbury who is recorded as being the owner of the parish in the *Domesday Book,* 1086. The entry for Bradford in that detailed book reads as follows:

'The same Bishop holds Bradford. In Edward's time it was gelded for 10 hides. There is land for 10 ploughs. One and a half hides of it are in demesne, and there are 3 ploughs there, 7 slaves, 8 villeins and 7 bordars [sic] with 8 ploughs. The Mill there returns 15/- per annum rent, and there are 20 acres of meadow and 3 acres of brushwood. It [Bradford] is worth £10.'

Whilst it may be true to say that the *Domesday Book* answers many questions about the parish in 1086, it leaves many more unanswered. It is not, for example, possible to ascertain with any degree of accuracy either the total acreage, or the population, or ever to know the precise location of any buildings which may be mentioned in the above entry. We are told that there was a mill which returned 15/- per annum rent, but where was it? It could have been where the present 'Old Mill' stands in Mill Lane but it could also have been at Limekiln (or Mill) Farm in the south-east corner of the parish. There is certainly evidence of early buildings in that area including what could well be the remnants of the site of a water-wheel and an ancient trackway leading to it.

Of the population it is not possible to say a great deal. 'Villeins' was a term used by the Normans for all villagers holding arable land and throughout the country they formed the largest percentage of the population, but nobody seems to know with any degree of certainty what was the status of the 'Bordars'. It is believed, however, that they were lower in the social scale but, like the villeins, they may have held a small piece of land and possibly the tenancy of a cottage. The slaves were of the lowest class with no legal rights at all.

Various formulae have been suggested for estimating the population of a parish from its *Domesday Book* entry, the most popular being to multiply the total number of households (i.e. villeins and borders) by five assuming that the slaves had no residence or family of their own. If this formula is adopted it gives a figure of seventy-five, to which should be added the seven slaves to arrive at a total population of eighty-two. Admittedly, to calculate the population on such a basis can, at the very best, be only rough and ready but in the light of what information it does give it would not be unreasonable to assume that the population of Bradford was approaching one hundred (including children) in 1086.

With regard to the acreage one must be even more vague. I have seen figures from as low as 48 acres to as high as 240 acres to the hide, so it is quite obvious that with such a variance it is very difficult to put a precise acreage to a hide in any partcular parish. The generally accepted figure, however, is now reckoned to be 120 acres to the hide. If this figure were related to Bradford Abbas it would mean that 180 acres were being kept by the Bishop for his own use, which land would be worked by the villeins and borders in lieu of rent. Of the total acreage a figure of 'ten hides' or 'land for ten ploughs' would give an acreage of 1,200 to which should be added the 20 acres of meadowland and 3 acres of brushwood to give a grand total of 1,223 acres, which is remarkably close to the present-day figure of 1,216 acres. This, in itself, poses another problem, for in 933 the

Bradford estate included the hamlet of Wyke farther to the east. If the Domesday survey covered only what is now the parish, when did Wyke cease to be a part?

For nearly another seventy years Bradford remained in the custody of the Bishop of Salisbury until in 1145 a Papal Bull of Eugenius III confirmed the estate to the Abbot of Sherborne—an association which was to continue unbroken for almost four hundred years and which was to add Abbas (a derivation of Abbot's) to the village name.

It may well be useful at this stage to show the development of the village name over the years:

933	Bradeford
	Bradan forda
998	Bradan ford
1086	Bradeford
1386	Braddeford Abbatis—which was subsequently reduced to the modern Bradford Abbas.

The first Abbot of Sherborne to have custody of Bradford Abbas following the Papal Bull of 1145 was Robert, who was succeeded by Peter, who himself was succeeded by Clement in 1155. Clement is of interest because it is during his term as Abbot that the village church is mentioned for the first time, when, in 1163 Pope Alexander III confirmed to Clement Abbot of Sherborne 'the manor and church at Bradford'. It is about this period that the first court records relative to Bradford Abbas appear and cases appear in the Dorset Feet of Fines in the years 1201, 1203, 1217, 1222, 1224 and 1268. I give below details of one of their cases which is a dispute with regard to the ownership of land.

'1203

At Westminster, five weeks after Easter between Ralph de la Buere, and Muriel his wife, plaintiff, and William Abbot of Sherborne, tenant, of 6^1/$_2$ hides of land in Bradford Abbas. Plea of homage was summoned between them, which land Ralph and Muriel claim for the Abbot and his successors by the service of one knight and a half, to be done therefore for all service. The Abbot acknowledged the land to be the right of Muriel, to hold to Ralph and Muriel and the heirs of Muriel for the Abbot and his successors for ever by the free service of four pounds yearly for all, save foreign service, besides the aforesaid service of one knight and a half, whereof the same Ralph and Muriel and the heirs of Muriel are quit, at Nativity of St John, twenty shillings at Michaelmas, twenty shillings at Christmas, and at Easter, twenty shillings.

'For the grant Ralph and Muriel gave to the Abbot and Convent one tun of wine at the price of forty shillings. And Moirice de London put in his claim in respect of that land.'

In 1285 Bradford Abbas was in the Hundred of Sherborne and the Rectory was valued at 10 marks, with the Patron being the Bishop of Salisbury.

CHAPTER II
Men of Property

It was during the reign of Henry VIII (1509–47) that one of the most significant events in the history of England took place and it was an event which came about directly from Henry's dispute with the Pope over his divorce from Katherine of Aragon.

This event has become known to history as the 'Dissolution of the Monasteries' which was in fact the breaking up of a religious way of life which had existed for hundreds of years. In 1535, the same year as the last Abbot of Sherborne was appointed, Thomas Cromwell, as Vicar General, sent Commissioners to all the religious houses in England to ascertain exactly what wealth in land, money, treasures and livestock these houses possessed. The purpose of these visits was twofold: first Henry desperately needed to swell the royal purse and the monasteries, upon whom he was casting his covetous eyes, were known to be immensely rich; and secondly there was a danger that if he allowed the monasteries to survive, they might well become pockets of Catholic resistance to the break with Rome. It is because of the dangers of internal strife that Henry VIII wished to ascertain the strength for him in these troubled times and so lists were made of those whom he could muster if required and what weapons were available. I have obtained a copy for the muster for Bradford Abbas in 1539, which I believe to be the first list of names ever drawn up for the village, or at least the earliest still in existence. It reads as follows:-

	Thomas Crisse	Has harness for man
AB	John Hodynet	Bill
	George Stere	Has harness for man
A	William Pondylde	Bow 4 arrows
B	Thomas Bartlett	Bill
B	John Mydleton	Bill
A	John Somer	Has bow-sheaf of arrows
	John Harris	Bill—sallet splints

B	John Smythe	Bill
A	Robert Harris	Has harness for man
	Thomas Master	Has harness for man
B	John Barttelet	
AB	John Bowe	
	William Poundfyllde	S + b box 4 arrows
	William Mede	Has bill splints
A	John Master	Has bow 12 arrows
A	Gryflyn Danythe	Bill
	William Daniel	Bow 6 arrows
B	Thomas Andrews	Bill
A	Edward Poundfold	Has bow 12 arrows
A	John Garrett	S + b bow 4 arrows
B	William Dyer	Bill
	Richard Harris	S + b sellet splints
A	Nicholas Calnerds	Has bow 4 arrows
	William Hadgard	Has bow sheaf of arrows
B	Thomas Hadgard	Sallet splints
B	William Fyller	Bow 6 arrows
B	Thomas Thomson	Bill
A	Thomas Ynyn	Bow 4 arrows

Key

S + b set to buy

A Archer

AB Able Billman

B Billman

Harness—general term for armour

With the country in a state of unrest, and with the threat of civil war—which fortunately did not materialise—it is not surprising that throughout the country many of the local squires were watching with more than a passing interest the development of Henry's policies towards the monasteries. One such squire in the Sherborne area, with considerable influence, was Sir John Horsey of Clifton Maubank. He, after all, owned much land adjoining the Abbot of Sherborne's and obviously it was of great concern to him into whose hands that land fell. He found therefore that it was necessary, entirely for his own benefit, to take a hand in the administration of the monastery at Sherborne and, being a member of the court of Henry VIII he was not slow in bringing pressure to bear or offering bribes in the corridors of power when he considered it expedient. It is a fact that he had great influence in the appointment of Dan John Barnstaple as Abbot of Sherborne in 1535 as the following letter, dated 9th May 1535, to none other that Thomas Cromwell, clearly indicates.

'I thank you for offering my friend, Dan John Barnstabull [*sic*] to be Abbot of Sherborne on the resignation of Dan John Meere, late Abbot. The Monastery are well pleased with the appointment. I cannot come to you now as I am appointed to look after the taxing of the Clergy. I will come, however, shortly, to make payment secretly, between your mastership and me, unto you of 500 marks (£333) according to my promise.'

That Sir John Horsey was a man of considerable foresight and a good judge of the political climate there can be no doubt for quite apart from being influential in having Abbot John Barnstaple appointed he had also obtained the much sought-after position as the Abbot's steward. This gave him an intimate knowledge of the Abbot's possessions, probably greater than the Abbot's himself, which meant that he could influence the Abbot's decisions to better his own aims.

For several years previously Sir John Horsey had been laying out large sums of money acquiring land in both Dorset and Somerset and obtaining a position of such trust in the employ of the Abbot that he was undoubtedly scheming to obtain his employer's possessions when the crash finally came. That he had laid his plans well is certain, for only three days after Abbot John Barnstaple surrendered the Sherborne monastery and its possessions to the King in 1539 it was none other than Sir John Horsey (for the sum of £1242) who was granted the reversion of the premises with their accruing rents in Sherborne, the Sherborne Abbey Church and churchyard, the manors of Bradford Abbas, Trill and Creech (in the Isle of Purbeck). Together with other lands it was estimated that Sir John Horsey at this time owned more than 18,000 acres. The value placed upon Bradford Abbas in the agreed price was £6 6s. 8d.

The transaction ended completely the relationship between the monastery at Sherborne and Bradford Abbas and so the land, which, if you recall, had been granted 'for all time' by King Athelstan in 933 was never to return to the custody of the church.

Sir John Horsey had thus obtained the lands for which he had plotted and for the first time the Lord of the Manor of Clifton Maubank was also the Lord of the Manor of Bradford Abbas and for the next 300 years this was to continue to be the case, during which time the history of the two parishes marched virtually side by side.

One may well ask who was this Sir John Horsey who amassed such wealth and influence. He was in fact the son of Sir John Horsey, also of Clifton Maubank who died in 1531. Upon his death Sir John Horsey's father had land from the Bristol Channel to the Dorset Heights, which included the manor of Horsey near Bridgwater from which the family derived its name and origins. The manor of Clifton Maubank came into the possession of the Horseys through marriage and it was Clifton Maubank which became the family seat. Sir John Horsey's father served Henry VIII well, and was included in the Commission of Peace sixteen times during his reign, sometimes for Somerset, sometimes for Dorset. He was nominated for both in 1514. His son was also a member of the Commission for Peace, three times for Somerset and twice for Dorset and both father and son were amongst the Commissioners appointed for gaol delivery at Dorchester in 1530. He and his son both held various other positions which of course largely explains the considerable influence they had in the district. The new master of Bradford Abbas had one brother, Jasper, who created the Digwell line of the family to which we shall come later, and three sisters: Agnes, who entered a convent, Dorothea and Elizabeth.

In 1539, therefore the star of Horsey was shining brightly. Sir John, who had married Joan Maudlin of Corscombe, had two sons, John, his heir, and Roger, and two daughters, Elizabeth and Eleanor.

Clifton Maubank was the family seat and being a man of great wealth and influence Sir John entertained many nationally known persons at Clifton House. However, he was only to enjoy the new addition to his possessions for seven years, as he died in 1546 to be succeeded by his eldest son John, who only a year later was made a 'knight of the carpett' by Edward VI. This John Horsey, in the same year his father obtained Bradford Abbas, had married Edith Stocker, a widow whose maiden name was Phelips. She was a daughter of Richard Phelips, Esq., of Corfe Mullen, the family which was later to become the owners of Montacute House. There is, even to this day, a connection between Montacute and Clifton House as the west front of the former is built with materials acquired at a sale when Clifton was being dismembered, in 1786. It is interesting that the purchaser of these materials was Edward Phelips Esq., a direct descendant of the family of Edith Phelips. To add further to the romance between the two houses it was this same Edith Phelips' new husband, Sir John Horsey, who is thought to have been responsible for building or rebuilding Clifton House into the magnificent structure it was until it was eventually taken apart, brick by brick, to become a mere shadow of the original that stands today.

Sir John Horsey and Edith Stocker (née Phelips) had one son, John, and two daughters, Elizabeth and Maria. From the time he succeeded his father in 1546 he continued to administer his vast possessions in a most satisfactory manner and was generally successful in increasing the family's wealth. Like his father he was influential and for several years was one of the county's members of parliament.

Upon his death in 1564 he was succeeded by his son, John, who was to prove to be the last of the five Sir John Horseys of Clifton Maubank. He was only eighteen years of age when he inherited his father's estates and it was considered by many that for such a young man to inherit such wealth might well turn his head. But it was not so, and while he was still only eighteen years of age he married into the House of Norfolk taking for his wife Grace, the daughter of Thomas Howard, Viscount Bindon. This was an extremely advantageous marriage even by Horsey standards but unfortunately the mistress of Clifton Maubank only enjoyed four years of marriage, for she died in 1568. There were no children of the marriage and being anxious to preserve the Horsey succession Sir John took a second wife. She was a widow, Dorothy, the daughter of Edward Gilbert, Esq., of London, and had nothing of the aristocratic background of the late Grace Horsey. But this second marriage also proved to be childless and the lack of an heir caused Sir John Horsey much more concern than the wealth he had inherited. However, like his father and grandfather before him, he was astute enough not to endanger the Horsey fortunes by any misdeeds or misdemeanors and like his father he became a member of parliament. He moved in high circles and was knighted by none other than Queen Elizabeth I during her 'progress to Bristow' in 1574. But for all his wealth and influence he was not so fortunate as the poorest of his tenants for he could not have the one thing he desired above all others—an heir, or even an heiress. And so when the time came for him to draw up his will he was still without issue and after making ample provision for his sisters, Elizabeth and Maria, he had to set about finding a successor to himself as master of Clifton House.

His choice was his cousin Ralph Horsey, of Digwell, Hertfordshire, a descendant of Jasper Horsey, Sir John's grandfather's brother, and it is from the time that Ralph came into possession of the Horsey wealth that the family's star began to dim, until it was finally extinguished.

Ralph Horsey became the master of Clifton House in 1588. Whether Sir John was aware of his cousin's weakness is not known but it can reasonably be assumed that he was not, as it was his dearest wish that his estates remain intact. Ralph Horsey wasted no time in moving to Clifton Maubank but what eventually caused the downfall of the House of Horsey is difficult to ascertain. It seems most likely that Ralph was a spendthrift, for his own father saw fit to advise him that 'if he should have occasion to sell any of his lands, not to part with the Hertfordshire inheritance'. He ignored his father's advice and disposed of his Hertfordshire estates, at the same time seriously encumbering the Clifton Maubank and Bradford Abbas properties, as well as several others. When Ralph Horsey died in 1612, Clifton Maubank and Bradford Abbas passed into the hands of his second son, Sir George, his eldest son, John having died without issue. Sir George, who had been knighted in 1581, was unable to stop the ever-accelerating decline of the Horsey dynasty and eventually his financial situation had deteriorated to such an extent that he found himself in Newgate Prison 'himself in want of bread and necessities, not sixpence in his pocket, nor knew where to go for a crown; that for two days he had not a farthing to buy bread for his servants, and lived only on water and oatmeal and threepence worth of sprats'. By 1639 he was living with his brother-in-law at Shroton but he was eventually outlawed for a debt of £10.

It is of passing interest, to mention that whilst Sir George was still resident at Clifton House he entertained Sir Walter Raleigh. An old record states: '26th July 1618. From Master Drake's they went on their journey to the house of Master Horsey. Raleigh was en route for London to face charges of treason.'

And so, in 1639, the Horsey's vacated Clifton Maubank and Bradford Abbas and the properties came into the hands of Sir John Hele. Of Sir John Hele not a great deal is known but according to one of his friends he was 'a person of very great estate, a personable gracious gentleman, his only fault was he loved the cup'.

In 1642 the Civil War between Charles I and his parliament broke out and Sir John Hele immediately took the King's side, and became a most active participant in the hostilities which followed. In 1643 he raised one hundred horsemen and four hundred foot soldiers and attacked parliamentary troops which were in Sherborne, driving them from the town, whilst in 1645 he was taking part in the seige of Bridgwater where he was taken hostage. He was later fined £6,000 for deliquency and died in 1647.

A most interesting item, however, appears in the will (dated 1643) of Sir John Hele in which he 'gave to the poor of the Parish of Bradford Abbas and the Parish of Clifton Maubank adjoining a yearly rent charge of 52/- to be distributed in white bread'. As a result of this it became the custom after evensong on the first Sunday of each month for thirteen men of the poor to attend at the Vestry of St Mary's Church and each to receive a loaf to the value of 4d. It seems that it became generally accepted that persons in receipt of parish relief were excluded from the benefits of the charity but whether or not this is what was intended by Sir John Hele is a matter for conjecture. The charity, however, is still in existence, although bread is no longer distributed. There are however funds available to help the needy in the two parishes in many other directions for the original terms have been altered with the full consent of the Charity Commissioners.

It is as well at this stage to examine how the village of Bradford Abbas was developing. From information available it would seem that the basic outlines of the 'old village' were already laid. Several of the cottages which now stand in North Street may well have been built or about to be built, whilst what is now known as 'The Cross' was more than likely the central point and meeting place for the villagers. There would also have been several cottages in Churchwell Street, Church Road and Westbury. It is also possible to obtain some idea of the population for in 1641, one year before the outbreak of the Civil War, all males of eighteen years of age or over were requested to take what was known as the Protestation Oath upholding the Protestant religion. The vast majority of the men signed the oath, even if only to avoid trouble, and by a fairly simple formula it is possible to obtain an approximate figure for the population.

A total number of males who signed the oath in Bradford Abbas was 113 (see Appendix A). This figure should be doubled on the assumption that there would be as many females over eighteen; the aggregate thus obtained is multiplied by 10/6 to include the numbers (generally calculated to be 40%) under eighteen. This gives a total of 376, which if one allows for a very small minority who may have declined to take the oath, would give a population approaching 400. There can be little doubt that both Bradford Abbas and Clifton Maubank saw many skirmishes during the Civil War, commencing with the battle of Babylon Hill in 1642 which in actual fact was only a minor skirmish in comparison with the battles that were to follow.

'Bedford then, having raised the seige and marched to Yeovil, within four miles of Sherborne quartered there that night and intended to be quiet the next day. But meanwhile the Cavaliers in the castle had received a reinforcement of 100 horse and 200 foot from Mr Richard Rogers of Bryanston, one of the Knights of the Shire at the beginning of hostilities. Accordingly on 7th September, Hopton with 400 horse and 200 musketeers or in his own words with "all the horse and dragons, and sevenscore musketeers" and accompanied by Captain Digby and Sir Francis Holles with their troops and by Lord Poulet, Sir John Stavel and Sir John Poulet issued from Sherborne about 2 o'clock in the afternoon and marched to Babylon Hill or Babe Hill, a mile from Yeovil, John, fifth Baron Poulet or Poulett of Hinton St George near Crewkerne, was Lord of the paramount Manor of Marshwood and exercised manorial rights in the parish of Lyme Regis. Shaftesbury calls him "a cunning, crafty old fox" and according to a Puritan tract before leaving Sherborne he had made a speech to his fellow soldiers wherein he gave "them order to kill men, women and children, without mercie; but to reverse such ministers as they could take what were well wishers to Parliament for to feed alive, and such like exquisite torments". And this same month at Wells he is reported to have said "with many imprecations, oaths and exacerbations, cavalier like (in the height of the fury) it was not fit for any Yeoman to have allowed him from his labours any more that the poor moitie of £10 a year; and when the power should be totally on their side, they shall be compelled to live at that low allowance, notwithstanding their estates are gotten with a great deal of labour and industry".

'Upon this people attempted to lynch Poulet, but a regiment passing at the time, most opportunely saved him. The hill, occupied by Hopton on 7th September 1642, looked down over Yeovil Bridge which the Parliamentarians held with a guard of foot and cannon. "So taking advantage of the ground, there being no coming up to him from the enemy's part but by two hollow wayes on each hand of him, Hopton placed a guard of 20 musketeers on his right; lined with all his dragoons the hedge which flanked his left; and drawing up his horse in battle array upon the summit of the hill, with the rest of the musketeers played from the side of the hill on the guard upon the bridge." Having spent an hour or more in

27

this position without such damage done to the adverse party, he acting upon the advice of his officers, resolved to retreat, and accordingly gave orders for the foot to march away, and the dragoons to march up to the house to make good the rear—it being by then within half an hour of sunset. But the foot were not clear drawn off the hill when Colonel Laudy espied the enemy marching out of Yeovil, by a secret way he had made over the fields, and that some of his horse had nearly ridden up to the top of the hill upon the left. Hopton, being advertised of this manoeuvre, resolved it was too late to retreat; ordered Lunsford to draw back the foot; and himself and drew up the horse and the dragoons towards the part where the enemy was advancing. He also commanded Edward Stawel with the troops of volunteers to march in the same direction, seconded by his own troop commanded by Henry Morston; and because they were both young soldiers, Col. Laudy to advance with them. Next to them he placed Sir Francis Hawley with his troops and kept Captain Digby's troops in reserve. Meanwhile the Parliament troops had their own difficulties to contend with. It was as much as they could do to put themselves into a posture of defence; to make good their approaches and guard their magazine. For the last few men were available and of those more pike men than musketeers; for the latter finding themselves the most employed on all occasions for the most part "slighted themselves away". However, they sent out these troops of horse and some musketeers, the cavaliers "braving us and calling us rogues and roundheads". The hill was difficult to ascend; Captain Ayscough took one way, Captain Tompson another, a little after him; and Captain Balfour (Sir William Balfour's son) a third with "our musqueteers [*sic*] after them as fast as they could". The way taken up the hill by Ayscough was so narrow that only two could march abreast; and when they were almost at the top they encountered Hopton's ambuscade of six musketeers on either side; but having won through these successfully, they arrived at the summit; Captain Ayscough and his troop being the first up, charged Stowel's troop through and through; and then engaged Captain Moreton's. But after the exchange of two or three brace of bullets and some sword play, Ayscough was forced to wheel about by the over pressure of numbers and retreat into the lane with the loss of four or five men. But almost immediately Captain Tompson with his troop joined him, and charging together, they threw the two Royalist troops of Stowel and Moreton into hopeless confusion. But Captain Balfour's troop meanwhile had not fared so well; for charging up the lane on the right—Lunsford having forgotten to station a party of volunteers there—they found no opposition, until they came among the volunteers upon the top of the hill. Here Balfour rode out from among his men brandishing his sword; whereof Lunsford giving notice to young Stowel, the latter rode forward to meet him. Balfour discharged his pistols at some distance, but Stowel reserved his until he might be surer of his mark; which he did so well that he fired the other's bluff at his breast; and with a quick blow of his sword made an end both of the duel and his adversary. At the same instant a bullet from Sir James Colborne's fouling gun also pierced Captain Balfour, whose troop being raw fellows, was immediately routed. But Hopton's forces being now thrown into confusion by the prowess of Captain Ayscough and Tompson with the assistance of 2,000 of Bedford's foot, beat a retreat. The Royalists lost fifteen or twenty horse; and of their foot between thirty and forty killed, but Major Bampfield who commanded them with about twenty of his soldiers were taken prisoners, Captain Joseph Hissey of Stow Payne was killed his commission being found in his pocket "himself being clad in plush" and young Lunsford escaped on horseback. Of the other commanders of Hopton's foot, Lieutenant Hall and an ensign were also killed. On the other side, fifteen or sixteen of Bedford's troop fell into the hands of the Royalists, whereof some were killed but the more part spared and taken prisoners to Sherborne. Had not night fallen shortly, the Parliament forces expected to have cut off most of the Royalist foot. They heard that "one of the Bartletts was killed" and Hopton hurt, and a Dorchester letter writer says untruthfully "Colonel Lunsford and Lord Poulet are certainly slain".

'The Royalists declared that the enemy "lost one hundred and forty of their men dead on the ground, buryed nine of their commanders next day in the church". Before Hopton's return to the Castle, Hertford had been reinforced by Richard Rogers of Bryanston with 1000 foot of the trained bands of Dorset." Local legend has it that the Royalists buried their dead in Soldier's Park, Wyke, in the Parish of Castleton.'

(*The Great Civil War in Dorset* by A.R. Bayley)

There can be little doubt that the village saw much of the forces of the King and Parliament, situated as it is between the two towns of Yeovil (for Parliament) and Sherborne (for the King), and in 1647 it is recorded that:-

'Parliamentary troops pulled down three dwelling houses of Hugh Hodges, an attorney, tenant of Sir John Hele's sequestered estate, and dispersed of the timber to rebuild some of those burned down on the previous Saturday night.'

It is not known whether these buildings were in Bradford Abbas or Clifton Maubank, Sir John Hele's estate covering both parishes. Having been fined £6,000 for delinquency and his estates having been sequestered, Sir John Hele died in 1647. A certain Henry Rogers became trustee for Hele's infant daughters and co-heirs, June and Dorothy, and eventually the estates were sold off. The new owners of Clifton Maubank were the Harvey family of Comb in Surrey, relations of the eminent William Harvey who discovered the circulation of the blood, and the first of that family to become the Lord of the Manor was Mr Richard Harvey. It is fortunate that a manuscript dated 1648 survives which would appear to be part of a 'sales brochure' which describes Clifton House and its environs and so gives an idea of the scale of the property to which Richard Harvey came to reside.

'The capital message consists of a faire yellowe freestone building, partly two and partly three stories, a faire hall and parlour, both waynscotted, a faire dyninge room and with drawing room, and many good lodgings, a kitchen adjoining backewards to one end of the dwelling house with faire passage from it into the hall, parlour and dyninge room and sellers adjoyngnge.

'In front of the house a square green court, and a curious gate house with lodgings in it staninge with the front of the house to the south, in a large outer court three stables, a coach house, a large barne and a stable for oxen and kine, and all houses necessary.

'Without the gatehouse paled in a large square greene, in which standeth a faire chappell; of the south east side of the greene court, towards the river a large garden. On the south west side of the greene court is a large bowling greene, with flower mounted walks about it, all walled about with a batteled wall, and sett with all sorts of fruit; and out of it into the fields there are large walkes under many tall elms orderly planted.

'There are several orchards and gardens about the house, 14 acres well planted. In the backside of the house there is a brewhouse, bakehouse, dayry house and all other necessary houses and lodgings for servants, and a faire double pigeon house and a cerne mill.

'The river runs through all the lands neere 3 miles, and encircle the house att a goode distance, saving at the east itt runnes by the garden next the parlour, in which river there is plenty of pike, carpes and other river fish. Behind the house, towards the north west, there is from the house an easy and dry ascent into the hill where the warren is and under the edge at that hill, and upon a part of that hill, very pleasant and many ashes and coppice walks by the river side also. And all the country north of the houses open champaign sandy fields belonging to Bradforde, very dry and pleasant for all kinds of recreation, hunting and hawking and profitable for tillage. To the south and west, in the front of the house is a deep riche soil, where eyeth the pasture and meadow and part of the arable, and the great coppice wood in which there is a competent number of deere belonging to the demeasnes into which there is a descent from the house which standeth upon a very sandy hill ground and hath a large prospect east, south and west, over a very large and pleasant vale.

'The house is seated from the good markett townes of Sherborne, 5 miles, Yeovil a mile, Ivelchester five miles, Searne six miles, Crewkerne seven miles, Somerton eight miles that plentfully yield all manner of provision and within twelve miles the south sea.'

When the new owner of Clifton Maubank and Bradford Abbas died he was succeeded by his son Michael. This Michael Harvey was commemorated on a tomb (now unfortunately destroyed) in Bradford Abbas Church which read as follows:

'From his youth he practised a religion not showily barren, but rich in good deeds and whose gate was always open to strangers, his neighbours and the poor, and his heart to all the good. Often elected to the supreme assembly of the senate he was ever found a defender of his country or her laws, and to friendships happily begun with great advantage he returned still greater benefits than those he received from them.

'He experienced the pious care of his most loving wife during the long weariness of a disease to which, through the fortitude of a Christian mind was equal, his mortal part succumbed.'

There is a similar monument (also destroyed) to Michael's wife:

'Who from her earliest years was ordered and adorned her life by true religion, sincerely faithful toward God, trustful towards men, equally calm in prosperity and adversity, thankful in health, perfectly resigned in sickness, liberally succouring the poor, excelling in kindness to guests and neighbours, a friend to all, an enemy to none.'

It is interesting to read in these inscriptions that Michael's 'gate was always open', and his wife was 'excelling in kindness to guests' for during their ownership of Clifton Maubank they entertained a man who was only a few years later to become infamous for leading a rebellion against James II, the Duke of Monmouth. He came from Exeter via Whitelackington en route for Longleat, and it was during the course of that journey that he came to dine with Michael and Rebecca Harvey.

Apart from this small event not a great deal is known regarding the ownership of Bradford Abbas by Michael Harvey except that as he was a supporter of William of Orange and the principles which he represented, it was rumoured that the land tax on the Harvey estate was much higher than on many other estates in the neighbourhood.

Michael Harvey died in 1711 and was succeeded by his son, another Michael, who was to prove to be the last of that family to be the Lord of the Manor for the two parishes. After having owned the properties for some thirty years or so he obtained an Act of Parliament to seal a part of his settled estates for the relief of the other portion. Like the Horseys before them the Harveys had run into financial problems, and he found it necessary to mortgage Bradford Abbas and Clifton Maubank to a certain Peter Walter Esq. of Stalbridge who decided to claim the estates just before Michael Harvey's death in 1748. It was unfortunate that Michael died when he did for had he survived John, Duke of Montague, who died in 1749, an estate worth £4,000 per annum would have passed into his hands.

The new owner of Bradford Abbas, Peter Walter, was a son of an elder Peter Walter, a London lawyer, Clerk of the Peace for Middlesex and Steward to the Duke of Northumberland and other noblemen. He had amassed a considerable fortune and it seems that it was his policy to lay out vast sums in acquiring estates.

From Peter Walter the properties eventually passed to his grandson Edward Walter and from him to Henry Bayly, Earl of Uxbridge in 1780. Henry Bayly, who was created Marquess of Anglesey in 1815, sold off the Clifton estate in 1825 to John Bridge Esq., but he retained the Bradford Abbas estates which later passed to his son. This second Marquess of Anglesey eventually sold the Bradford Abbas estate to William Clayton Esq. in 1852.

With the sale of the Clifton Maubank estate in 1825 the Lord of the Manor of Clifton Maubank no longer held any authority in Bradford Abbas and so after almost 300 years, during which the two estates were owned entirely by wealthy men, the history of the two parishes separated.

CHAPTER III
Hard Times

At the beginning of the nineteenth century the population of Bradford Abbas was 480, consisting of 211 males and 269 females. There were 82 houses making up the village of which 4 were uninhabited. Of the population 153 were employed on the land while a further 309 were employed in trades and manufactures.

The late Mr Harry Warr, in his *A Short Account of Bradford Abbas* (Chaffins) relates with regard to these trades and manufactures that many were employed in flax dressing, some in twine making, others were working in cork, whilst on the site of the present Old Mill in Mill Lane there was a large flax mill which employed a large number of girls including many from outside the parish.

The main streets of the village were North Street, Higher Westbury, Westbury, Grope Lane, Church Road, Churchwell Street and Mill Lane, with the trading centre of the village being at The Cross at the bottom of North Street, where in the early years of the ninteenth century stood a fine market cross. The main building in the village was, of course, the church. There was no parish room or village hall, and the school was in a small cottage in Churchwell Street. The cottages in which the villagers lived were no more than hovels and the only house of any substance used solely as a dwelling was the vicarage, now St Mary's House.

The Rev. Robert Grant, writing about his arrival in the village in 1828 to take up his duties as Vicar wrote:

'The County of Dorset, at the period when I entered on my ministry in the Parish had acquired an unenviable notoriety with respect to the temporal condition of the peasantry. Generally speaking they were ill paid, ill housed, ill fed and ill clad. And when sickness was added to poverty the burden which they had to bear was necessarily much heavier. My Parish formed no exception to the hard state and circumstances of the labouring classes in the County. The hard-earned wages of the ordinary farm labourer average 7/- per week, with some trifling perquisites.

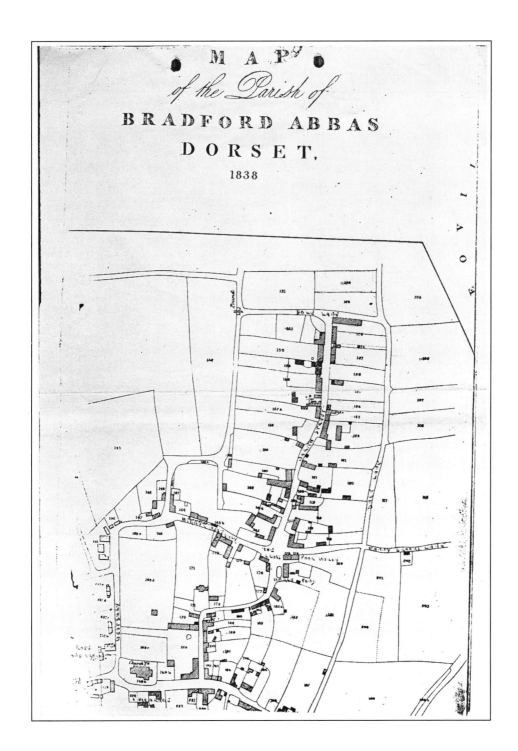

Map of Bradford Abbas, 1838.

Their cottages were rented very high. It is true such articles of food which were available to him, such as butter, cheese and milk were very much cheaper than in other parts of England. Butcher's meat was never seen except when sent to a sick person by any one, and pig meat very rarely on the poor man's table. Potatoes were their main article of food, which at that time were good and cheap. I have known them as low as 5/- a sack. Yet notwithstanding their comfortless and inconvenient dwellings, especially as regarded their sleeping apartments, when husband and wife and children of both sexes and of all ages would occupy the same room, their slender sustenance, their many privatations, their various sufferings, the endurance and patience with which their lot was borne were as extraordinary as they were praiseworthy. No wonder they were demoralised if not brutalised. The women and girls who were old enough to handle the needle contributed their share to the general stock, by sewing gloves, which were manufactured in the neighbouring town of Yeovil. But their contribution was but small seeing that they were only paid three halfpence for a pair of gloves, besides having to find their own needles and thread. The best work woman could only make from three to four pairs of gloves in one day, and even then, they had to work by candlelight when the day shut in. The stooping over their work was always very prejudicial to their health.'

It is not surprising, therefore, that with conditions for the vast majority of the villagers being so bad, there was much agitation for reform, and rioting became an almost everyday event in some cities and towns. Both Sherborne and Yeovil were seriously affected by the movement for reforms and several persons from Bradford Abbas took part in these riots—one villager in fact took such a leading role that he was fortunate not to end up on the gallows. The Rev. Grant suggests that there was a lurking 'spirit of mischief' amongst some of the working classes, 'which manifested itself in incendiary fires in the Parish of which there were no less than 7 in 6 months. With the exception of one, which was an act of revenge, they never could be traced to their foul source.' And he goes on to say:

'And yet the greater part of the inhabitants turned out and worked with a will to subdue the flames. Although there was no disloyal feeling in the place, there was a large amount of drunkenness and immorality, so much so that there was scarcely a meeting of the magistrates held without one or more of my parishioners being brought before them. How indeed could it be otherwise when we consider the gross ignorance that prevailed at that time.'

It is not surprising that the Rev. Grant mentions 'drunkenness' and 'ignorance' for with regard to the former he speaks of four beershops and a public house, all of which were in the village at the same time. Many of the older inhabitants of the village today will readily relate that their parents have told them that there were four public houses in the village towards the end of the century, and in my first book I named them as the Seven Bells, the Fox, the Manor and the Rose and Crown. However, bearing in mind that Seven Bells ceased to be a public house in the early years of the century it would have meant that there could only have been three at any one time. However, to my surprise the story handed down from parents to children has proved to be true as I have now discovered at the bottom of North Street near the Cross—the Hare & Hounds. I have successfully located four of these Inns; the only one whose location I do not know is the Manor. Although it was well advertised, its situation was just given as 'Bradford Abbas'.

It does make one wonder how four public houses could survive in a village the size of Bradford Abbas and indeed some of these establishments did not survive for so many years as by 1880 there was only one such house left—the Rose & Crown.

However, whilst the population was 480 in 1801 the village continued to grow despite the hardships of its inhabitants, until it reached its peak in 1841 with 652 persons in the parish, a figure which incidentally was larger than the population in 1961. As one would expect, the number of dwelling houses had also increased. Twenty-five additional cottages were erected in the ten years between 1801 and 1811, and by 1851 there were 128 separate dwellings compared with 82 50 years earlier. In fact by 1861 the number of dwellings had reached 139, although by that date there was a most definite trend towards depopulation.

In his book *Forty Years in a Country Parish* the Rev Grant mentioned the ignorance of the villagers due to their lack of education and goes on to say that of the two churchwardens, both persons of some standing in the village, one could barely write his name whilst the other could not write at all. This situation continued until the latter years of the century, when some members of the Parish Council still made their X's in the minute book.

Sickness and disease was also a problem, in particular to those who were already on the poor relief as the Rev Robert Grant records.

'The Parish authorities contracted with a medical person for attending the poor when sick, and supplying them with medicines; cases of midwifery and broken limbs being excepted. The remuneration at the time I am writing about was, I believe, £40 per annum. Of course, so paltry a sum was beneath an experienced practitioner's notice. Indeed except for the purpose of extending his practice, no one, except a young man, would undertake such an unremunerative office. But the hardship which the system of "farming" the sick entailed upon the poor was very great; for the parish doctor was not obliged to visit anyone without an order from the Overseer; and unless the sick person had already been in receipt of parish pay, he was loath to give the order, for it would make the applicant a pauper, and consequently entitled to some allowance. The consequence was that great delay occasionally took place. The parish officer would put off giving the order from day to day, in order to see whether the sick person became worse. I have known a very severe case unattended to for a fortnight; and when on my urgent interposition, the doctor came it was too late.'

This is only one instance but one must ask the question—just how often did this happen?

Under the Poor Law (the new Poor Law was passed in 1834) life for those who fell onto parish relief life was far from easy. The Vestry, which was virtually the village government until the formation of Parish Councils, was the sole tribunal before which claimants for relief brought their cases. As those who constituted the Vestry were personally interested in keeping the poor rate as low as possible they were naturally though wrongly swayed by motives other than those of justice and humanity. A book was kept in which the names of the persons who applied for relief were entered, with the decision that was reached in each case. The Chairman of the Vestry in the early years of the nineteenth century was a local farmer, the Vicar being absent most of his time from the parish. He did not look kindly upon the poor and was according to the Rev. Robert Grant something of a dictator and although it may be coincidental, he had the right name—King.

It is not known what the amounts paid in relief amounted to as the records have long since been destroyed but one can be sure that the payments made were not over-generous. The Vestry accommodated those who had no roof over their head in the village poor house, which was situated at the corner of the Cross and Bakehouse Lane. The Vestry were paying 1/- rent per annum for the premises and although the premises were destroyed a number of years ago a description of them survives.

'It was a long narrow building, which once had been used as the village bakehouse, in which there was a public oven heated on certain days for the purpose of baking bread for those persons who could not do so at their own homes. It was divided into certain small compartments, or cabins, separated from each other by very light partitions. Little light and still less air, penetrated these wretched dwellings.

'Some were literally on the ground floor, and some above which were open to the thatch. From three to four families, besides two or three old couples, were the inmates. The filth, the noise, the smells are not to be described.'

I suppose, by the standards of the times the Vestry could be given the benefit of the doubt and it could be said that they were doing their best but it cannot be forgotten that the people who controlled the Vestry were those who were basically footing the bills so they cannot have been enthusiastic about laying out too much money in parish relief.

Times were very hard, of that there can be little doubt, but what of the people themselves—what did they do to help themselves? Everything in the parish records indicates that they did the best they could and were very loathe to accept 'charity' as they called it, a tradition that still pertains today particularly amongst the older villagers. The families were much larger in the nineteenth century and families of ten or more children were not uncommon. In fact ten children was a little on the low side and twelve to fourteen was more usual. There was certainly a great deal of sex outside marriage and 'shotgun' weddings were quite common. However, there were also many more widows and widowers in the 30-40 age group, most of whom usually remarried and embarked upon a second family. There were many children who died young (in one year seventeen children under the age of 10 were buried.) How the families accommodated their children is another mystery. One couple, Henry & Eliza Gill, had twelve children and although they were living in a small cottage in Westbury (which still stands) they still found room to accommodate a lodger. What the conditions must have been like in these houses with all those children is beyond imagination, but the Gills were not exceptional and there were many others like them. And yet they seemed to do everything properly; their children were baptised and confirmed and are generally recorded as having, most of them, lived a reasonably satisfying life by the standards of the times. Many lived to a good old age, and it is not uncommon to see regular burials of persons of 80 or 90 in the church registers.

However, the men in particular were not entirely satisfied with their lot and this showed itself in particular with regard to health. The Rev. Robert Grant records that this manifested itself in friendly societies. During the period of his incumbency he witnessed the birth and death of three such societies and the birth of a fourth, which was to survive well into the twentieth century. These societies, however, did not always receive the recognition from the hierarchy of the village that one might expect as is recorded by one leading villager.

'I am unable to form an opinion respecting their general utility and individual benefit to the members. Unquestionably there is a certain amount of good in a national, as well as a private point of view. When enrolled, according to the Act of Parliament, some of their rules are calculated to enlist the members on the side of law and order; they are likely to regard themselves with greater self respect; they have, so to speak, a stake in the national faggot. The benefit accruing to the individual is too obvious to be dwelt upon, but like most other matters in this chequered state of things no small evil is mixed up with the good. In the first place I have reason to know that some of the members have had recourse to borrowing money to enable them to pay up their monthly contributions; and when the club breaks up and the division of the spoil takes place, whilst a certain number, no doubt, are benefited by making a proper use of their share of the deposits, not a few employ them in paying the debts that they have contracted, whilst others waste them in excess of riot. Another serious evil is when such Societies have been set to foot by either the publican, or by parties connected with the public house where the monthly meetings are mostly held, when it is compulsory on the members to spend a certain sum in drink, which of course offered a great temptation to spend more than was required by the rules. The annual feast moreover is a great drawback from the good of the Societies. Seldom if ever, do these annual gatherings take place without a large amount of intemperance, and sometimes quarrelling.'

Certainly throughout the nineteenth century, intemperance was a problem but the friendly societies were also useful in so far as members of a society who fell sick could at least receive a limited income to help them over their difficult times. They were also the first organisations in the village which gave the villagers anything of a social life as in the early years of the century everything revolved around the church and it was not until 1886 and the arrival of the Rev. Gordon Wickham that any social organisations other than the friendly societies were formed.

However, as happened with many Dorset villages, a process of depopulation had set in by 1855. This was not apparent to those in the village at the time, as in the ten years from 1841, when the population was at its peak, it had dropped by only 31. The process accelerated so rapidly however that by 1901 the population was as low as 394, compared with a peak of 652, and the number of dwellings had dropped from 139 to 78. In 1851 there were 13 farms in the parish and by 1901 only 4.

There were very good reasons, of course, for the decline in population but Bradford Abbas was lucky in so far as it did not decline as much as many similar villages and many people managed to obtain work other than on the land due to the coming of the railway through the village.

The largest farm in the village consisted of 600 acres upon which 19 men were employed whilst, the smallest was a mere 18 acres upon which one man was employed. These farms, however, were most uneconomical due to their scattered nature, with pieces of the farm often being at opposite ends of the parish. And so, when William Clayton Clayton became the owner of the parish in 1852 he became responsible for changing the farming structure of the village. Like his predecessor the Marquis of Anglesey, William Clayton Clayton did not reside in the parish but whereas the Marquis of Anglesey employed an agent during his period of ownership William Clayton Clayton put his son, Albert Clayton Clayton in charge of the parish and insisted upon him becoming a resident of Bradford Abbas. The new owner of Bradford Abbas was, by profession, a barrister at Lincoln's Inn, but his financial circumstances were always such as to render him independent of a professional income. He was looked upon as a powerful speaker and a forceful writer and was the author of a learned legal work *The Origin of Tithes*. According to his obituary, 'though born in the last year of the century he was never what may be termed "old fashioned" for he always kept his mind open for the reception of new ideas and liked to hear fresh and improved plans of sanitation and education'.

One of the first matters he considered upon attaining the ownership of the Bradford Abbas estate was the completely uneconomical situation created by the 13 farms in the village, and he almost immediately embarked upon the break-up of these farms and the creation of larger holdings, the eventual number being 3. He had 3 substantial farmhouses built, Coombe House, Manor Farm and North Farm, and by 1860 he had completed this process. The most impressive of the three farms was Coombe House. Although this policy created a certain amount of unemployment it was not as bad as was first expected. But what Mr Clayton had done was, essentially, an economic necessity and there can be little doubt that if he had not followed this policy himself a future Lord of the Manor would have done so. I do not believe that Mr Clayton wished to create unemployment and some of his other actions in the village tend to contradict that view. He was for example responsible for the opening of the present old school in 1856, which he built at his own expense, an action which does not bear out the belief of some people at the time that he was accelerating or anticipating the decline of the village. There was, in any case, a general decline in the rural population of the country, and in particular Dorset, at this time, so it is quite reasonable to assume that his policies in fact saved some jobs which may have been lost had the small farm system survived. Even in those days it was hardly possible to survive on a farm of just 18 acres. However, there was another factor which came into play which was most fortunate; only eight years after Mr Clayton became the owner of the parish the present railway line which bisects the village was laid, and opened on 1st June 1860.

This was at almost the exact time that the three big farms were created and so many who lost their livelihood on the land took employment with the railway company. The railway track completely altered the landscape of the village as it cut straight through the middle of the built-up area, and it was necessary to build an embankment, the soil from which came from a cutting which had to be created at the eastern end of the parish.

About 100 men were employed in building this stretch of the railway but very few of them were local, most of them having come from various parts of the country. While they were working on this section of the track, however, they resided in the village, many of them in tents alongside the railway. They were a rough and ready lot of men. Several of whom were fleeing from justice and many others who had left their wives, but the Rev. Robert Grant says that during their stay in the village there were 'no unusual deprivations'. They certainly had several brushes with the village hierarchy, however, usually over religious subjects due mainly to the Vicar requesting them to attend church services and their reluctance to do so. When they left the village a few pregnant women were left behind but rough and ready as they were there was no serious outbreak of crime during the period of their stay.

It was hoped that a station would be built in the village and it is believed that the railway company were anxious to provide one and were only dissuaded from doing so by the inexplicable opposition of certain members of the parish. They did find it necessary to build a junction at the eastern end of the parish, but it did not allow passengers to embark or disembark, and was only to serve for ten years or so, for it was replaced by the present Yeovil Junction and the old track demolished. Even the buildings which were built at this junction and some cottages in the area have now been destroyed and the cutting through which the old track passed is now probably the most deserted part of the parish; every time I have walked that way I have had only rabbits, birds, butterflies and the occasional fox for company.

One unfortunate effect of the coming of the railway, however, was that it caused the destruction of many cottages due to sparks alighting thatched roofs and although the railway company, on occasion, paid compensation, they were not over-generous. These cottages were never rebuilt and to a large extent their destruction was responsible for the decline in the number of dwelling houses I have mentioned earlier. I would, however, mention at this stage that the railway which bisects the village was not the first track in the village. The Great Western line which ran from the Pen Mill to Weymouth over the so-called Bradford Viaduct and which passes through the western edges of the parish was laid in 1849.

CHAPTER IV
Better Times

Bradford Abbas laundry staff, c. 1908. The laundry was situated in a cottage at the Cross. The young gentleman on the far right, Mr Harry Gillham, is still very much a part of the modern village.

The coming to the village of Rev. Gordon Bolles Wickham as Vicar of Bradford Abbas and Rector of Clifton Maubank in 1886 was to mark a step forward in the life of the parish. One of his first actions was to build a parish hall, entirely at his own expense. He was also the instigator of the Men's Club, a youth club, an evening continuation school, and other social activities. In 1894 the village had its first Parish Council, which in effect took away all the Vestry's civil powers and the Rev. Wickham himself

became the village's first ever representative on the Sherborne Rural District Council.

By 1901 the population of the village had dropped from its peak of 652 in 1841 to only 391 but it was a village that was coming alive. In 1900, Mr Harry Warr was appointed Headmaster of the Village School and through his efforts and those of the Rev. Wickham the villagers were beginning to have the drudgery taken out of their lives. In 1914 Mr Albert Clayton Clayton died and the estate was purchased by its principal tenant, Walter Wyatt Paul who was to be the last of the Lords of the Manor. He was to own the estate for almost 40 years and it was during this period that the population again showed signs of increasing. Although the rate of increase was inevitably slowed down by the two world wars, the trend has generally continued upwards throughout this century except for the last ten years or so when it has remained reasonably static. The major problem which, as landowner, Mr Wyatt Paul had to face was the continual agitation for extra housing which would, of course, have to be built upon land owned by himself. As early as 1913 the first murmurings could be heard and the Vestry decided to set up a committee to ascertain if there was a demand for additional cottage accommodation. What the results of the committee's deliberations were, are not recorded and I am doubtful if they ever bothered to investigate the matter. The Parish Council also showed little enthusiasm for housing for according to a minute of 17th April 1913, 'Mr King brought forward the question of housing accommodation and after discussion nothing was done in the matter.'

The coming of the First World War, however, put a stop to any question of additional cottages being built as many men left the village to serve in His Majesty's forces, but it appears that there was not much enthusiasm for enlisting on the part of many of them. As early as 1st September 1914 the Rev. Gordon Wickham wrote in his monthly address to the village, 'So far the response from this village has been inadequate and I earnestly appeal to our young men to consider carefully wherein their duty lies, and act promptly,' and on 8th March 1917 a Parish Council minute reads:

'National Service; A circular was read from the County Committee as to the formation of a village committee for the purpose of canvassing for volunteers for national service. After considerable discussion it was ultimately agreed that the

Chairman write to the County Committee in the following terms as expressing the opinion of the Council. "After due consideration the Council are of the opinion that there is no spare labour available in the Parish.""

To be fair a good number of the village men did enlist but I cannot say that I am altogether surprised at the reluctance of many others particularly if they had read of the carnage that was occurring in France at the time. The Vicar posted a list of those who were serving in the armed forces on the wall of the village hall freely stating that he would like to add names to the list as the months went by but whether it was an attempt to shame some men into enlisting or intended as a roll of honour I know not. I do know, however that he kept the villagers advised as far as possible of the activities of those who were away fighting in foreign lands.

During the war the village housed some Belgian refugees and German prisoners of war were kept in the Old Mill in Mill Lane, and were put to work on local farms. The children and others were active in making clothing etc., for the troops at the front.

Fortunately, although there was loss of life, the men from Bradford Abbas killed in action were few and there can be no doubt that when the flag was flown from the church tower and bells rang out on 11th November 1918 there were many glad hearts. Welcome home parties were held, but only after a certain amount of argument and in the formation of two separate committes, and were enjoyed by all who were present.

With the end of the war and the return of the men to the village the mumblings for new houses began again and although there was constant agitation during the 1920s it had little effect, as the local councils, parish and district, did not appear to be giving the needs of the villagers in this direction any priority whatsoever. The anxieties of the villagers manifested themselves at the Parish Council election on 11th March 1931 when 10 nomination papers were handed in for the seven seats. At the subsequent election over half of the sitting members were defeated, even though 8 council houses at Emlet had just been completed; the villagers felt that the number built was far from enough for the needs of the inhabitants.

The whole matter exploded into the open a couple of years later in the pages of the press when Mr Wyatt Paul stated that he had great objections to selling any land in the centre of the village and, if forced, would consider placing the village in the hands of an auctioneer for sale. He went on to say that if the Council (i.e. Sherborne Rural District Council) wanted to build houses for Yeovil they could build them on the outskirts of the parish on the Babylon Hill road.

The threat to sell the village may well have been quite serious as quite apart from being the major landowner in the parish, he also owned farms at Cattistock, Hassocks (Sussex) and Brighton, so his farming activities in the parish were by no means his only source of income. But the Sherborne Rural District Council was under pressure from many directions to provide more dwelling houses as a letter from Bradford Abbas Mothers' Union clearly indicated: 'We, of the Mothers' Union, feel that the present overcrowding and the number of couples unable to marry in consequence of the shortage of houses is a serious blot against the administration.'

Quite apart from the village organisations, who were bringing pressure to bear, the passions of many individual villagers were also aroused and they were far better educated than their ancestors and not afraid of answering back even to the Lord of the Manor himself. One parishioner, describing himself as 'Evictus' aptly summed up the problem and the feelings of the villagers in a letter to a local newspaper:

'In your last week's issue I noticed a reference to the landowner of Bradford Abbas threatening to put the village up for sale if he were forced to sell some small portions (not quite two acres) of his land for building purposes. When one considers that nearly twenty applications have been made to the Bradford Abbas Parish Council and many of these from persons living in the village, it is about time the Council asserted their powers to compel the sale of sites and build houses for people who are inadequately accommodated in rooms and old fashioned houses at exhorbitant rents, which to say the least do not come up to modern standards of rural housing. The gibe that it would mean 'building' for 'Yeovil' can be met with the rejoiner how many from Bradford Abbas are living in houses provided by Yeovil Council. Anyone knowing the proposed building fields cannot but think that the tenants of those would not be inconvenienced, by having to give them up. As the Parish Council would have the electing of the tenants for the new houses and nearly all would be Bradford Abbas folk, a more convenient site to be near their own people instead of, as if proposed, living in the wilds of Babylon Hill would be more appropriate. The Rural Council should not be intimidated with threats about selling the village and flimsy excuses about accommodation letting of land but boldly pursue a policy of getting better homes for a rural community who are in urgent need of them.'

When this letter was written the 8 houses in Emlet had already been built, and these were shortly to be followed by the four in North Street and a further six in Westbury, with a further six planned but not proceeded with, due to the outbreak of the Second World War.

It would be easy to condemn the Rural District Council and to say that it was slow in building houses but the facts are that apart from the difficulties of obtaining the land and the necessary finance, the question of the water supply was another major obstacle. There was no mains water supply at this time and most of the water came from wells and more often than not was found to be unsuitable for human consumption. There were particular problems with the Emlet houses which took a long time to resolve and many private houses in the parish were also from time to time advised to boil their water before using it. The inadequacy of the supplies manifested itself in a terrible way in late 1935 and early 1936 with the death of a young girl, Sybil Elsie Gosney, aged 7. An enquiry was held as a result of a personal investigation by the County Medical Officer of Health into a mysterious throat malady which had affected nearly 40 residents of Bradford Abbas. Sybil had been ill for only two days when she died. It was therefore reported in the press on 6th December 1935:

'A family of five all in the neighbouring hamlet of Wyke and two further cases were reported there yesterday. Five patients have been sent to hospital and two from Bradford Abbas. Mr W. Patch, Postmaster of Bradford Abbas, and a Parish Councillor told me today: "The villagers are demanding an enquiry into the existing conditions and water supply. Many of our wells have not been cleaned within the living memory."'

The school was closed on 9th December 1935 as was the village hall, but worse was to follow with the deaths of two other children, Doreen Rand and Victor Chant, reported in the local newspaper:

'Grey mist overhung the village on Friday and accentuated the note of sadness caused by the funerals of two children in the afternoon at St Mary's Church. The school children were absent from each, as it had been considered advisable to avoid any gathering of children.'

The Medical Officer of Health made a statement in which he said:

' "For the past few weeks there has been an epidemic of sore throats affecting the children of Bradford Abbas. There have been in all about twelve cases with two deaths.

' "Bacteriological investigation proved that the disease was Vincents Angina, a malady of the throat. Investigation showed that the cause of the spread was the proximity of the children at school and that the disease was spread through the agency of the school. Suitable measures have been taken to disinfect the school which has been closed and will remain closed until the epidemic is safely in hand.

' "It is anticipated that the epidemic may last for another week or so, but now that the school, the Sunday School and the Village Hall are closed and the parents of children have been advised to keep their families to themselves, it is not thought the further extension will be a grave one.

' "The disease is no way mysterious nor is it anything like as widespread as might be imagined from the reports furnished by other sources. With regard to the suggestion that on the whole this is caused by diphtheria, bacteriological examination has shown that while diphtheria has been present in 2 or 3 of the throats the real dangerous element of the complaint was the organism of Vincent; and the diphtheria is not regarded as the really dangerous element."

Eventually the disease abated, the school reopened and village life returned to normal but the problems of the village water supply did raise its head from time to time and was eventually to result in the school being closed again shortly after the end of the Second World War.

In 1939 the world was at war again so the question of more houses being built in the village was shelved and the villagers turned their minds to the problems the war was to create. As early as 31st March 1938 the village was preparing itself for the conflict which was to come and a talk was given to the Parish Council on what precautions would be necessary and that was followed by a public meeting in the Village Hall when a large number expressed their willingness to act as volunteers for the A.R.P. should war come. When the war did come, the impact was felt in Bradford Abbas within a very few days when about 100 children from St George's Roman Catholic School, Westminster Bridge Road, London, arrived in the village as evacuees. They were billeted with various families and the Village Hall was commandeered for use as a classroom. It is to the credit of the teachers of both schools that there was very little friction, since the school was very overcrowded and the children were basically of two different religions.

Very soon the Rev. G. Kendrick was recording in the Deanery Magazine the names of the men of the village who had left for service in the forces and this was a practice he was to continue throughout the war as well as reading out their names at Evensong on the last Sunday of each month. A local Defence Committee was formed, led by Mr B.C. Forder, and a Home Guard which in the early years was commanded by Mr A. Turnbull, and later by Mr. W. Dunster. The headquarters of the Home Guard were at Ruskin House, where all the stores and equipment were also kept. The Air Raid Precautions squad was initially lead by Mr Turnbull and later by Mr Freddie Mear who was ably assisted by the Vicar. Other positions of importance were as follows:

District Food Officer	Miss M. Henfrey
First Aid Post	Tudor Cottage, Church Road
Billeting Officers	B.C. Forder & Miss M. Henfrey
Rest Centre	Mr R.C. Day

Meticulous records were kept of the manpower in the village and who could do what and even what vehicles etc. were available.

'TRANSPORT

2	Lorries	50 cwt Manor Farm
2	Tractors with trailers	Manor Farm
		Wyke (no lights)
1	Tractor with iron wheels	no use on the road
		Wyke
13	Waggons	7 Manor Farm
		3 Wyke
		3 Mill Farm
8	Carts	Manor Farm
5	Putts	3 Wyke
		2 Mill Farm
18	Horses	10 Manor Farm
		6 Wyke
		2 Mill Farm
2	Light Horses	1 Wyke
		1 T. Patch
2	Delivery Vans (Motor)	T. Patch
		1 Mill Lane
1	Delivery Van (Horse)	T. Patch

20	Motor Cars	Wyatt Paul (2), Forwood (2), Rev. F. Nesbitt, Rev. G. Kendrick, Miss Benson, Miss Henfrey, Messrs F. Purchase, Dawling, Davern, H. Gillham, R.C. Day, Gale, Frampton, Dunster, Weller, Bryant Blackmore.	*Bradford Abbas Home Guard Unit, 1940.*
1	Sidecar	F. Purchase	
1	Motor Bike	R. Loxton	

'TOOLS

Saw & Cross Cut Saws   Manor Farm
Yeoleas
Wyke

Picks, Shovels, Crowbars   Manor Farm
Wyke
Yeoleas

Ladders	Forder (3), Blackmore (2), H. White, Nelson, E. Fowler, Mear, W. Patch, Rev. F. Nesbitt
Rakes	Blackmore, E. Smith, B. Garrett, E. Fowler, F. Gill, Mear, F. Purchase, F. Cox
Stirrup Pumps	Village Hall (2), E. Smith, B. Garrett, Rev. Kendrick, Mear, W. Patch, Rev. Nesbitt, F. Purchase, Forder, D. Purchase.'

In case of emergency the Grange was to be the Emergency Food Distribution Centre and rations were to consist of biscuits, corned beef, soup, condensed milk, tea, sugar, margarine to the total value 6/- per head. The total number of persons to be catered for was 321 and the number of houses was 112.

However, for all the preparations made the village suffered no war damage nor was it even attacked but the siren did sound on several occasions when enemy aircraft were in the vicinity, as the following extract from an old village record shows: 'Due to an air raid alarm the children went into trenches at 9.50 a.m. the all clear sounded at 10.25 a.m.'

The trenches were dug for the children in June but prior village records also show that the School Managers had proposed a scheme for the dispersal of the children in the event of an air raid as follows:

'SCHOOL

Junior Infants	Children under desks, Roman tortoise formation, along south wall.
Senior Infants	As above, but along the north wall.
Juniors	As for Senior Infants

School windows to be covered inside with fine mesh wire netting. Glass above partition to be protected. Stirrup pump considered necessary.

'HALL

All children to leave building, which is constructed of wood. Accommodation as under:

In Mr Samway's building adjoining school garden

N. End Pig Sty, no windows 8½ x 18 feet

Along east wall – std IV – 20 children

S. End Fowl House no windows $9^1/_2$ x 11 feet
Along east wall – boys of Std V, VI, VII – 20 children
Centre of field – Cowstall, double $17^1/_2$ x 20 feet
Along north wall of south part and south wall of north part – Girls of Std V, VI, VII – 30 children
Owing to possibility of nervous disorders amongst children of Std V and upwards separation of sexes considered essential.
The cowstall at present is open to cattle and requires cleaning. Cattle should be prevented from entering in future.
Passage through boundary wall of paddock to be made.
Five buckets with water to be set outside Hall. Stirrup pump desirable.
Other buildings suitable for extra children:

Stable at north end of Mr Samway's yard	20 children
North Stable at Vicarage	10 children
Church Tower end	20 children
Choir stalls	20 children

It was just as well that there were no bombs dropped on Bradford Abbas and that the children were not required to go into the cowstalls or the pig sty, and it was with some relief amongst parents when the trenches were dug and the emergency procedures suggested by the School Managers were not implemented.

Some of the village girls worked on the land as 'Land Girls' and some went to work at Westlands. However even with the help of the Land Girls the local farmer Mr Wyatt Paul still had difficulty in getting in his crops and in 1941 he had to employ children on his farms as the following letter of thanks to the Headmaster indicates.

'Being much indebted to the Education Committee, and yourself, for allowing me to have 33 of the schoolboys and girls for potato picking and not only planning the holiday for so doing but granting another week for those who were employed, I feel led to write you a letter of thanks.

'You will be interested to hear that they worked well under one of my foremen. Without their help there would have been a great part of over 30 acres potatoes still undug. Their help has been a national asset, under present conditions, to what I regard as a national effort in my increase of 50% potatoes and sugar beet with a depleted staff, and the potato section have been overcome [achieved] by the schoolchildren, thus enabling me to get on with the wheat sowing and sugar beets, while the latter will not be delivered even now before the factories close unless more labour is available from somewhere.

'These particulars were added to emphasis how much the help rendered is appreciated by me and the staff.'

It seems, therefore, that just about everybody in the village was 'doing their bit' but as the war progressed and things got a little easier the village began to get back to normal. The last of the evacuees who had arrived in 1939 left on 22nd March 1944 and the Home Guard held its final muster with a little jollification on 9th January 1945, at which thanks were expressed not only to the platoon itself but to the A.R.P. wardens and all others who had been in responsible positions throughout the war years.

With the cessation of the hostilities the men began to return to their homes and welcome home parties were held. But soon the old agitation for more houses begun and it became an issue, if not the main issue of the 1950 election for the Sherborne Rural District Council, which resulted in a comparative newcomer to the village defeating the long-standing member. But he won on a popular theme because what was largely holding up the erection of more houses was once again the inadequate water supply, which had again resulted in the school having to be closed for a considerable period. In his election address, the victor, Mr Percy Pettitt, had said, 'My chief concern is that an adequate water supply be installed as soon as possible, and the facts of the case are that until this is achieved, sanitation and housing cannot possibly be considered.'

The new councillor set about his duties with enthusiasm and not a little skill and he attended not only the normal council meetings but many others outside the district with a view to getting a mains water supply installed. Within two years he was successful. This paved the way for the building of homes but, of course, the necessary land had to be purchased. Mr Pettitt related to me how he went to meet Mr Wyatt Paul to endeavour to obtain land. After much discussion there was no sign of Mr Paul's obstinacy of fifteen years earlier and after having, as farmers are wont to do, described the difficult times through which the farming industry was passing, he agreed to sell part of his field, Emlet, to the Sherborne Rural District Council. This land, upon which Queen's Road is now built, was purchased for the sum of £591 (including £29 for legal expenses). And so by 1953 Queen's Road was built. This was a massive development by

Mr Tom Gosney with his 'fiddle'. He spent his life working on the land and now resides at Ambrose Close.

Bradford Abbas standards and Mr Pettitt had carried out his duties so successfully that 41 local people needing council houses were housed and he had to go outside the village to obtain further tenants in order that all the 52 houses were taken.

In 1954 Mr Wyatt Paul died and his estate was sold by auction at the Digby Hall, Sherborne on 8th July 1954. At this auction many of the villagers took the opportunity to buy their homes, which they had until then been renting. The cottages were not expensive, not even by 1954 standards, nor was the land, but once the auction was completed the village was no longer virtually owned by only one man, but was now broken up into much smaller lots. I suppose if any man could now be called the Lord of the Manor it is Mr Ronnie Loxton who became the largest landowner in the parish, but the death of Wyatt Paul closed a chapter in the history of the village.

From 1960 onwards those who had shown sufficient foresight at the 1954 auction and had purchased land were, with the aid of the rapidly rising values, able to realise their investments at considerable profit, which had the effect of almost trebling the size of the village. In the early 1960s Ambrose Close, South View, Wessex Drive, Cross Roads, Grope Lane and Manor Close estates were built; since that time almost every available plot in the present residential area has had a dwelling house erected upon it. Not too long after this building boom it became necessary to build a new school which was later followed by a new Village Hall and a Sports and Recreational Club.

CHAPTER V
The Vicars, the Villagers and their Church

The Church of St Mary the Virgin lies at the southern end of the parish and is a good and typical example of early fifteenth-century design with some slight traces of earlier work and an early twentieth-century addition. The walls are of local rubble with ashlar and dressing of Ham Hill stone whilst the roofs are leaded, except the chancel, which has stone tiles, and embattled. The present church consists of chancel, nave, north vestry, south vestry, north aisle, south chapel, south porch and west tower. It is undoubtedly the west tower which is the most striking feature of the church and may most easily be described as a Dorset version of the fifteenth-century Somerset style.

However, Bradford Abbas has not always possessed such a beautiful church as it does today for the original church would probably have only been of timber construction as well as being very small. It is not even known for certain when a church was first built in the parish but local legend has it that the earliest church dates back to very shortly after AD 705 when St Aldhelm was appointed Bishop of Sherborne. St Aldhelm was instrumental in the area around Sherborne in encouraging village settlements to have their own churches and there is no reason to believe that he overlooked Bradford Abbas in pursuing his policies. When the first stone building was built is not known but the easternmost wall of the chancel is believed to be twelfth century but this wall has been repointed and repaired on so many occasions that it appears to be no different to any of the other walls. This first stone church would however, have been very small and about the size of the present chancel. It was probably this very small building which was mentioned in a Papal Bull of 1163 by Pope Alexander III who confirmed to Clement, Abbot of Sherborne, 'The Manor and Church at Bradford'. This is the first written record of the

St Mary's Church,
Bradford Abbas.

parish church and except for one very short period when it was in the care of King Edward II the church remained in the ownership of the abbots of Sherborne until the 'Dissolution of the Monasteries' in 1539.

The abbots would have been responsible for the maintenance and enlargement of the church as well as having the power to appoint the vicars. The first recorded vicar of Bradford Abbas was Richard Alewy (or Alewyn) who was instituted on 13th October 1310, but he was certainly not the first vicar of the parish as it is recorded that he obtained the incumbency on the resignation of the previous vicar, who is not named, and it could well be that there were a number of other vicars who served the parish when it is considered that a church was known to have been here since 1163 and possibly as early as 705. Very little is known of Richard Alewy except that he owned some land which was the subject of a dispute some years after he had resigned the living, in 1315, to reside in Somerset. He was succeeded by Henry de Brandeston, who was instituted on 31st January 1316, and was the first of a number of vicars to have a French

background, which was very common in Dorset villages at this time. De Brandeston resigned the living in 1331 and was succeeded by Roger de Fernham who was instituted on 16th June 1331. Then followed William de Pennell (instituted 1337) who in turn was succeeded, or so it is believed by Richard de Killatrum. However, according to the old records Killatrum came into the living upon the 'death of Roger ....' so it is possible that there was in fact another vicar between Pennell and Killatrum. Killatrum, who was instituted in 1348, died the following year and this may be of some significance for 1349 was a year in which the Black Death was prevalent throughout the country and could well have been the cause of Killatrum's death. His successor, John de Mullebron died in 1361 and

The interior of the Church as it is today, looking eastwards.

again his demise could also have been due to the Black Death for in that year the disease was again rife throughout the country.

John de Mullebron was in fact the last vicar to have a Norman background and upon his death William Play took up the living and was to become the longest serving vicar up to this time, for he remained in office until his death in 1399—a total of 38 years. He was succeeded by Edmond Kymerich who was to care for the parishioners' religious needs for the next 21 years until he, like his predecessor, died in office.

The west tower of St Mary's Church.

William Haselgrove took up the living and it was probably during the latter years of his ministry that the idea of rebuilding and enlarging the church was first conceived. The church, as it was at this time, was only the size of the present chancel, but the new church was to be extended to include a nave, south porch, a south chapel and a short north aisle. This work was put under way by William Bradford, Abbot of Sherborne 1436–59 and was continued by his successors John Saunders (whose initials can be seen on a shield in the south chapel) and Peter Rampisham, with the whole scheme being completed in 1485, at about the end of the War of the Roses. After the completion of the first part of the enlargement, it was decided that a west tower should be added which meant that the north aisle had to be extended. When this work was completed the church appeared very much as it does today, with the exception of the north vestry which was not added until 1911.

The most striking feature of the new church was undoubtedly the west tower and it is usually described as a Dorset version of the fifteenth-century Somerset type. It is of three stages and four storeys and its four angles are adorned with octagonal buttresses decreasing in dimension as they ascend to be crowned ultimately with elegantly carved pinnacles. The angle containing the staircase to the belfry and roof is the most prominant and elaborately finished. The buttress containing the staircase is of some interest for on a closer inspection the present buttress appears to have been rebuilt, possibly when the bells were originally installed, as on its western side it meets more or less head on with the east wall of the tower and does not project in the same manner as the other buttresses. It can also be seen that the eastern battlement on the tower wall does not meet up uniformly, and neither does the beading, ornamented with carved roses, which runs around the top storey of the tower.

It may be worth mentioning at this stage that there is some evidence that prior to the building of the west tower, there was a tower on the south side and that the present south vestry was the base of that tower. There is certainly a stair turret in the south-east corner of this vestry. Until recent years there was a fifteenth-century door attached to the entrance to the stair turret with strap hinges but this seems to have disappeared. Towers on the south side were not uncommon in the late fourteenth and early fifteenth century and it could well have been built when the enlargement of the church was commenced and later pulled down when it was decided to build the west tower. I have also read that the present 'priests' porch' was built to give direct access to the vestry from the churchyard to replace an earlier entrance in the west wall of the vestry which would no longer have been of use to priests wishing to enter the vestry without being seen. There are the remains of hinges in the west wall of the vestry which indicate the earlier presence of a door, but the question still remains as to whether there was a south tower and if so, when it was built and when demolished.

What prompted such a large scheme to be undertaken is uncertain but tradition hands it down that the local wool merchants had indicated their willingness to contribute and that the opportunity of obtaining financial assistance encouraged the abbots to loosen their own purse strings. However, William Haselgrove must have only seen the very early beginnings of the enlargement plans for in 1438 he exchanged livings with Richard Engeland, Rector of Corscombe. Richard Engeland was vicar for only one year and upon his resignation Thomas Wotton moved into the parish. He resigned in 1449, to be succeeded by Richard Lymyn, who was instituted on 26th July of the same year. William Larder was instituted on 14th January 1450 and he continued in office until his death in 1463, to be succeeded by Nicolas Kennell who also died in office in 1477. He was succeeded by Thomas Taylour, who for some reason or another, also went under the name of Thomas Cooke but he resigned in 1479 to be followed by Richard Wygynton, who was the encumbent at the time of the completion of the enlargement scheme.

With the exception of the north vestry, the exterior of the church was as it is today, but the interior would have presented a very different spectacle. There were 4 altars (the piscinae still remain) and the roof of the nave was decorated with alternative red and white roses, whilst the main and intermediate beams were painted in the barber's pole style. The roof of the chancel was adorned in blue and dotted with stars. No tie beams or collars were erected to support the roof which was thought unusual and eventually resulted in the roof bending. The walls were plastered and above the screen was an overhanging wooden gallery, above which, on a beam, was the crucifix with the attendant figures of Our Lady and St John. The pews faced north and south and there were also a number of carved and painted angels in the roof, holding either shields or scrolls.

Richard Wygynton only preached in the completed church for two years before he resigned and was succeeded by Thomas Laurence who died in

1494, to be succeeded by Andrew Kerver, instituted on 14th September of the same year. There is no record of what happened to Kerver for the next recorded vicar was Gilbert Style who succeeded to the incumbency in 1526 on the death of Nicholas Ponfold. There is also no record of when Nicholas Ponfold came into the parish. Gilbert Style died in 1529 to be succeeded by John Babcary who resigned in 1538. The reason for Babcary's resignation could well have been political for by this time Henry VIII had moved well away from the Church of Rome, the dissolution of the monasteries was imminent and Sir John Horsey was scheming to obtain possession of the abbots' lands. He was ultimately successful and became patron of Bradford Abbas church the following year. Thomas Maister was instituted as vicar in October 1538 and it has been suggested that he had lived in the village for a number of years before taking the living. This may well be true as a Thomas Maister certainly appears in the Tudor Subsidy roll of 1524.

During the early years of Maister's ministry the crucifix in the church, together with its attendant figures, was removed to be replaced later by a royal coat of arms, which unfortunately no longer survives. It is also known from a report made by the Dorset Commissioners that the church possessed:-

'First iij chalices of silver
j pair of vestments
j cope of crimieson velvet
j peyre of vestments whereof one is of sylk. The rest of dorneck
ij old copes
iij alter clothes of dyaper j of locorum
I ten one hundred of led in weight
Half a hundred of candelstyck metal
v belles in the tower
viij fowelles
ij corporas
iij corporae clothes
The church use: apoyneted by the said commisseners the worst chalice,
I cope of crymeson velvet with all the tables clothes and surplesis, the rest comytted to the charge of them under uryten.
Thomas Maister, Vicar
John Somer

Nycholas Syller Churchwardens
John Garrett
Lyonnel Frances William Doynyell—Parishioners'

John Somer & Nicholas Syller are the earliest recorded churchwardens and this return by the Dorset Commissioners is also interesting for the fact that they mention that the church had 'v belles in the tower'. It is doubtful, however, if any of these five bells survive. There are, at present, seven bells in the tower encased in an old wooden frame, the details of which are:-

INSCRIPTION	DIAMETER	WEIGHT	NOTE
W & C Powell, bell founder Cullompton 1832	2' 6"	5. 1. 6.	D
My sound is good my shape is neate Twes Kingston cast me o complete	2' 8"	6. 0. 10	C
Save the Lord 1783	2' 9"	6. 3. 15	B
Rev. Robert Grant, J. Custard W. Arnold, Wardens 1832	2' 11½"	8. 1. 1.	A
G.M.I.T. C.W.T.P., Anno Domini 1665 J.G. Vassall Col. C. Duff, H. Warr Churchwardens	3' 4"	10. 1. 6.	G
Robert Grant, Vicar J.J. Newman, J. Vincent, Churchwardens AD 1859	3' 7"	13. 2. 21	F

The seventh bell, which is above the others, is only 17 inches in diameter and 13½ inches high. It has a jumbling of letters on all sides of it and was recast by Messrs Gilbert & Co., Croydon 1889.

It was during the period of Maister's incumbency that the first entries were made in the church registers:

'17th April 1572   BURIAL of William Vincent
14th May 1572   BAPTISM George, sonne of John
                Parsons
19th September 1572   MARRIAGE John Adams &
                Elizabeth Barrett'

In later years it appears that a curate, John Chaunte, was employed for the registers are regularly signed with his name.

In 1585 the Rev. Masters (the 'i' had now been dropped from his name) resigned and went to live at Chilton Cantelo in Somerset where he died. In his will, dated 21st January 1585, it was evident that he did not forget the village he had served for so long and several interesting items appear:

'I give to the parish church of Bradford Abbas tenne shillings
I also give to the poore folke the said parish of Bradford Abbas thirteen shillings
I give to the prisoners of the gails at Jerchester (Dorchester or Ilchester) three shillings forepence.

'Codicil—To the daughters of Thomas Masters I give four bushelles of beans, four bushelles of bread, four bushelles of pulse. To the poore of Yeovil I give tenne shillings and sixpence. I give George Masters one bedestead at the vicarage at Bradford.'

Following the departure of Masters, George Punfold was instituted in June 1585. He was vicar of the parish for 48 years and was most likely to have been the first vicar to have preached from the Jacobean pulpit which is in the church today for it is dated 1632 and carries the initial PGRM. He died in 1633 and is believed to have been the first vicar to have been buried in the village churchyard.

From the death of Punfold the succession of vicars becomes very confused. In 1643 it is recorded that George Stirr (or Sterr), vicar of Bradford Abbas, was buried in the churchyard, and his name also appears on the Protestation Return for 1641, which he did not sign as it says that he was living in Somerset at the time, and from further researches I have found that he was an absentee vicar who was employing a curate, John Penney. It is therefore reasonable to assume that he succeeded Punfold, but

The pulpit in St Mary's Church. It bears the date 1623.

there are doubts as to who succeeded Stirr. From a minute of the Dorset Standing Committee of 26th April 1648, Mr Pullham seems a likely candidate:

'It is considered that Martin Kellway and George Ring do sequester, gather and collect all the tythes and profits of the vicarage of Glasen Bradford in this county, lately belonging to Mr Pullham, clerke (a delinquent), late vicar of that parish, and at the same time to pay unto such orthodox and able minister as they shall pain to officiate in the church of the said parish, the sum of 20s per sabbeth, and to give an account of the remainder thereof unto this committee when they shall be thereunto required; and it is further ordered that William Lovelidge, the present curate there sett to officiate by the said Mr Pullham forebeare to officiate any longer in that church as he will answer the contrary at his peril.'

Within a very few months it was to become apparent why the Standing Committee did not wish William Lovelidge to officiate in Bradford Abbas church, for a minute of that committee on 14th June 1648 states that charges laid against him will be heard a week later and indeed, on 21st June another minute records:

'Upon a full hearing and debate of the charge of scandal against Mr William Lovelidge, clerke, vicar of Glasen Bradford in this county, this committee do judge him sequestrable by ordinance of parliament for drunkeness and ale house haunting which was proved against him by sufficient witnesses heard via voce, [who] therefore do out him of his vicarage.'

The Standing Committee also saw fit, later the same year, to resolve that Mrs Lovelidge 'shall have and receive the full gifts of all the tythes and profits of the vicarage of Glasen Bradford' and yet another minute, dated 27th November 1648, relates:

'Upon the petition of Magdelen Lovelidge, wife of William Lovelidge, clerke, it is order that the said Magdelen shall receive 8li yearly out of the vicarage of Glasen Bradford for the gifts and profits thereof, assigned to her by a former order of 21st June last for maintenance of herself and children, which so sum of 8li from the said 21st June, according to the ordinance of parliament, by Robert Pittman, who is authorised to sequester and receive the profits of the said church and to give account to this committee of the remainder, when he shall thereto be required. And whereas we are informed there was tythe wool due to Mr Lovelidge at the time when he was ousted of the said vicarage, it is further ordered that the said Pittman shall have authority to demand and gather the woole so due as aforesaid and deliver the same or the value thereof unto the said Magdelen Lovelidge as is ordered.'

It is quite possible that with the removal of William Lovelidge the parish did not have a resident vicar for a number of years and there is no record of Robert Pittman being formally instituted although he was obviously carrying out the normal duties of a vicar and reaping the rewards, but it is also possible that during these troubled times the spiritual affairs of the parish were carried on by lay readers. It is also believed that it was about this time, when the Civil War was at its height that the fine preaching cross which stands a little to the west of the church was badly mutilated by Cromwell's troops. It was from the steps of this cross that travelling friars would have preached to the parishioners. In *The Stone Crosses of Dorset* by Pope a detailed description of the cross is given:

'The very fine perpendicular Cross, the remains of which now stand some 18 feet from the north west buttress of the tower, was probably built about the same time as the church, 1484. It is of the same stone as the church viz:-
Freestone from Ham Hill below Yeovil and is in a very fair state of preservation. It is constructed as an octagonal plan with a calvary of two steps. A massive socket and 7 feet six inches remain of the original handsome shaft. On the west face of the shaft is a niched and canopied male figure, 2 feet 4 inches in height,

The late fifteenth-century preaching cross in St Mary's churchyard. Friars used to preach to the local residents from the steps of this cross. It was badly defaced during the English Civil War, 1642–9.

standing in a corbel and much defaced, but sufficient is left of the clothing to favour the conjecture that it may well be of St John the Baptist.

'On the east face a female canopied figure, possible that of the Virgin Mary, to whom the church is dedicated and on the north and south sides are indications of crocheting and the fixing of other figures.

'The shaft is beaded into the notice which is 15 inches square. The socket which is cut from a solid block of stone, set up on a deep moulded plinth, 4 feet 4 inches square, is octagonal on its upper bed, squared by four angled shafts with caps and bases, on the tops of which may be seen the iron davels of which the figures or ornaments were fixed to the shaft. On the four sides of the socket are sculptured panels, on the west side a quartrefoil with a rose in the centre, and on the north and south sides are quartrefoils with blank shields in their centres. It has a good moulded weather drip. The basement, which is octagonal and measures 4 feet on each face and 1 foot 9 inches in height, has a deep projecting weather drip and a good set off.

'It is faced with solid worked stone, but is much worn and out of repair. The step which stands on the basement and supports the socket is also octagonal measuring 30 inches on each face and is 20 inches deep; it has a good moulded weather drip, with a fillet and a deep plinth.

'This cross, which must have formed a very beautiful and striking object is of the same type as those at Stalbridge and Rampisham and was doubtless erected about the same date.'

It has also been suggested that Cromwell's men were responsible for removing the statues from the niches on the west side of the tower. Two of these niches are at present occupied; one showing a figure wearing what appears to be a doctor's cap and dressed in a rich lace mantle down to his feet, and the other a figure similarly dressed but holding a book. I believe that the Roundheads are wrongly blamed as it seems more than likely that the other niches were never filled and the absence of corbels tends to support this view.

It was not until 1660 that Robert Butt was formally instituted as vicar although it is most likely that he was regularly officiating for some time before his institution as he was already signing the registers two years earlier. Robert Butt died in 1669 to be succeeded by Charles White, who has the distinction of being the longest ever serving vicar (64 years). It was during the early years of the Rev. White's ministry that the Monmouth rebellion took place. Three people left the village to take part in this

The figures in the niches on the west wall of the tower.

rebellion. One, on the side of James I, died of wounds received in the service of the king and his body was returned to the village where a floor slab in the chancel commemorates his death. The other two joined the rebels and it is not known what happened to them.

Rev. White was also the last vicar of Bradford Abbas not to hold the Rectorship of the adjoining parish of Clifton Maubank, for when he died in 1733, he was succeeded by Rev William Preston, who was already Rector of Clifton Maubank and he administered the two parishes, as is still the case today. According to his tombstone, now disappeared, the Rev Preston 'had a just sense of virtue, the alone source of sterling glory. His such was a faithful mirror of the duties of his spiritual successors. To throw his character into miniature he was a uniform comformist to the religion of nature, and the established religion of Jesus.'

The Rev. William Preston, who died on 11th April 1742, aged 73, is however, best remembered for the founding of a charity school in 1738 when he gave some lands at Nether Compton, Dorset, for the support of a charity school and his benevolence is commemorated on a stone plaque at the base of the tower. Unfortunately the plaque cannot be seen due to the siting of the organ.

Preston was succeeded by Thomas Paget who was a Fellow of Corpus Christi College, Oxford, Rector of Poyntington and Headmaster of Sherborne School for Boys—as well as being a proctor. He was a close friend of John Wesley and although he was bound to celibacy by his fellowship he had, while at Oxford, secretly married 'the daughter of an alehouse keeper in a place called Magpye Lane' and raised a large family before being asked by the college authorities to resign. When this scene was exposed he was obliged to seek haven with his father who ordered that his family should be brought from Oxford to Poyntington, Dorset, in a wagon which was sent for the purpose. Paget settled at Poyntington where he started up a private school which was quite successful. He was appointed Headmaster of Sherborne School a year after taking up his duties as vicar of Bradford Abbas, leaving a son to run his private school. There is no doubt that he preferred his scholastic duties to his priestly ones and it was rumoured that he was diverting boys from Sherborne School to his own private school. It is likely, therefore, that Bradford Abbas saw very little of him which was probably just as well for he was not a popular man and was described by one of his contemporaries in unfavourable terms.

'It is certain there was a collegian, pedantic stiffness or affected stateliness in his deportment which, as a schoolmaster, excited an awlful deference from his pupils, but as a member of society rendered him rather disagreeable appearing in the garb of spiritual pride.'

Thomas Paget resigned as vicar in 1751 and gave up his scholastic duties in the same year whereupon he became vicar of Mells, Somerset, where he remained for the next 32 years until he died, at the age of 78, in 1783, and an elegant white monument was erected in his memory in Mells parish church.

Narcissus Whittaker, a former vicar of Fifehead Magna, was Paget's successor but he died in 1767 to be succeeded by Conyers Place, who at the time of his institution on 21st March of the same year was already Rector of Marnhull. He owned property in London and other parts of the country and was really an absentee vicar. When he died in April 1778 (it is thought of small pox) he was buried at Marnhull. He was succeeded by Edward Matthew West who was the great grandson of Peter Walter of Stalbridge who had ousted the Harvey's from Clifton Maubank. He was not an absentee vicar but it was during the period of his incumbency that, due to him failing to appoint a headmaster of the school founded by Rev. William Preston, two parishioners, Mark West and William Read, invested monies in the 4% Annuities of 1777, and thereby founded a second charity school in the village which was to cause many difficulties in the future. There is a plaque at the base of the tower commemorating the foundation of this school but again it cannot be seen due to the position of the organ. One of Rev. West's sons was buried at Bradford Abbas while another son, Henry, distinguished himself at the Battle of Trafalgar 1805, where he was wounded but later received a gold medal and 50 guineas from the Committee for the management of the patriotic fund. Edward West was 62 when he died and was buried at Bradford Abbas and in the following year his wife was laid to rest alongside him.

He was succeeded by someone I have seen described as 'a bird of passage', Edward Smedley, who it seems employed a curate throughout the whole period of his incumbency. The curate appears to have officiated at all services except weddings which the vicar always conducted himself. He died in 1825 and was succeeded by David Williams who had previously been an usher at Sherborne School for Boys where he had been summoned by the Governors and rebuked for 'undue severity towards the boys in the foundation'. He was very much an absentee and, like his immediate predecessor, he also employed a curate, Edward Walter West, throughout the whole term of his incumbency and even then, services were only held every other Sunday as on the other Sundays the curate was preaching in another parish.

In 1824 an Act of Parliament was passed in which the two parishes of Bradford Abbas and Clifton Maubank were to be officially united and which confirmed a situation which had existed for all practical purposes since 1733. This act also provided for the building of a new vicarage house to be erected in Bradford Abbas, the materials for which were to come from the old rectory at Clifton Maubank which was to be demolished, and also for the occupier of Manor Farm, Bradford Abbas, to be responsible for the repairs to the chancel in the church, a situation which still exists to this day. The erection of a new vicarage meant that St Mary's House, which was the vicarage, reverted to being a farmhouse and the new vicars were to reside in what is not quite correctly called the Old Rectory.

In 1828 Rev. David Williams resigned to be succeeded by the Rev Robert Grant who was instituted on 15th May 1828 but who did not, in fact, conduct his first service in the church until June 1829. During this period the curate, Rev. Edward Walter West, continued to care for the spiritual welfare of the parish, the delay in the Rev. Grant's arrival being due to the new vicarage house not having been completed. The Rev Robert Grant, who was born in 1796, was ordained deacon in 1819 and a priest in 1829, by the Bishop of Oxford. He was a BCL of Oxford and a Fellow of Winchester College. His first incumbency was at St Paul's, Southsea where it was said he was 'greatly beloved by members of his congregation'. He was to retain the living for 58 years.

On taking up his duties, however, the Rev. Grant found that the religious life of the parish was not at all to his liking. The church was in a dilapidated condition and the sittings appropriated to the poor were rotten and could not be used in wet weather, resulting in small attendances at services. But the church building was not the only thing in a state of disrepair; the religious outlook of many of the parishioners was also in need of attention. As I have mentioned, the previous vicar had employed a curate who, says the Rev. Grant, 'was a faithful servant of the heavenly father and discharged the duties of his calling according to his ability, but although he was armed with two swords, the ministerial and the magisterial, he exercised little or no influence.'

It comes as no surprise, therefore, to learn that the Rev. Grant encountered difficulties in his dealings with certain sections of the community, the first such difficulty arising when he claimed his right to be the chairman of the vestry meetings, which resulted in him dethroning the previous chairman who had only gained that position through the curate not discharging his duties correctly. He also found, quite obviously to his disgust, that there were a large number of dissenters, who he says were 'not violent or bitter' but did attend a chapel rather than a church, although there were some who attended both, as the services in both establishments were arranged so as not to clash. The chapel referred to was pulled down in the mid-nineteenth century whereupon services were held in a cottage. However, it is quite obvious that he was far from happy with the position for he wrote:

'In small rural parishes, dissent is far from being an unmixed good. Even a faithful and zealous clergyman finds it an obstruction to his ministerial influence and usefulness . . .

'The system on which I have all along acted is this—to consider every inhabitant of the parish as part and parcel of the flock of which I am the regularly constituted pastor. Even with respect to those who do not avail themselves of the ministrations of our church I consider that they are still under my pastoral charge. I have never denounced dissent, still less dissenters personally, from the pulpit. I have only denounced error in doctrine and in practice.'

But probably the greatest resistance came from the bellringers, who it seemed had become almost a law unto themselves.

'The ringers in my parish had been accustomed, I believe, to no control whatever, when the curate who was my predecessor went out of the parish, his place was supplied by the ringers, who used to ring the bells. Drinking and smoking took place in the belfry. On one occasion, after the celebration of a marriage, I requested the ringers to ring only one short peal as the noise of the bells was very stunning, the church being near to the old vicarage house, the mistress of which had been recently confined and was seriously ill, having lost her infant. This they promised to do. They rang one peal though not a short one. To my surprise and dismay, about noon, the bells struck out again which greatly disturbed the invalid. I was in the act of preparing a sermon and I rushed out, pen in hand, and ordered them to stop immediately. This, however, they did not do, chiefly I believe, because when the bells are in full swing they can only be stopped gradually. As soon as they were still I spoke to them strongly, reproved them for having broken their word and for having behaved disrespectfully towards me, and unfeelingly towards one who was most near and dear to me. The first person who broke the silence was W.C. who was a sort of spokesman for the rest who said I had a right to only one bell, a tinker, which was the Clergyman's bell, which was rung by himself when he entered the churchyard immediately before the service and that the rest of the bells belonged to the parish, suiting his action to his word he added, "That is your end of the church where the pulpit is and this is ours." Although my spirit was stirred, I was able to control my temper and said, "Oh, that is the law is it, I shall call you the village lawyer," which caused a titter among the rest. "Now I will tell you what the law is. This church and churchyard is my freehold as parson of the parish, and no one has a right to be here, except for the purpose of religious worship, as for the performance of other religious duties. And to show you that I have the right and authority on my side I order you all to quit the belfry immediately." I spoke firmly and I dare say I looked as one having authority, and after taking down all their names and telling them that they should not ring again until they asked my pardon, with my pen in my hand I made them all quit the belfry. I drew up a set of rules, which I subjoin for the benefit of any of my brethren in the ministry who may read these pages, and which I required them to sign before the bells were rung.

'RULES TO BE OBSERVED BY THE RINGERS
1. The Ringers to be chosen and appointed by the Vicar and Churchwardens.
2. Leave is always to be asked of the Vicar, or in his absence of the Churchwardens for the bells to be rung, when a written order to the sexton will be given without which he is not to let the belfry door be opened.
3. On two evenings a week the bells may be rung. No peal to begin after nine oclock.
4. No drinking or smoking to be allowed in the belfry or churchyard.
5. The bells are not to ring on a Sunday evening or when a corpse is lying in the parish. Some of the ringers will be required to chime for the services on Sundays. These rules to be signed by the ringers.

I had hoped that matters would go on smoothly and pleasantly but I was disappointed. A custom obtains in this, as in most other parishes viz: to ring out the old, and ring in the new year at midnight. They were not required to ask permission to do this. On the following morning, at noon, whilst visiting a dying person, I was much surprised and annoyed at hearing the bells ringing. I accordingly went to the Churchwarden, who was a respectable and well conducted person, and popular in the parish, and requested him to accompany me to the belfry, which he willingly did. On arriving there I found that the door was bolted inside, whilst the key had been left in the door outside. I, as well as the Churchwarden, ordered them immediately to leave off ringing and to open the door, upon which one of them said "If you will allow us to ring another peal we will." I replied "I make no terms with rebels. If you do not open the door within five minutes, I will have every one of you put in the Ec-cle-si-as-ti-cal Court," making the word as long as I could. I added "Although you have bolted us out, I have locked you in." After a few minutes the door was unbolted, and we went in.

In order to show them I was not afraid of them I bolted the door and took out my pocket book to write down their names. The first person to whom I addressed the question "Why did you not open the door when we ordered you?" replied "I did not know it was your voice" I replied "I can almost believe that, for you never come to church." This repartee caused a laugh at the man's expense from the rest of the party and then I said "If any other man in this belfry will have the effrontery to say the same I promise you I will take no further notice of the matter." No one however, did. The first person who addressed me reminded me that when I first came into the parish I told him that I was fond of bell ringing. I said it was quite true and that I was still fond of it, at the proper time.

'The result was that I forbade them to ring for six months. They all signed a paper expressing their sorrow for their conduct. The fact is, it was a trial of strength and by blending firmness with good nature I established my authority and the ringers have given me no further trouble.'

Having won this 'eyeball to eyeball' confrontation with the ringers the Rev. Grant's relationship with his parishioners improved and he was able to advise the Bishop of Salisbury, 'I am living on excellent terms with the respectable and influential persons in the parish as indeed I am with all parishioners.'

In 1830 the Rev. Grant was married and his new bride came to live in the parish. On 4th November 1832 his first child, Robert George was born, followed by other children in quick succession, Edward, Fanny, Emily, Louisa and Augustus. Robert his eldest son died on 12th April 1835 but on 17th May 1840 his wife, Frances Mary, also died, leaving the Rev. Grant a widower, which he was to remain, to bring up a young family. This was a terrible shock to the Rev. Grant but it is to his credit that at this time of his own personal suffering he did not neglect the needs of the parishioners. Of course, he was more affluent than most others in the village and in 1841 was employing five servants but nevertheless it must have been a very difficult time for him. His wife was buried in St Mary's Churchyard where 47 years later he was to be buried alongside her.

There was, however, work to be done in the church and a board that used to be in the vestry intimates that the church was 'renewed' in the year 1842, as a result of a grant from the Incorporated Society for Promoting the Englargement, Building and Repairing of Church and Chapels, resulting in 183 additional sittings; 172 of these were declared to be free, and unappropriated forever.

In 1853, the restoration of the chancel was considered necessary in order to obtain a greater uniformity and increased accommodation. As a result, the wall above the screen which divides the chancel from the nave was removed and the existing chancel arch removed. The walls were also scraped, thereby removing several coats of yellow wash and in a few places the remnants of red and green paint. The circular altar rails were replaced by parallel bars which stood in front of the Harvey monuments on the north and south walls of the chancel, and two large square pews which also stood in the chancel were taken away. These were replaced by long low pews. Being in the chancel, the Lord of the Manor, Mr William Clayton Clayton, in a letter dated 7th April 1858 made it quite clear that these were to be under his control.

'To prevent any misunderstanding hereafter I wish to state that I shall consider the new pews in the chancel, Bradford Abbas Church, as exclusively subject to my disposition and that the incumbent and churchwardens shall not have any power over same. On this condition only I allow them to be erected.'

The Old Rectory, formerly The Vicarage.

It was hoped to carry out more work on the church at this time but due to lack of funds this was not possible, even though the building was in far from good condition, and it was only seven years later that more maintenance work became a matter of urgent necessity. The roof badly needed strengthening and some new timbers were inserted, whilst at the same time the gallery at the west was removed and the pillars scraped of numerous coats of whitewash. The pews were altered so as to face the east and the doors on the pews in the chancel were removed. The walls were scraped of mortar and stuccoed, whilst the organ which had previously been at the west end was moved to the north corner of the north aisle.

I have not been able to determine with any degree of accuracy when the church first came into possession of an organ but I would think that it must have only been a few years prior to 1865, as this was the year that the

St Mary's Church, c.1880. The figure in the top hat is believed to be Henry Arnold, at one time the oldest parish clerk in England.

gallery was removed as it was felt that it was no longer of any practical use now that the church orchestra, who used the gallery, had been disbanded with the advent of the organ. The last leader of the orchestra, Henry Arnold, was, at this time a comparatively young man and quite remarkable, devoting virtually all his life to the welfare of Bradford Abbas church. He was a shoemaker by trade, with a shop in the village, and he had first become associated with the church in 1815, when at the age of eight he became a member of the church choir, and with the exception of two years, 1830 and 1831, which he spent in London, he was continually with the church until his death in 1902 at the age of ninety-five. At one time in his life it was his proud boast that he had missed only seven services in forty-five years, and at the time of his death he held the unique distinction of being the oldest parish clerk in England. He in fact served as parish clerk for a record seventy years, and until a few months before his death he was still energetic enough to think little of walking to Yeovil once or twice a week, usually attired in top hat and frock coat. For visitors to the church he was a mine of information and when he went to his maker, Bradford Abbas lost a good and loyal friend.

In 1857, or thereabouts, the Rev. Grant, employed a curate and so less was seen of him in the village than in the early years of his incumbency. The first curate which he employed was his own son, The Rev. Edward Pierce Grant who was later to become the vicar of Portsmouth and he was to be succeeded by the Revs. F. Salmon, C. Neal, C.F. Powys, D.C. Miller, and J.W. Valentine, who was still curate when the Rev. Grant resigned the living in 1886. The Rev. C.F. Powys was of particular interest for he was a brother to the famous Powys, the west country author, who later went on to become vicar of Montacute where he was buried on his death. Shortly before he left the parish, the Rev. C.F. Powys married. He was presented with a 12-inch silver salver, suitably inscribed as it was said that his pastoral care was much appreciated, and when he returned from his honeymoon the village, including the school, took a holiday. It was reported at the time that 'everybody appears to be looking at the arches, flags etc., which have been erected to welcome the Rev. C.F. Powys and his bride'.

It was during the Rev. Grant's incumbency that the railway was built through the village and his relationship with the navvies makes interesting reading.

'In the year 1860, the Salisbury and Yeovil Railway which intersects my parish was commenced. About 100 navvies were employed in the formation of it between Sherborne & Yeovil, a large proportion of whom resided in the village. At the same time the Great Western was working their line from Yeovil to Weymouth. As there was a large number of men employed, a meeting was held in Yeovil, and a subscription entered into, for obtaining services of a scripture reader. The first that was appointed was the son of a clergyman. Upon his entering on his duties in my parish, he reported to me that his reception was anything but favourable; that the navvies would not listen to him, because he was a parson and was in their opinion, a white clover. He assured them that he was not a clergyman, although he was the son of one. I recommended him to wear a black choker which he did and they then listened to him. I had not hitherto any experience whatever with this peculiar class of labourers. When they were working on that part of the line which was very near to the vicarage house, I used to meet them going to and returning from their work, when a mutual greeting took place. A large number of them, when they ceased from their work for their midday meal, would sit under the wall which enclosed the vicarage premises. On these occasions I would speak to them in a kindly way, and distributed tracts, which they almost to a man received. I also gave them permission to draw water to supply their tin cans from my pump instead of going to the river for that purpose. I also wrote a few letters for some who could not write. On becoming more acquainted with them I spoke to them about their religious state, but at first without any encouragement from them. On one occasion when I was walking on the ridge of a deep cutting, I heard one of the gang pointing me out as the parson; upon which one of his mates said "I was not wanted," or words to that effect, "as there was no heaven or hell". I mentioned this to the scripture reader who had succeeded the first, and who was more suitable and acceptable to the navvies, in as much as he was not so well-bred and educated as the former one. He was an Irishman and had been a Roman Catholic but had been brought to see the cross of that Church and had renounced them. He had been evidently accustomed to argue, and was not only sharp-witted, but possessed also an excellent temper as well as a quiet humour. He informed me one day that on reading to them, when they were resting from their work, one of them, probably the individual whom I overheard to say that there was no heaven or hell, made the same statement. On which, the scripture reader challenged him to a discussion on the point, which was agreed to. What the arguments were which the scripture reader produced I know not, but the result was that, in the judgement of the navvies who acted as umpires, he obtained a complete victory over his opponent who failing to overcome him by fair words proceeded to threaten him with violence, a sure sign of a bad cause. This, however, the other navvies, much to their credit, would not permit. They said he had been fairly beaten, and protected the vicar from any rough treatment.

'On one occasion, on a Saturday afternoon, when they were paid their wages, as I was walking through the village, I met a female relative who was staying with me, walking in great haste, who asked me to give her my arm, as a large number of the navvies were coming down the street, which rather alarmed her. On my escorting her, a huge fellow came up to me and seized me by the arm. Some bystanders explained, "That's the Parson." "I knew it" he said, "I'm not going to hurt him." Although I felt a little uncomfortable from being in the grip of such a powerful man, I quietly said "Well my friend, what do you want." He replied "I shall come and see you tomorrow", meaning I suppose that he would come to church. "You must not come in this trim" I said, partly alluding to his dress and partly to his manner, which impressed me with the idea that he had been drinking, although he was not intoxicated, "go home and put yourself to rights." He walked on with us still holding me tight by the arm. After a little time he released me from his grasp. He did not, however, fulfil his promise of coming to see me the next day. After he had left I spoke to another navvy who was standing at his door and asked him what his name was. A very unwise question, this, by the way, for not a few, it may be suspected, having left their native place, some of whom have fled from justice and others have deserted their wives and children. Unquestionably, as a body, they have got a bad name. But I am bound to say, that during the time they were living in my parish, there were no unusual depredations committed, although there was a large amount of immorality. Very few remain for any length of time in one and the same place. "I am not going to tell you my name" was the man's reply. "Well" I said, "I really do not want to know your name but I asked the question merely to get into conversation with you." I then asked him what was nearly as unwise a question, where he came from? At first he demurred to answer it. Presently he said, "Do you know where Hampshire is?" "I ought to" I replied, "for I lived for many years, particularly the early part of my life, in that county." He then commenced a sort of cross examination. "Do you know where Portsdown Hill is?" "To be sure I do for my father lived very near to it." "Do you know where Cosham is?" "Yes, just at the foot of it." "Well I don't live there when I'm at home. Do you know where Bedhampton is?" "Yes," I said with some feeling "for this lady's father and mother and other relatives lies in Bedhampton Churchyard." We thus got into conversation. I mention this simple circumstance to show that it requires a certain tact and knowledge of human nature, to get on with this particular class of our countrymen. One is more likely, especially a clergyman of whom they seem to be somewhat suspicious and on their guard, to get them to listen to you, particularly on religious subjects by introducing any ordinary topic instead of hugging religion, if I may say so, by neck and shoulders. This remark recalls to my recollection a more affecting instance. It was thought desirable that there should be a Chaplain appointed, as well as the Scripture reader. The Clergyman who was appointed although a conscientious and good man had a shy and awkward manner, and was consequently ill-fitted to deal with such a class of persons. He informed me one day that there was a young man dangerously ill and that on visiting him he evinced no desire for his ministrations, and when he offered to read or pray to him, he civilly declined his offer, and that he had, in consequence, ceased to visit him. Without any presumption, I hope, on my part, I said I would go and see him and try whether I could succeed better than he did. I accordingly went, and found him sitting up, but evidently in a sinking state. He was quite young and of interesting appearance. I had heard from the Chaplain that he bore a very good character, which the persons at whose house he lodged, confirmed. I spoke to him about his bodily health, and as I saw at a glance that he was in a rapid decline, I suggested that he should try what a change of air might do, especially that of his native place, and that if he would consent to go, I added there would be no difficulty about sending him, provided it was not very distant. He told me it was in Sussex. On hearing which, I said that Sussex was a County, the very name of which always sounded very pleasantly in my ears, for my first curacy was in that County. I then told him the name of the Parish, or rather Parishes, for I had charge of two. He said he knew the place well, for they were not far off his own Parish which was Hastings. The ice being broken, we got into conversation; and on asking him about his relatives he said that he had none that he knew of, that he was brought up in the Parish workhouse, although he believed he had a sister in London. Having thus got the ear of the poor fellow, and I may add, won his confidence, for he saw that I was interested about him, I then spoke to him about his soul. He listened to me with seeming interest and I then offered to read to him and to pray for him, which he readily assented to. I then left him and promised to call and see him the next day. Some alarming symptoms, however, manifested themselves in the course of the night and on being asked whether he would wish to see me, he said he would wait till the morning probably from a desire not to disturb my rest; but before the morning he died.

'On the Chaplain resigning his office, I undertook to give the navvies a service on Sunday afternoons, at the 'huts' as they were called, a temporary dwelling on the side of the line. I had previously ascertained that such a service would be acceptable to some of the occupants.

'Accordingly, I went up in my gown, attended by the Scripture reader and by the Clerk of the Parish, who was a good singer. I also took with me some hymn books. From 8 to 12 as far as my memory serves me attended. We first sang a hymn, in which several of the navvies joined, and after offering up a short prayer, I read and expounded some plain and impressive passage of scripture. I concluded by offering up a short prayer. They were very attentive, and after thanking me expressed a hope that I would come again.

'An incident occurred, which may appear almost of too trivial a nature to be mentioned, but I do so to show that however rough in their exterior most of the navvies are, some of them are not devoid of what may be termed good manners, or good breeding. On rising from my knees, after having prayed, as there was no stool, still less, no hassock, the sawdust with which the floor was covered clung to my trousers, which one of the navvies near me wiped off with his slop. I also supplied them with small testaments which the British and Foreign Bible Society had most liberally placed at my disposal, and which after writing their names in them, they thankfully received.

'As the numbers increased and the room was too small to accommodate them, and particularly as the time of the year had become more favourable for holding the meeting in the open air, I did so, and the attendances became larger. One Sunday after I had offered up the opening prayer, I observed two navvies coming towards me from the huts. One of them had a pipe in his mouth. They came close to me, and sat down on a form. The passage of scripture on which I was about to speak was from Matthew XVI 26. "For what is a man profited, if he shall gain the whole world, and lose his own soul" or "what shall a man give in exchange for his soul?"

'I mentioned the different kind of losses to which we are more or less liable, such as the loss of health, which might be restored; the loss of property which might be replaced; the loss of character which might be regained; and the loss of liberty which might be recovered. With respect to the last loss, I said that a man might break the laws of his country and be sent to prison; on which the navvy with the pipe in his mouth said "That's very true, I've been there before now." I was tempted to say "You will go there again if you do not take care", but I restrained my tongue and quietly said "I will thank you not to interrupt me." He kept on muttering something, and I spoke to one or two who were steady men, to try to silence him, or remove him, but they shook their heads. As I proceeded to speak on the loss of the soul in hell he said "That's not in your book". Whether he meant there was no such place as hell I know not. However, as I saw that he was bent on mischief, I closed my Bible, and asked them to join me in prayer, which they all did, with the exception of the disturbing navvy, who was becoming more noisy. After this interruption and especially as the other navvies did not protect me from it, although on speaking to them afterwards they told me they did not interfere, because he was a quarrelsome fellow and there would have been a serious row if they had interfered. In consequence I gave up, I hope not in an improper spirit, holding any more open meetings. Indeed the cold weather was setting in, so I offered to give those who were disposed to come, a short afternoon service in the Church, which several attended, and they behaved very well.

'After the line was finished, and the navvies had dispersed, the Scripture reader showed me a letter which he had received from one of the two navvies who had been mentioned above, written from Kent, and after stating that he had tried to stop his mate, who interrupted me, from attending the service at the huts, he knew he was not in a proper state to do so: he went on to say that the text which Mr G had read, and began to explain, and the short prayer which he offered up were never out of his thoughts and that he hoped he was a converted man; that he read daily the New Testament which I had given to him and that he endeavoured, so far as lay in his power, to make others think and care about their souls. He concluded by desiring to be remembered to me and added that if he ever came to Dorsetshire he would call on me to thank me in person. But I never saw him, or heard anything more of him.'

It was during the period of the Rev. Grant's incumbency that two interesting plaques were unveiled in the church and which can be seen in the north aisle—one commemorates the death of William Clayton Clayton, Captain of the Queen's Royal Lancers who died whilst playing polo in India in 1876 whilst the other, which was unveiled on 15th April 1869, is in memory of Major General George King. It had been given by the officers of the 15th Prince Albert's Light Infantry in which regiment he had served for 33 years. The plaque itself shows the Indian, Crimean and Turkish medals as well as the Legion of Honour, his sword and the regimental badge. It is, however, interesting to learn that this distinguished soldier died at Bradford Abbas due to the mortification of one of his toes, resulting it is believed from cutting a corn too deep. The Rev. Grant became a Canon and for 33 years Rural Dean but he spent the last few years of his life at Southsea, where he eventually died. He had a book of poems *Kapiolani and other poems* published in 1848 which was followed in 1873 by his *Forty years in a Country Parish* which is now an extremely rare book. It was said that he was a proud and pious man, and having read some of his writings I would go as far as to say that he considered himself to be a very superior person.

His successor was to be the Rev. Gordon Bolles Wickham who was to prove to be extremely popular and who was remembered with

The Rev Gordon Wickham, c. 1912.

considerable affection for many years after his death by the parishioners with whom he worked. Rev. Wickham was the eldest son of a Rev. Frederick Wickham, and was educated at New College Oxford, where he gained a Batchelor of Arts degree in 1872 and a Master of Arts Degree in 1873. He had been ordained as a deacon in 1873 and as a priest in 1874. He was the incumbent at Crookham from 1875-83 and when he left that parish he was presented with a handsome oak chair, which contains some seventeenth-century material, and which is now in the chancel of Bradford

Abbas church. From Crookham he became Assistant Commissioner of St Agatha, Portsmouth and a Winchester College Missioner at Landport. He was recommended to Winchester College (Patrons of the Church) by the Rev. Grant and he conducted his first service in the parish on 15th August 1886.

From the time of his arrival he did great work, not only improving the fabric of the church but also improving the lives of his fellow villagers. He was never slow in lending his support to the labouring classes and ensuring that they had the rights to which they were entitled. Within a few months of his arrival he built, at his own expense the first ever parish hall, created the Men's Club and each Christmas invited the fathers and mothers to dine at the vicarage. He was a bachelor when he arrived in the village but in 1887 his banns were called and on 7th June of that year he married Miss Sidney Kerr, daughter of Lord Frederick Kerr, in the parish church of Crookham, Hants. Their honeymoon was spent at Henley on Thames and the reception given to them on their return to the village gives an indication of how quickly the Rev. Wickham had gained the hearts of his parishioners, as the following newspaper report of the event shows:

'Bradford Abbas was *en fête,* the occasion being the return of the Vicar, the Rev. Gordon Wickham with his bride. From an early hour the village was astir and from one end to the other triumphal arches were erected all bearing suitable inscriptions. The white ensign was hoisted on the church tower, and the bells rang a merry peal as the down train passed through the village to the junction.

'On reaching the bridge below the vicarage, the carriage, kindly lent by Mr J.T. Stacey, was unhorsed, and the bride and groom were drawn through the village from end to end, escorted by a body of the Vicar's Sunday class, arranged on each side of the carriage, together with the children of the school, and many other parishioners. The Bradford Abbas Brass Band at the head led the procession. Bouquets were presented to Mrs Wickham by Mrs Hugh Lang, Miss A. Lang, Miss L. Lang and Mrs Collier. There was no doubt as to the kindly feeling which the event evoked and it seemed as if "God Bless the Bride and Bridegroom" (which was the text of one of the mottoes) was really the heartfelt wish of the Parish. On reaching the vicarage, a fresh surprise awaited the Vicar and his bride. The outer porch was decorated with a "Welcome", the inner with the silver anchor and "Our Navy" and Mr C. Read's two sons acting as side boys received the bride as an Admiral's daughter. Mr Simeon Lang representing the Committee appointed to carry out the reception then stepped forward and presented in the name of 120 subscribers an illuminated address and a very handsome time piece. The members of the band at the same time, through their bandmaster (Mr Beare) presenting a chased cigar tray. The following is the wording of the address. "We the undersigned inhabitants of Bradford Abbas and Clifton Maubank, have experienced with pleasure in uniting together to present you and your beloved wife with a very humble present which we offer you both with our best wishes for your future happiness; and we sincerely trust you will both have good fortune to live a very long life in our midst. We also hope that by the assistance of Mrs Wickham you will become even more attached to your parishioners (if possible) and they to you.

"'We ask you unitedly to accept this timepiece as a token of our united love for you both and we earnestly wish you health, wealth and prosperity, a long life and a happy one."

'The inscription on the clock ran thus: "Presented to the Rev. Gordon and Mrs Wickham on the occasion of their marriage, by the inhabitants of Bradford Abbas and Clifton Maubank as a token of love and respect."

'The Vicar, who was obviously much touched by the heartiness of the reception, tendered his thanks on his own and his wife's behalf, for these unexpected proofs of affection and said that he hoped by God's help and the prayers of those committed to his charge they might be long spared for a life of usefulness in the Parish.'

Mrs Wickham, like her husband, took a great interest in parish affairs and together they must have made a formidable team. The big disappointment of their lives was that they were unable to have any children, but Mrs Wickham did much good among the young mothers and was a Sunday School teacher for many years whilst the vicar carried out his pastoral duties, with which he was to have major problems, particularly in regard to the fabric of the church.

The last work of any consequence on the fabric of the church had taken place in 1865 and this had only been something of a temporary arrangement. The timbers used in 1865 were of oak, but they were not dry and free of sap as they should have been with the result that by 1890 they were in much worse condition than the original beams after their four centuries of use. This was particularly true in the chantry where much damage had occurred. The wall plates and feet of the beams were much decayed, as was much of the boarding, part of the graining and much of the latest work. The condition of the roof in the north aisle was rather better but the remainder of the roof was bad, with the lead being no longer as weatherproof as it might have been. It was decided that the whole of the roof needed new boarding which was to be of pitch, the old oakboards with their decorations being preserved to still show under the new work, and the lead was to be recast and relaid. At the same time the tower needed a thorough repointing and the pinnacles were to be made more secure, while the peal of six bells, which were particularly useless, were to be quarter turned and hung on entirely new fittings at a cost of £90. The dilapidated floors in the tower were to be removed and the ringers were, in the future, to operate from the first floor instead of the base of the tower, which space was to be filled by the font which was to be moved from its position opposite the south door and where it is again now situated.

The total cost of all this work, it was estimated, would amount to £1400, but in actual fact by the time the restoration had been completed the cost had risen to £1592. For a village with a population of under 600 inhabitants (excluding Clifton Maubank) it seemed an almost impossible amount to attain, but nevertheless the parishioners set about the task with great energy, enthusiasm and determination by arranging concerts, rummage sales and a unique 'American Sale' which was held at the Victoria Temperance Rooms in Yeovil and which created considerable interest throughout the neighbourhood. By April 1890 the restoration work was underway, the main contractor being Mr John Andrews of Thornford with Messrs C & B Benson as the architects. Whilst the work was in hand the church was partitioned and all services, with the exception of the Holy Communion were held in the Parish Hall. The Holy Communion services were held in the part of the church where no work was being done in order to avoid the necessity of procuring a licence to celebrate it in the Parish room.

By the end of the year almost all of the money required had been raised and the work, apart from a few roof decorations, completed. Of the total cost of £1592, £800 was contributed by Arthur W. Bridge Esq., of Clifton Maubank and a further £200 by the Lord of the Manor, Mr Albert Clayton Clayton, who had also faced up to his responsibilities laid down in the Act of Parliament of 1824 by having the chancel roof restored at the same time at his own expense. It seemed, however, that almost every household in the parishes of Bradford Abbas and Clifton Maubank contributed in varying sums to as low as 6d with every person's contribution being shown separately in an account which was published by the Rev.

Wickham. It was a truly magnificent effort when one considers that the average weekly wage of the labouring classes was under 10/- per week, but it must be said that without the £1000 contributed by Mr Bridge and Mr Clayton it is extremely doubtful whether the parishioners themselves would have been able to raise the necessary finance for a number of years. Quite apart from his considerable financial contribution, Arthur Bridge also gave to the church the west window which depicts various events in the life of Christians—Birth, Baptism, Resurrection and Ascension—in memory of his wife Anne, who died on 14th November 1890.

The 11th December 1890 was the day set aside for the re-opening of the church and the events of that day were to be long remembered:

'Almost before dawn had broken the music of the bells was heard from the tower and the merry peals were repeated at intervals throughout the day. Raised on the tower and fluttering in the breeze was St George's Cross.

'The opening service was preceded by a dinner to which all the workmen who had been engaged on the church's restoration had been invited. This was provided in the Parish Hall and about 60 sat down, Mr J.J. Ring presiding. At the conclusion of the dinner the Rev. Gordon Wickham entered the hall accompanied by the Venerable Archdeacon Sauter. Addressing the workmen, Rev. Wickham said that it was his wish that everyone who had put a finger in the building should be there that day for dinner and he regarded the presence of so many as a token of the goodwill which existed between himself and them. He thanked the contractor and architect for the way in which they had each carried out their respective work, which had been done well and effectively and he trusted that the men who had taken part in the work had always born in mind that they were doing the same for God Almighty (Applause). Archdeacon Sauter said he was extremely glad to be present this day. He remarked upon the beauty of the church and observed that it must have been a pleasure to workmen who cared for that sort of work to have taken part in the restoration. He trusted that as the church was restored in the outward fabric, God's spiritual church would get built stone by stone and perfected; and he prayed that they might all be living stones in that temple (Applause). Mr J.J. Ring thanked the Rev. G. Wickham for his great kindness in providing that excellent dinner. He remarked that if Mr Wickham had never done anything else to make his name remembered he had, in the restoration of that church, done enough to make his mark for four hundred years (Applause).

'The opening service was fixed for 3.30 but some time previous to this the pretty little church which had undergone such a thorough transformation was crowded with a congregation including not only residents of the parish, but persons from most places in the neighbourhood. The Lord Bishop of the Diocese and many clergy assembled in the schoolroom where they robed. Among the clergy present were: Rev. Archdeacon Sauter, Rev. C. Powell (East Coker), Rev. C.R. Tate (Trent), Rev. C.H. Mayo (Longburton), Rev. Rowland Hill (Dorchester), Rev. A.B. Rose (Melbury Osmond), Rev. Canon Lyon (Sherborne), Rev. A. Phillips (Yeovil), Rev. J. Going (Hawkchurch), Rev. J.A. Laurence (Closworth), Rev. E. Hogg (Melbury Osmond), Rev. W.P. Oakley (Chetnole), Rev. S.E. Davies (Broadwindsor), Rev. H.T. Baebe (Yeovil), Rev. H. Dodington (Leigh), Rev. W. Roxby (Thornford), Rev. W.E. Colgrave, Rev. E. Young, Rev. G.A. Beinman (Sherborne), Rev. R.S. Macdowell (Yetminster), Rev. T. Blathwaite (Lillington), Rev. J.H. Maclean (Chilfrome), Rev. A.D. Hill (Dounton), Rev. J. Powys (Montacute), Rev. A.P. Wickham (Montacute), Rev. E.W. Goodden (Nether Compton), Rev. Canon Ravenhill (Buckland Newton), Rev. J. Warrington Strong (Sherborne) and others.

'A procession formed at the schoolroom was headed by the Bishop, the Rev. Gordon Wickham carrying the pastoral staff, and Mr Lawrence Cotter of West Coker, the Cross.

'While crossing the road to the church, Psalm CXVIII 19-29 was sung. Arriving at the west door, the Bishop knocked upon it, and having repeated a portion of the service and received a reply from the congregation assembled therein the door was opened by Mr Whittle, Churchwarden of Clifton Maubank, and the procession proceeded up the church to the chancel. The opening prayers were pronounced by the Bishop. After the singing of Psalms 24 and 150 the Rev. C.F. Powys read the lesson (52nd chapter Isaiah). The other portion of the service was taken by Rev. A.D. Hill. After singing the hymn "Lift the strains of high thanksgiving" the Bishop delivered an appropriate discourse founded upon the words "Behold how good and pleasant it is for brethren to dwell together in unity" etc. (Psalm 113). The hymn sung during the offertory was "Holy offerings rich and rare".

'The service was a most hearty one, the singing being especially bright. The choir (Choirmaster J.J. Ring) had received assistance from residents in the parish and from the neighbourhood. The musical accompaniments were by Miss Grosvenor on the harmonium, the organ not being in perfect condition. Tea was served at 5 o'clock for visitors and at 6 o'clock for the choir in the Parish Hall.

'An evening service was held at which the Rev. Archdeacon Sauter preached at 7 p.m.'

The evening service, therefore, brought to a close a day which will live for ever in the annals of Bradford Abbas and for many years afterwards the

Rev. Gordon Wickham held a special service on this day, but this is a custom which no longer survives.

The villagers, now had a church of which they could be proud even though it did not regain its former beauty, and the interest created by this major restoration was reflected in the increased attendances at the church services each Sunday.

Like his immediate predecessor the Rev. Wickham was also to experience some difficulty with the Vestry meeting where every effort was made by some members to call meetings at times when many villagers were unable to attend and it is to the Vicar's credit that although the Lord of the Manor and the principal farmer in the parish were the main culprits, he in no way condoned their behaviour. In 1892 he wrote not only to some of the members of the Vestry but also to a local newspaper as follows:

'I was glad to be able to answer some days ago to a suggestion that a meeting should be held to request the summoning of the Vestry at an hour at which labourers could attend, to the affect that Mr Clayton had sanctioned the hour of 7.30 p.m. on Thursday March 24th. Notice to this effect was posted *as usual* by the Assistant Overseer, Sunday, March 13th.

'On Sunday March 20th, a second notice written by Mr Walter Paul and signed by the Overseer was posted, summoning the Vestry at 9.00 a.m. on Saturday March 26th. Considering this to be practically a denial to the labouring classes of their privilege of voting I have no intention of sanctioning the same by my presence in the Chair. May I be allowed to say that if, as I am told, the first notice was illegal, then the Overseers appointed last year were not legally appointed, and had no power to sign the second notice.

'I am sending a copy of this protest to the local papers.

Yours faithfully
Gordon Wickham.'

It was acts like this that endeared the Rev. Wickham to the parishioners and this was to show itself in many ways, particularly in regard to church activities.

As happens today, much care was taken to decorate the church for the various religious festivals, and, having seen a photograph of the decorations in the last few years of the nineteenth century I have nothing but admiration for the loving care which the decorators must have taken to achieve the results they did. An account of the decorations for the Harvest Festival service of 1891 still survives:

'The decorations, although not elaborate were very neat and effective. The font had received considerable attention at the hands of Mrs Clayton and proved very attractive. At the base were several decorative plants, ivy and maidenhair ferns relieved with begonias whilst the sides hidden with small sheaves of wheat, oats and barley, with greenery trailed around. The bowl had a bedding of moss, ivy etc., and an edging of white cactus dahlias, a small sheaf of wheat, oats and barley standing in the centre. The rood screen was trimmed with wheat, oats and bunches of red berries, a large sunflower plant stood on each side. On the top of the screen was a very neat and tasteful arrangement of fruit and vegetables. In the middle stood a cross composed of wheat and berries with some carrots at the bottom, and at each end was a miniature sheaf of wheat, the space between being filled with parsnips, apples, vegetable marrows etc. Great credit is due to Mr James Bragg to whom this part of the decoration was entrusted.

'Marguerites, ivy and decorative grasses were used for the altar rails, at each end being a dish with a collection of apples, red currants, honey, geraniums and barley.

'The cross on the communion table was embellished with oats and barley, bunches of grapes hanging from the front, whilst on each side was a vase of roses. On the window sill above the table had been placed an 8lb loaf, given by Mr Patch, which was surrounded by beetroots, apples and parsnips. The pillars of the church were adorned with garlands and the window sills afforded space for collections of all kinds of fruit, flowers and vegetables, with which they were filled. Several small sheaves consisting of cereals were here used, as well as sunflowers, asters etc.'

It was the custom at this time to give the harvest festival goods, which had been donated by parishioners, to the Yeatman Hospital in Sherborne, and this continued to be the case for many years until it was changed a few years ago. The life of the church was bubbling with enthusiasm during these early years of the Rev. Wickham's incumbency with excellent attendances at services, a successful Sunday School, a good choir and a strong team of bellringers. Christmas in particular was a very active period and quite apart from the normal church services on Christmas Day, the Sunday School prizes would be presented, a football match played, and a tea for the footballers, church helpers, Sunday School and bellringers, provided by the Vicar and his wife. On Boxing Day there would be a fathers' tea, usually given by Mrs Wickham and a couple of days later a mothers' tea. Summer outings were also arranged with the children being taken to and from the railway station in farm wagons. On 17th December

1894 the Rev. Wickham was elected as the village representative on the Sherborne Rural District Council, a position he was to hold for several years and therefore he became the first ever District Councillor for the parish. He did much good work during his term of office, although at one stage he was disqualified from office for his failure to attend meetings. A by-election had to be held and he was promptly re-elected.

It was also during the Rev. Wickham's incumbency that the village received its first royal visitors. Mrs Wickham, before her marriage, had been a lady in waiting to Princess Louise, the granddaughter of Queen Victoria, and Princess Louise visited the vicarage on 27th September 1898 with her husband Prince Louis of Battenberg. Following lunch the royal couple went on a tour around the village before returning to London.

In early 1895 a chiming apparatus was presented to the church by a Miss Gertrude Hatfield (who also paid for the reflooring of the nave the previous year) which continued in use until very recently. In February 1896 the impressive stained glass window in the south chapel was unveiled and dedicated by Canon Lyon. It had been given to the church by Miss J. Minet, and her sister Miss S. Minet, who, whilst not residents of the parish came every year for a holiday and had a great love of the parish church. The window, the work of Powell & Son, Whitefriars, London, consists of two lights one representing Aldhelm, first Bishop of Sherborne AD 705 (who it is believed may also have founded Bradford Abbas church) and the other William of Wykeham, a former Lord Chancellor and Bishop of Winchester, who also founded New College, Oxford. Aldhelm is depicted holding in his hand a model of his saxon church at Bradford on Avon, while Wykeham holds a book. Both hold a crosier in the left hand, that of Wykeham being copied from the original which is preserved in his church of St. Mary, College of Winchester, in Oxford. Particular care has been taken with the bordering of the vestment—that of Aldhelm being copied from an ancient missal now in Lambeth library while that of the Bishop of Winchester shows carefully painted miniatures, in full length, of episcopal figures. The colouring is rich and pleasing and every detail bears inspection.

In 1897 the church was fitted with its present, and in fact only clock. It was given to celebrate the diamond jubilee of Queen Victoria by Messrs Edward and Albert Clayton in memory of their parents, William Clayton Clayton, Lord of the Manor, Lay Rector and of Elizabeth his wife. This generous gift is recorded on the north aisle with a fine brass plaque, but even so it did not meet with the approval of the labouring classes of the village, for the clock has only two faces—one on the south wall facing what was to be later the vicarage and the other facing east towards where Albert Clayton Clayton, then the Lord of the Manor, resided. The locals felt quite strongly that there should have been a third face, i.e. northwards—but the Clayton brothers did not agree.

By late 1902 it was realised that some urgent work had to be carried out on the floor of the church and that as the floor was deteriorating rapidly, urgent repairs would have to be carried out. It was known during the 1890 restoration that such repairs would be necessary at some time in the future but nobody had taken the matter very seriously. In due course a tender for the repairs from Messrs Lang Bros to the sum of £104 10s was accepted and the work was commenced. Once again the villagers started to raise monies to meet this amount but for some unaccountable reason the enthusiasm which was so apparent 13 years earlier was now lacking and despite constant appeals by the Vicar it was almost three years before the account was settled, by which time the Rev. Wickham was appealing for more money to restore the lead on the tower roof and the rotten timbers below it. However, it seems that the eagerness was returning for the tower was restored, as was necessary, and the money required was raised without any great difficulties.

In 1904 the fine old lectern was presented to the church by the Lang Brothers who were the village carpenters. It has a swivel top and was carved in their workshop which at the time was in Westbury, but is now a private house. Five years later, in 1911, it was found that the weight of the chancel roof was causing the north wall to bulge which would necessitate the taking down of that wall as well as a portion of the west wall. This, in itself was of no financial concern to the villagers as such, for any repairs in the chancel were the sole responsibility of the Lord of the Manor, Mr Albert Clayton Clayton. Mr Clayton fully accepted his responsibilities and, as well as stating his intention to have the chancel repaired, he also indicated that he was willing to move his seats, which by prescriptive right were in the chancel, to the main body of the church. To the Vicar and the Church Council, however, the necessary work to be carried out on the chancel seemed an ideal opportunity, if the necessary finances could be obtained, to add an organ chamber to the north of the chancel and so appeals were once again made for funds not only in the village but throughout the neighbourhood. The appeals were responded to, although there were some who were not in agreement with the proposed organ chamber and the extension of the edifice was completed late in 1911 at a total cost of £520. The work was carried out by Mr Wilfred Andrews of Thornford (the son of Mr John Andrews who was the main contractor for the 1890 restoration) and Messrs Lang Bros of Bradford Abbas. The new organ chamber was built to correspond to the south vestry, including a similar stair turret, and apart from the Ham Hill stone used, there was also stone taken from Mr Clayton's quarry in the parish. This was the last major addition to the church and the last major scheme to be carried out during the Rev. Wickham's incumbency.

The other project attempted by the Rev. Wickham which he himself had to finally admit was a failure, was the production of a village magazine. This magazine was largely devoted to news of the church but also contained other items of parochial interest, very much like the modern Pennant, but more elaborately produced. Unfortunately, it was a financial disaster and although for some time the Vicar met the losses out of his own pocket, the time came when he had to call a halt, and the magazine folded into oblivion.

With the outbreak of the First World War the Rev. Wickham made a patriotic appeal to the young men of the village pointing out quite directly that the call to the colours in Bradford Abbas had not been adequately heeded and asking all those who were able bodied to consider very carefully their duty and to act promptly. Several did respond and a roll of honour was kept and shortly after the end of the war a brass plaque was unveiled at the base of the tower listing six names who had fallen during that great conflict:

'Col. Frederic Walter Kerr—killed in action Hodge, October 31st 1914
Pte. William Gordon Wickham—1st Canadian, France, July 2nd 1916
CPO Albert Symes—H.M.S. Hampshire. October 3rd 1915
Cy. S.M. Arthur Burrough—2nd Scots Guards, Fest Hubert, France, May 16th 1915
Pte. Hubert Glover—D.C.L.I, France. September 2nd 1916
Pte. Hobart Smith—2nd Dorsets, Mesopotamia, December 9th 1916.'

It must be recorded however, that the first two names on the plaque were not natives of the village, but relatives of the vicar. It is ironic that also at the base of the tower is a carved wooden crucifix, given to the church by a German prisoner of war who was held captive in Bradford Abbas during the Great War, and is in fact the only crucifix in the church.

In 1918 C.P.L. Frith of Clifton Maubank presented to the church a statue of the Blessed Virgin and Child, which stands above the entrance to the south porch, and which was to prove to be the last gift to the church during the Rev. Wickham's incumbency. On the night of 19th December 1920, the Rev. Wickham, who had been suffering ill health for some time, died peacefully in his sleep, at St Mary's House, aged 71. His death was, however, quite unexpected; even though he had been liable to attacks of cardiac weakness very few realised he was as ill as he actually was. He was buried in St Mary's churchyard, close to the church he had served so worthily and amongst many friends with whom he had worked. His gravestone is a simple cross topped by a cherub which unfortunately has been damaged by vandals in recent years.

The death of the Rev. (he was in the last few years of his life a Canon) Gordon Bolles Wickham turns the final page on one of the most interesting periods in the history not only of the church, but also of the village, and it would be a difficult task for any incumbent to live up to the standards set by his illustrious predecessor. However, the villagers were not to be disappointed as they soon realised after the appointment of the Rev. John Godfrey Vassall, who was instituted as Vicar on 1st July 1921 by the Archdeacon of Sherborne. He was the 14th child of the Rev. William Vassall of Hardington Mandeville and had been educated at Charterhouse and Keeble College, Oxford, where he became a Batchelor of Arts in 1901 and a Master of Arts in 1905, the same year in which he was ordained priest. He had been curate of Christchurch, Isle of Dogs, before becoming a missionary and then a curate again at Sydenham and later St John's, Dulwich, from which position he resigned to take up his new situation at Bradford Abbas. He was a bachelor and when he came to Bradford Abbas he brought with him his sister, Amy, who acted as his housekeeper. Amy Vassall was quite a character in her own right and became well known throughout the village and although her nature was not all it should have been and she was not always as polite or discreet as would have been desirable, she, like her brother, was well liked. The new vicar soon proved himself to his parishioners by taking part in the social life of the village and it was not uncommon for him to pay for village

*The west door of
St Mary's Church.*

outings out of his own pocket and it was he who first allowed the vicarage
garden to be used as tennis courts.

In 1925 the bell frame in the tower collapsed and the church council
decided that as well as having the frame repaired they would authorise a
complete overhaul of the bells and the bell chamber. Two of the bells were
recast by Messrs Mear and Stansbrook of London whilst the old bell
frame, which was described as 'an interesting old relic' was repaired by the
village carpenters, Messrs Lang and Mr Wilfred Andrews of Thornford.
The cost of the work was £451, and the money was raised by voluntary
contributions, a fête and a bazaar.

The bells were rededicated by the Bishop of Sherborne at a special service on 20th May 1926, which was well attended and was followed by a reception. An amusing entry, in the Rev. Vassall's handwriting appears in the parish records three days after the rededication ceremony, which immediately brings to mind the Rev. Grant's difficulties with the bellringers a century earlier:

'23rd May 1926. We had a tremendous dose of bellringing. My churchwarden Mr H. Warr being the chief culprit. The Vicar will have to use his control and authority if this continues.'

I am pleased to record, however, that the Rev. Vassall encountered no further difficulties in this direction.

He was also very surprised, late in 1925, to be handed by a villager (who is unknown) a scrap book which had been originated by the Rev. Wickham and in which were various newspaper cuttings and notes made by the late vicar. It was mainly an ecclesiastical record of the Rev. Wickham's incumbency. As the Rev. Vassall was not aware of this unusual record, there was a gap covering the period from the death of the Rev. Wickham until the time that the book was recovered, which, the Rev. Vassall did his best to fill, writing up his record of those years most carefully. His handwriting appeared to me to be of a painfully tedious nature and it did not surprise me to learn that in July 1926 the Rev. Vassall left the village to go to Droitwich Spa for 2 weeks' treatment for chronic rheumatism, from which he had been suffering for some considerable time. Following the advice of a London specialist, he immediately went into a nursing home in Yeovil on his return to the district, where he remained until 6th December 1926 when he left the nursing home to go to Hurst Manor, Martock, for further rest and recuperation. In fact he was a very sick man but he eventually took up his duties in the parish again although his attendance at the church was spasmodic and the vast majority of the services were taken by Rev. A.W. Douglas, who had become Priest in Charge of the parish during the vicar's absence.

In 1929 the Rev. Vassall presented the church with an altar of Ham Hill stone in memory of his brother and to this gift he added various other items including a handsome cross and ornaments of silver upon copper. On 10th April 1933 he tendered his resignation as he was now confined to a wheelchair and had not, in fact, officiated at a service in the church for over 8 months. He left the village for Martock in July 1933 but before leaving he was presented with a cheque for £50. He died on 4th April 1938 and was buried at Martock but before his death he had requested that his sister, Amy, should make several presentations to Bradford Abbas church including his own private communion set, and before evensong on 10th April 1938 the bellringers, with half the bells muffled, rang a quarter peal of grandsire doubles in memory of their late and popular vicar.

He was succeeded as Vicar by the Rev. Eric Campbell Douglas who took up his duties on 19th October 1933. He had been ordained priest in 1910 and had held various previous curacies as well as having served with the British Expeditionary Forces in France in 1917, and as Chaplain to the Forces from 1918-26. At the time of his appointment to the living at Bradford Abbas he was Chaplain to the missions to Seamen Training Ships at Greenhithe. The Rev. Douglas built up a close relationship with the Brothers of St Francis at Batcombe, where his brother was resident, and several of them became regular visitors to the church as well as taking part in other village activities. They also performed short plays in the churchyard after evensong on several occasions, which were attended by many villagers, as old records show:

'21 July 1935: The Churchyard of Bradford Abbas made a wonderful setting for one of the *Little Plays of St Francis* by Laurence Houseman this evening. The play acted was *A Mess of Pottage* and the actors were some of the brotherhood of St Francis of Assisi. Brother James made a perfect Brother Juniper and won the hearts of the audience. Brother Knott played the part of Father Mattes with real sympathy and understanding and Brother Oswald appeared as Brother Rufus. The brothers in their Franciscan habits against the grey walls of the old church brought back the days of old, and the audience was enthralled. When the play was ended, Brother Douglas, Prior to the Brotherhood, mounted the steps of the old Churchyard Cross and gave a simple talk to the people. Old England was revived, and few will forget the evening.'

The link between Bradford Abbas and the Franciscan Home at Batcombe was further strengthened when the Rev. Douglas was appointed Chaplain of their home at Lenthay (now destroyed) and a gift of candlesticks and a cross was made by the Church Council to the Franciscans.

In 1934 the Rev. Douglas wrote a brief history of St Mary's Church which was to become the first guide to the church which could be read by visitors. With regard to the fabric of the church the only change made during Rev. Douglas' period of office was the installation of electricity which was dedicated on 10th February 1935, thereby replacing the oil lamps which had been the only source of lighting for so many years. The Bishop of Sherborne also visited the Parish on 20th June 1936 to consecrate an extension to the churchyard in respect of land given by Mr Wyatt Paul.

In March 1936 the Vicar advised the Church Council that he had received a most generous offer from a retired vicar, Rev. Frank Nesbitt, who was residing in the village, who wished to give an organ to the church in memory of his late wife Mrs Florence Nesbitt. This offer was gratefully accepted. It was formerly dedicated on 17th September 1936 having been placed in what is now the north vestry. The organ had been built by Messrs J.W. Walker & Sons, and was considered at the time to be of the most modern design, of a particular fine tone and extensive range. It is still in use in the church at the time of writing, the only addition being a small brass plaque in memory of Mrs Farmer, who was for many years the church organist.

Another matter which came to the attention of the church council in 1936 was the state of the Michael Harvey memorial, which I am sorry to record is now no longer in existence other than in shattered fragments in the churchyard. However, at this time the concern was that it had fallen to the floor of the chancel and broken. It was subsequently examined by an expert who reported that owing to the dampness of the chancel the iron supports had rusted through. The monument was replaced on the wall, however, but it fell again on several occasions until it was no longer re-erected. A similar occurrence happened to another monument on the facing wall, that of Susannah Harvey, wife of Michael, of which no trace now remains. It was, of course, during the period of Rev. Douglas's life in the parish that the coronation of King George VI was celebrated and on the day of the great event the Rev. Douglas was to act as Chairman over the dinner that was to be held. The highlight of the day was undoubtedly the carnival procession, which followed a service in the church and I find the Rev. Douglas's notes on the day's events more amusing than those that appeared in the press:

'During March and April a committee was formed to arrange local celebrations for the coronation. Mr Underdown was Chairman. It is very doubtful whether the celebrations are fully in harmony with the majority of the villagers' wishes. Some £60 was collected and £40 of this was to be expended on a meat and beer supper for all who wished to go—an allowance of 3/4lb of meat per head was agreed on, although many of those who had experience of catering were alarmed at the amount. The meetings were not always harmonious and were similar to those arranged for H.M. George's Silver Jubilee local celebration. The Chairman had little control and, as in the Peace Celebrations, the Rose & Crown habituées rather controlled matters.

'On the day the following points are note worthy:-

'Time of events on the whole took much shorter time than the Committee anticipated.

Coronation procession in North Street, 1937.

'Carnival started at Yeoleas at 2.30 pm. and marched past the Church, Old Council Houses, down North Street, up Westbury and were in the field next to the school at 3.15 pm. The judging took 20 minutes. Various childrens' sports took place before tea. Tea lasted only 25 minutes. Supper for the Parish:

Time advertised	6.30 pm.
Time started	7.15 pm.
Supper finished	7.43 pm.
King's Health	7.45 pm.

Chairman (Vicar) had no control over proceedings. Unnecessary speeches were made by Messrs Mellish, Underdown and Patch, though the speech of the last named was all right, the other two became a mutual and self advertisement society! As a result of this the men's sports had to be cut short owing to lack of time.

'MEMO: On occasions like this, speeches are undesirable, especially, as it was arranged that there should be no speeches except the Royal toasts.

'Catering—The butcher appears to have done himself remarkably well!! 209lbs of beef and ham were ordered for 260 people; uncooked, but when this was cooked by him it only weighed 116lbs (including wrapping, ham bones and innumerable skewers) and it was decided afterwards that it would have been much cheaper to have bought cooked meat. 17lbs of meat were left over, consequently 90lbs of cooked meat was enough for 260 people. The meat was not well cooked and the butcher said that accounted for the wastage; the butcher annexed all the dripping.'

The Coronation celebrations were the last big event in which the Rev. Douglas participated, for at the Parochial Church Council meeting of 10th September 1937 he announced his resignation and advised that he would be leaving the village by 1st December. The period of his incumbency had, therefore, been the shortest of any vicar of the parish for almost 200 years and was to set a fashion that has continued until the present day when, with the exception of his immediate successor, vicars have only stayed for a few years. He was succeeded by the Rev. George Vincent Kendrick who was instituted by the Bishop of Sherborne on 15th March 1938. He had been ordained priest in 1910 and had spent most of his career in New Zealand before he came back to England.

The early years of Rev. Kendrick's incumbency were marred by the war and the restrictions that those difficult times imposed but through the Deanery Magazine he kept his villagers informed of all the latest news of those who had left the village as well as keeping a roll of honour on the altar of St Mary's Church of all those who were serving their country.

In 1951 the roof of the church was again causing problems and repairs were becoming absolutely essential. A fête was held to raise funds which was very successful and, with the sale of lead, met the amount of £633 8s 4d necessary for repairs. At the same time the clock was cleaned and the numerals painted in gold leaf. It was while funds were being raised for these repairs that the Rev. Kendrick received an envelope containing a £5 note and a piece of paper on which was written:

'For better roofs, than England's sky
Between her earth and heaven apply
To crevices where rain may creep
Or where else it's help may keep St Mary's people dry.'

In May 1952 the Rev. Kendrick resigned, and this was to precipitate a situation in which the two parishes of Bradford Abbas and Clifton Maubank were entered into plurality with Thornford and Beer Hacket, and the Rev. J.W.D. Perkins, Rector of Thornford was appointed as Priest in Charge to replace the outgoing Rev. Kendrick. This was a state of affairs which met with little or no approval and it only added salt to the wound when it was later decided that the incumbent should reside at Thornford (on the grounds that it was the centre point of the plurality) and that St Mary's House should be sold. There was a considerable amount of agitation and dissatisfaction by the Bradford Abbas Parochial Church Council and the churchwardens (Mr T. Patch and Miss R.M. Benson) wrote a letter to the Archdeacon of Sherborne which contained the following points:

'1. On what authority are the two livings being amalgamated.
2. Why have the accredited representatives of the parish received no notification of such a proposed amalgamation?
3. Why have we received no notification that the new Rector of Thornford is to be the new Vicar of this Parish? It seems extraordinary to us that a man can take over a parish by just walking in and saying "I am your new Vicar." '

After going on to say that the new Vicar would be given a welcome the letter concluded by saying that things would have been much pleasanter if only someone had had the courtesy to say what was happening and that the whole matter had been handled highhandedly and was not conducive to the smooth workings between the ecclesiastical authorities and the laity. But the Bishop of Salisbury withstood all the pressures put upon him and the plurality became permanent and St Mary's House was sold. So for probably the first time in its history, the village was without a vicar they could truly call their own.

The villagers themselves, and to their credit the Church Council, were not, however happy about the plurality and when the idea of a Free Will Offering scheme was mooted, rumours spread around the village concerning the proceeds of the sale of St Mary's House. It was felt that with the money received from that sale there should be no need for the Free Will Offering scheme, which was resented by many of the villagers who were not aware of the facts of the situation. The Rev. J.N. Perkins, who had already announced his resignation as Priest in Charge, therefore brought these rumours to the attention of the Parochial Church Council as a result of which he issued the following statement—one of his last acts before leaving:

'To clear away any misunderstanding I want to make clear two things:
1. What happened to the Capital obtained from the sale of the Vicarage and
2. What happened to the sum of money obtained from the Parish Fete held in 1951.
'Let me deal with the sale of the vicarage first. The money raised by the Church Commissioners on the sale of the vicarage has been incorporated into the capital of the benefice and can be withdrawn at any time a parsonage house at Bradford Abbas is required to be built or bought. But in no sense is the capital so obtained, or the interest from it, available for church expenses, nor has it put up the incumbent's stipend by one penny. It is held in trust for the parish by the Church Commissioners and cannot be used for any other purpose than the one stated. Secondly as regards the proceeds of the parish fete organised so efficiently in 1951. This was, of course, before my time but I have ascertained the following facts which I laid before the Church Council last week and was accepted by them. The summer fete was arranged initially to pay for the renovations to the church roof but in fact the work was put in hand before the fete took place and the whole cost had been paid by the generosity of a number of private subscriptions. The result of the fete was that money raised totalled £154 15s 2d. To this amount was added the money realised from the sale of lead bringing the total to £366 of which

£300 was invested in the Globe Building Society and is known as the Fabric Fund. A balance of £66 was allocated to a minor Fabric Fund (B) and has largely been expended already on repairs to the building and the new boiler. I hope these facts will clear the air of any possible misunderstanding as to what was done with these moneys. I may add that £100 from the Fabric Fund (A) has now been allocated to cover repairs that require to be done in the next few months.

'I hope therefore, it will be clear that, to cover our day to day expenses some such scheme as the Free Will Offering envelopes is absolutely necessary. No church to my knowledge exists solely on its Sunday collections.

John N.D. Perkins.'

Whether this statement made any difference or abated the rumours I know not but the Free Will Offering scheme which had been launched earlier in the year had a response from only 42 persons out of 240 who were advised of it, which the Church Council considered 'as somewhat of a disappointment'.

With the departure of the Rev. J.N.D. Perkins in April 1955 an attempt was again made to end the plurality but it was to no avail as the Rev. C.G. Kerslake was appointed to the joint benefice and he took up his duties with effect from 21st June 1955.

The Rev. Kerslake was a native of Wiltshire and he enlisted in the army at the age of 16, seeing active service in France during the First World War. He was ordained a Deacon in 1924 and became a Priest while Curate of St Michael's, Bristol. In 1935 he became a missionary to the Seaman's Chapel at Antwerp and a year later he became Vicar of St Anthony in Monaga until 1944. During the Second World War he served as a naval chaplain for three years with the Fleet Air Arm in the Middle East and then as Chaplain of a hospital for naval psychiatric cases. He was a Master of Arts of Oxford University. He was married and his varied experience at home and abroad included such diverse activities as street corner preaching in the Old Kent Road, acting as a member of a Government Advisory Committee on Education, building the first stone church at Foyid in Egypt, as well as holding services for Coptic Christians in an Egyptian village. He also served for several years as a member of Melton and Belvoir Rural Council.

He was obviously a well-experienced man and he soon made many friends in the plurality and took part in the various social events, and it came as a shock when he died suddenly at Thornford Vicarage on 2nd May

1956, aged 56. The funeral service took place at Thornford where he was buried in the churchyard.

Again the agitation for the cessation of the plurality arose and again the efforts were unsuccessful for on 1st July 1956 the Rev. Donald Blackburn was appointed Priest in Charge. The Rev. Donald Blackburn was a native of Liverpool but had spent most of his life as a missionary mainly in the Middle East but also in China and had only returned to England earlier in 1956, to be honoured with the award of the OBE in the Birthday Honours list.

In 1957 the tower and the pews of the church were repaired, and a year later it was decided, through the generosity of Mrs Richardson of Coombe, to have the font removed from the west door of the church to its present and probably original position opposite the south door. This in isolation was by no means a memorable event as such, but what is of interest is that when the font was removed a small, sealed bottle was found. When the bottle was opened it was found to contain two pieces of notepaper and two silver coins. The first paper had been written on, in Greek by the Rev. Robert Grant in 1842, and with it a silver sixpence dated 1841. It read:

'St Matthew 16:18. This church was renewed and this font repaired on October 27th in the year of Our Lord 1842. This bottle (and coin) were deposited by the Rev Robert Grant, Vicar of the Parish and Fellow of Winchester College. George Masters and John Sherring (Churchwardens). The population of the Parish of Bradford Abbas, Males 308, Females 344. Clifton Maubank, Males 27, Females 23.'

The second paper with a silver shilling dated 1889, read:

'18th November 1890. This font was remove to its present position during the restoration of the church roof in 1890. Enclosed in glassbottle was found a coin of 1842 and a statement by the then Vicar, Rev. Robert Grant which are now replaced. The front was in 1842 opposite the south door. The population of this Parish at the last Census in Bradford Abbas 510, Clifton Maubank 80. Total 590. Gordon Bolles Wickham, M.A. New College, Oxon, Vicar. Albert Clayton, William Whittle, Churchwardens. Robert H. Cooper, Sidesman.'

These papers and coins were replaced in the font and a third paper added together with coins of the reign of Queen Elizabeth II including a halfpenny contributed by a child from the village school. The third paper which was inserted by the Rev. Donald Blackburn, includes the names of the churchwardens, the builder, the architect, the headmaster of the village school and the two masons who found the bottle, Mr L.E. Trott and Mr Courtenay Newis.

It should be mentioned at this point that the font is believed to date from the time of Henry VII which means that it was probably installed just after the extension of the church had been completed and is a fine example of perpendicular work and in form very unusual. In Paley's *Baptismal Fonts* published in 1844 the following description is given:

'It is octagonal and round the bowl, which is panelled with quartrefoils runs a richly sculptured wreath of foliage under the cornice; it is supported by a central shaft panelled in the lower part and in the upper, three have the figure of a bishop and the fourth is a lamb upon a book, under canopies with primroses.'

Very shortly after the font had been placed in its present position, tragedy struck the church and all the good work of the past nearly came to nothing. On a February evening in 1959, Mrs Ruby Gosney (née Cox) was walking from her home in Line Path down around the church corner when she suddenly noticed flames shooting up inside the church. She immediately gave the alarm and the news quickly spread that the church was ablaze. Within minutes a number of parishioners were fighting the flames before the arrival of the fire fighting appliances from Sherborne and Yeovil. The fire was soon under control, but the firemen removed quantities of smouldering debris from the building. The damage was not, fortunately, as extensive as was at first thought and was restricted to the north aisle where parts of the organ were either unsalvageable or damaged and two pews together with hymn books, hassocks, and part of the flooring were no longer of any use. The fire had been caused by an electric soldering iron being inadvertently left switched on by one of the workmen engaged in overhauling the organ. Fortunately the cost of putting the church in order was met by the Insurance Company with whom the Church Council had insured the building.

About a month after the fire it was noticed that some of the paving stones in the chancel were sinking and beginning to break up, which prompted the Rev. Blackburn to have them raised, resulting in the entrance to a vault being found. It had been sealed off with tree trunks which were black with age and mortar. Upon their removal the tombs of Edward West, Vicar 1777-1812, and his wife were discovered whilst below these tombs were the seventeenth-century lead caskets which are believed to contain the remains of two of the Harvey's of Clifton Maubank. Late in 1959 whilst there was scaffold around the church as it was being cleaned, a survey of the building was carried out which showed that the church in general was in good condition although some of the leadwork needed some repair.

On 23rd January 1960 the Rev. Donald Blackburn announced his resignation as he wished to return to the Middle East and when he actually left the village on 26th February he was presented with a painting of the church in appreciation of his services.

It was to be seven months before a new incumbent was appointed again after some more unsuccessful attempts to end the plurality. The new Priest in Charge was to be the Rev. L.J. Chesterman, a married man with two daughters, who on accepting the living at Bradford Abbas resigned his position as Vicar at Whitwick, Leicestershire. During the seven months before his appointment the Rev. William Carroll, a curate of Sherborne Abbey had administered the spiritual needs of the village and during the short period of seven months he had become extremely popular and upon his leaving he was presented with some book tokens. However, the Rev. L.J. Chesterman was not to be Priest in Charge for very long for on 12th March 1962 the Parochial Church Council was informed 'that the Archdeacon of Sherborne (The Ven. D.R. Maddok) had visited the three parishes and had found [*sic*] the strong opinion that Bradford Abbas should become independent, with its own Vicar.' And so, on 9th April 1962, the Church Council were further advised by the Rev L.J. Chesterman that the Diocesian Pastoral Committee had agreed that in view of the present and impending growth of the village, the former plurality should not be renewed and that an independent vicar should be appointed, and a vicarage house acquired. This brought great pleasure to the parishioners, enhanced later in the year when it became known that Rev. George Rowland Buchanan, who had been a curate at Sherborne Abbey for the past three years, was to be the new Vicar.

The Rev. Buchanan was inducted into the living, his first, on 29th January 1963 and he took his first service as Vicar on Saturday 2nd

February 1963. He came to reside in St Mary's House which had been re-purchased for use as a Vicarage by the Church Commissioners. Rev. Buchanan set about his duties with a great deal of enthusiasm and quite apart from his spiritual duties he took a great interest in the school, the village hall and other organisations in the parish but in May 1963 he was to face a problem which reminded me very much of the Rev. Grant's comments regarding dissenters. A visit from two young Americans resulted in the Reverend issuing a circular letter to all the parishioners as well as making a statement to the Western Gazette:

'On Wednesday afternoon I was called upon by two young Americans who informed me that they were based in Yeovil and were about to conduct a house to house visitation of my parish on behalf of the Church of Latter Day Saints.

'It subsequently appears that the visitation had, in fact, started some days ago. I felt it my duty as Vicar to this Parish to inform all of my parishioners, irrespective of their Christian denomination of something of the background of this American religious society, which, despite its name is not a Christian Church.

'In a circular letter to all parishioners I pointed out that "The Church of Latter Day Saints" does not belong to the Christian World Council of Churches and is not in communion with any Christian Church. I advised all Christians in Bradford Abbas to witness to their faith by firmly, but politely, having nothing to do with the two young American 'missionaries' of this strange and unorthodox American 'religion' which is not Christian.'

Whether these young men did gain any converts I cannot be certain but certainly, and no doubt due to the efforts of the Rev. Buchanan, it would appear that their mission was unsuccessful.

Rev. Buchanan had in fact become vicar at a crucial time in the history of the village for not only was it expanding rapidly but there were major problems such as providing a new village hall as well as a new school. The Vicar was Chairman of both of these organisations and did much good work. In his church activities he instigated the formation of a St Mary's Guild, which consisted of two groups of ladies, one group being responsible for decorating the church and cleaning the brass ornaments and the other group undertaking embroidery and repair work on the church linen. He also revived the ailing Mothers Union, formed a St Mary's Fellowship which was open to all women over 18 years of age, and a similar 'Mens Christian Fellowship', all of which met monthly. He followed all of these activities by forming a Bible Reading Fellowship and played a leading role in the formation of a Wolf Cub Pack.

In 1965 as a result of the ecclesiastical boundary revision the hamlet of Wyke became part of Bradford Abbas thereby ending its long church association with Castleton Parish, of which it is still a part for civil purposes. This, in effect, was only making official what had already been a fact of life, for generations of people from that hamlet had been worshipping in Bradford Abbas Church. Also, later in the same year the Harvey memorials which had been in the church for over two centuries were taken down. They had been creating difficulties, mainly through corrosion, for many years, and had become badly cracked.

It came as something of a surprise, in 1967, when the Rev. Buchanan advised the church council that he was leaving the Parish to move to the living of Wishford Magna and Little Langford. The Rev. Buchanan and his wife said farewell to the village at a ceremony in the village hall where they were presented with a 1760 grandfather clock and an antique corner cupboard.

On 1st September 1967 it was announced by the Church Patrons (Winchester College) that the Rev. Gerald Squarey was to be the new Vicar. He was at the time a curate at St Leonards, Heston, having previously been an assistant curate at All Saints, Poplar. He was educated at Sherborne School and so was not unfamiliar with the area. He was instituted to the living by the Bishop of Sherborne (Rev. V.J. Pike) and inducted by the Rural Dean of Sherborne (Canon S.B. Wingfield Digby) and it was not only villagers who attended these ceremonies but also a large contingent from his previous parish in Middlesex. The Rev. Squarey quickly became very popular in the parish particularly amongst the younger generation to whom he became affectionately known as 'Batman' due mainly to his never being seen without his clerical habit. It came, therefore, as something of a surprise when in the Autumn of 1973 it became known that he was leaving the village to move to Corfe Castle.

He was succeeded by the Rev. John Mentern who was appointed Priest in Charge and not Vicar as talk of plurality was again in the air and sure enough, when he retired in 1985, he was replaced by the Rev. David Greene who was already administering to the needs of Thornford and Beer Hacket. This, in effect, meant that the village was thrown back to the plurality days—St Mary's House was again sold and at a vast profit, of which no benefit fell to the Parish.

CHAPTER VI
The School

The story of the school starts during the years of the incumbency of the Rev. William Preston, who, a few years before his death in 1742, purchased certain lands in the parish of Nether Compton, the rents from which he used to fund and maintain a Charity School for the instruction of twelve poor boys from the parishes of Bradford Abbas and Clifton Maubank. In his will, dated 5th April 1738, he devised these lands to Michael Harvey of Clifton Maubank or in the event of his death, to his wife Rebecca Harvey, who were to administer the land as they saw fit. The Harveys, who only survived William Preston by a few years, fortunately did not dispose of the lands but continued to use the income therefrom in the way they knew the Rev. Preston intended thereby keeping the school in existence. Upon the deaths of Michael Harvey and his wife, or it may have been earlier as the Harveys ran into severe financial difficulties, the lands passed into the hands of the Rector of Clifton Maubank (who it so happened was also the Vicar of Bradford Abbas) and his successors, as had originally been suggested in the Rev. Preston's will.

Where the school was situated and what subjects the children were taught are matters for speculation, but more than likely the school would have been no more than a room in a cottage and the subjects only reading, writing and probably religious knowledge.

It appears that all went well with the school until the year 1779, when the schoolmaster Mr. John Brooks died. For some reason, the then Rector, Rev. Edward West, was dilatory in appointing a new master which created a certain amount of friction in the parish, and in particular between the Rector and a principal inhabitant, Mark West. He went so far as to threaten the Rector with chancery or to seek out the heirs of the late Rev. Preston to prevent the rents becoming the Rector's own. An advertisement was, in fact, placed in the newspapers for the heirs, but nothing came of it, as whether through fear or otherwise the Rev. West saw fit to appoint a new master. The Rev. West's appointment of Mr. George Snook as the new headmaster did not meet with the approval of Mark West, as it turned out that the income from the Nether Compton lands was been paid to a Schoolmaster who was teaching the children in what was no more than a Sunday writing school. And so Mark West and another inhabitant, William Read, invested £300 in equal shares in the 4% Consols of 1777, the dividends from which were to be used for the purpose of establishing a free school, in which the poor children of Bradford Abbas and Clifton Maubank could be instructed in reading, English, writing and common arithmetic. What happened, in fact, was that the boys were taught reading, writing and arithmetic, whilst the girls only learnt reading, spinning and knitting, and that they learnt to write at the Sunday School.

The £300 stock had been invested in the name of five trustees—Mark West, William Read, James West, Mark Fooks and Thomas Thompson and these same five people also became Governors of the new school. They appointed a Mr Robert Newman as the Headmaster of their school and he set about his duties almost immediately. In 1785 a further £50 of the same stock was acquired, thereby increasing the school's income from £12 to £14, exactly the same income as Preston's school, with the extra income being used to increase the number of children attending the school from twelve to fourteen.

In 1794 the Trustees of Read and West's Charity were granted a lease, at 2/- per annum, of premises upon the lives of Mark West (aged 14) and Edward Thompson (aged 7) for 99 years. It is of some importance that in granting this lease neither the Lord of the Manor (the Earl of Uxbridge) nor the trustees made any reference whatsoever to Preston's School, so presumably at the time there were two schools operating. The premises which the Trustees now held were undoubtedly on the site of the house in Churchwell Street which is still called the Old Schoolhouse, and is currently the home of Mr and Mrs Gordon Barber. It consisted of two tenements, one being fitted up and used as a schoolroom and the other as a dwelling house. Where Preston's School was situated at this time is not recorded. It could still just have been operating as a Sunday writing school.

By 1800 the Rev. West saw fit to make an important change in the constitution of the Preston foundation and he made a full settlement of the lands in Nether Compton, in his own name, that of Rev. John Williams and three others. So Preston's Charity, which since its foundation had been administered by successive individuals was now placed in the hands of five trustees, as of course, Read and West's had been since its inception.

According to the Deed of Assignment the Trustees of Preston's Charity were to hold the land.

'In trust to let the same, and to apply the rents as follows: that is to say, to pay the yearly sum of £8 for teaching eight poor children, inhabitants of Bradford Abbas and Clifton Maubank in reading, writing and arithmetic, and other useful learning and in the principle and doctrines of the Church of England as by law established: and it was agreed that the master should be appointed by the said Rector and Trustees, by writing under their hands and seals, subject to removal by them for any of the causes thereinafter mentioned, and that he should declare himself, and be known to the majority of the said Trustees to be a member of the Church of England and the said Trustees were to apply the residue of the rents annually for teaching poor children, inhabitants of the said parishes to read, knit, sew and other usual acquirements as the mistress and Trustees should think proper, and also for instructing them in the Catechism of the Church of England, the number of such children to be proportioned to clear remaining rent, at about 8/- per annum for each child; the mistress to be nominated and to make such declaration as aforesaid; and it was agreed that the Rector of Clifton Maubank should from time to time, have the exclusive nomination within one month after any vacancy occurring, in default of which the Trustees or either of them, might appoint and the master and mistress were not to receive any money or other presents upon the entrance of the said children or any other account whatsoever, except their salary from the said rents, but were to be at liberty to take other scholars into the said school, receiving pay for them, the number to be regulated by the Rector and Trustees; and the said scholars were to attend at the parish church of Bradford Abbas on Sundays, and other usual days, and to be accompanied there by the master and mistress; and it was agreed that the said Rector and Trustees should once a year, or oftener, if necessary meet at the school house, to examine the management and make sure rules as they should think proper for any irregularity or neglect, to remove the master or mistress, and appoint others in their stead, and to expel any of the children upon sufficient cause, and that a book should be kept in which should be entered the names of the children with the date of their entry and departure and the ages at such times, respectively, and also proceedings of the said Trustees: and it was further agreed that, if after a lapse of time any alteration in the application of the said rents should seem more for the benefit of the said poor children it should be lawful for the said Rector and Trustees by deed, under their hands and seals, to direct such alteration by such writing to direct the application either in apprenticing or clothing some of the said poor children or in some other manner for their benefit.'

So now the two charities were to be administered on very similar lines and one may well consider that the Rev. West had arranged this with a view to the amalgamation of the two schools, for on 18th March 1800, Mr John Custard was appointed Schoolmaster at a salary of £8 per annum, and he was to take up his duties with effect from Lady Day. The two schools, therefore, it would seem were now under one roof, even if they had not been before, and they operated successfully in this manner, for nearly thirty years. During these years John Custard enlarged and improved the premises largely at his own expense, and also presumably carried out his scholastic duties to the satisfaction of all concerned. In 1829, however, the Trustees of Read and West's charity gave Mr Custard notice to quit the premises, which they were entitled to do, as they considered that he was becoming neglectful of his duties as schoolmaster, having become 'more addicted to book binding than book teaching'. There is no record of the feelings of the Preston Trustees regarding the proposed dismissal of John Custard, but the Rev. Robert Grant, who had only been in the parish about a year, made it his business to try and resolve the state of affairs which had arisen. He held an 'amicable meeting' with two of the Read and West's Trustees, namely Mr Mark Fooks Snr and Mr Mark Fooks Jnr, and on the Rev. Grant's undertaking to personally ensure that John Custard did not neglect his scholastic duties the question of his dismissal was dropped. It seems that the Rev. Grant was successful in his efforts for the question of dismissal was not raised again and the school continued to operate successfully so that by 1835 not only was John Custard teaching 20 boys and girls, as well as 4 private pupils, there was also a Schoolmistress teaching 27 girls, 7 of whom were her private pupils.

In 1835, however, disaster struck and the schoolhouse was burnt down. This obviously created tremendous difficulties, but until such time as a new schoolhouse could be built, John Custard taught the boys and girls in his private house, and the Mistress agreed to do the same. For carrying out these duties the salaries of the Master and Mistress had now reached £10 per annum. As a result of the burning down of the schoolhouse the Rev. Grant after consulting with his fellow trustees of Preston's Charity, suggested that the two charities be put on a more permanent foundation by uniting them, and thereby avoid the possibility in the future of either being rendered useless by the withdrawal of the assistance of the other. This seemed to be a logical move to all concerned particularly as the two foundations had virtually been operating as one for a number of years, and after consultation with Edward Thompson and Mark Fooks Senior, two of the Trustees of Read and West's Charity, provisional agreement was reached. In order to be fair to all parties it was agreed that the Trustees of both charities should be equal in number (the number for Read and West's Charity having been unaccountably reduced to four) and that should any dispute arise between the two bodies of Trustees the Lord of the Manor was to act as arbitrator and his decision was to be binding.

The Trustees who were party to these arrangements were:

'PRESTON CHARITY
Rev. R. Grant
Mr B. Cooper
S. Pretor Esq.
Rev. J. Parsons
John Goodden Esq.

READ AND WEST CHARITY
Mr Mark Fooks Snr.
Mr Mark Fooks Jnr.
William Fooks
Edward Thompson
Jonah Hannah'

In order to obtain complete unification of the two charities it was agreed that an application should be made to Lord Anglesey, the Lord of the Manor, for a new lease of the school premises as there was only one life (Edward Thompson) remaining on the present lease, and for any new lease to be vested in the name of both charities. Through his agent, Mr Castleman, Lord Anglesey indicated his willingness to meet with the Trustee's wishes as far as he could and a meeting was arranged between Mr Castleman and two representatives of each charity. All appeared to be going well and the signing of a new lease seemed to be no more than a formality. But at the same time the appointment of a new Headmaster had to be considered as John Custard was now an elderly man and largely on the initiative of the Rev. Grant it was more or less agreed that George Custard, who was well qualified for the position, should succeed his father. That this would have been a popular appointment there can be little doubt as a petition signed by a number of parishioners was presented to the joint trustees indicating that it was their wish that George Custard should be the new Schoolmaster. George Custard was willing to accept the appointment and he indicated that he would be prepared to spend £200 in addition to the £200 insurance money in rebuilding the burnt-out schoolhouse. However, before all the details of George Custard's appointment had been finalised, Edward Thompson revealed that he had received an anonymous letter in which both the Thompsons and the Fooks were spoken of in a most improper manner, and he had reason to believe that it had been written by the prospective new schoolmaster. George Custard freely admitted that he had written the letter 'in a moment of irritation' and he very much regretted having done such a thing. Mr Thompson forgave him for his 'indiscretion' and so it appeared that all difficulties had now been overcome.

And so, in October 1835 the Rev. Grant and S. Pretor Esq., for Preston's Charity and Mr Mark Fooks Jnr and Mr J. Hannah for Read and West's Charity went to Stalbridge for a pre-arranged meeting with Mr Castleman to discuss and hopefully finalise the new lease, but, on their arrival, and to quote the Rev. Grant's own words, 'much to our astonishment and regret' they ascertained from Mr Mark Fooks that his brother William would not agree to any new arrangements whatsoever and had, in fact, gone so far as to try and discuss the matter with Mr Castleman the evening before the meeting with the official representatives of the Trustees was to take place.

What caused this sudden dissension on the part of William Fooks is not really known but it could well have been connected with the anonymous letter written by George Custard as the Rev. Grant records: 'In order to leave nothing untried I proposed to leave Mr George Custard out of the question and get the best master we could. This proposition was not acceded to and so we returned leaving the matter as it stood.'

In January 1836, the Rev. Grant had a meeting with a Mr Smith, one of His Majesty's Commissioners, who agreed that the uniting of the two foundations was beneficial to all, but even Mr Smith was unable to attain any sort of agreement even though he emphasised that the parish would be the loser if the schools were to become disunited, as the salaries arising from each charity would be quite inadequate if efficient Schoolmasters were to be engaged. By 1837 the school premises had been rebuilt on the same site as the burnt out school and John Custard occupied them again as

Schoolmaster, but in May of the same year he died after an illness of only two days. The appointment of a new Schoolmaster was, therefore, now a matter of some urgency and after some difficulties over the wording of an advertisement a Mr Edward Thorne was engaged.

Mr Thorne was a young married man from Fordingbridge and it seems that despite the tragic loss of his young wife, he carried out his duties efficiently and it was the cause of some regret when in 1846 he tendered his resignation to take up a new appointment at Martock.

One further attempt was made, in 1844, to resolve the question of the new lease, as there was a possibility that the premises might be sold, but no further progress was made. Mr Thorne was succeeded by Mr William Priddle from Tintinhull, who was a bachelor and came to live in the village with his sister. Mr Priddle, however, was induced to resign as 'he was failing to give satisfaction'. The Trustees met at the vicarage on Grants Hill on 27th February 1854 for the purposes of formally accepting Mr Priddle's resignation and for the appointment of his successor. The minutes of this meeting still survive and make most interesting reading.

'The resignation of Mr Priddle of his office as schoolmaster was accepted. It was communicated to the Trustees that Mr Clayton Clayton had most liberally offered to make up the salary of the new schoolmaster to £70 per annum. It was resolved that this generous offer be accepted and that Mr Grant be requested to communicate to Mr Clayton their high sense of his liberality, his regard for the welfare of the poor inhabitants of the parishes of Bradford Abbas and Clifton Maubank. It was further resolved that on the recommendation of Mr Clayton Clayton, after having inspected the testimonial forwarded by the Principal of the Highbury Training School Institution, with which they were satisfied, the United Trustees have appointed Mr Ring as schoolmaster, providing he complies with the terms mentioned in his appointment, and that the power of removing him or dismissing him rests with the Trustees of both Charities. It was further resolved that in case any question should arise respecting the conduct of the master involving the probability of his removal, that the Trustees of both Charities shall have due notice of assembling to deliberate on the point, and that the question of removal shall not be decided but by an equal number of the Trustees of both Charities, and in the event of an equality of votes, that the point be referred to the Lord of the Manor for his decision.

It was further resolved that in consequence of the increase of the master's salary through the liberality of Mr Clayton, the children of mechanics and

The village school which was officially opened on Easter Monday, 1856.

labourers, who shall be educated, may be admitted in the school without any limitations as to the numbers as regards to the boys school, but the master is at liberty to take any private scholars on his own terms.'

Mr John James Ring promptly moved into the school premises in Churchwell Street, the Lord of the Manor furnishing it for him and providing new desks for the children, but the school was only to remain there for about two years for on 6th June 1855,

'The foundation stone of the new school which is to be built by the new Lord of the Manor William Clayton Clayton Esq., was laid with some ceremony by Miss Grant, daughter of the Vicar. John Goodden, Esq., publicly thanked Mr Clayton for his liberality and Mr James Vincent, Mr Clayton's steward acknowledged the compliment in the absence of that gentleman.'

It had been quite obvious that new school premises were required, particularly as the benefits of the school had now been thrown open to the children of mechanics and labourers, and the premises then in use were too small. So it must have given great pleasure to the teachers and children alike when they moved into their new and more spacious school on Easter Monday 1856. Mr Clayton had built the school at his own personal expense—about £900—and the old school premises were retained as the offical residence of the headmasters. In consequence of an exchange of land a few years later the new school premises came into the hands of Winchester College, who continued to allow them to be used as a school rent free, although it was later decided to charge a nominal rent of 1/- per annum, a position which I believe still continues at the present time.

The master, Mr Ring, could now divide the school into four classes and arrange the timetable so that the two higher or two lower classes be grouped together for his teaching.

It was only four years after the move into the new premises that the first prizes were awarded in the school, and a description of this ceremony which took place on 1st July 1860 reads:

'The first and second classes in the boys' and girls' schools, amounting to upwards of 40 were examined on 16th and 17th instant by the Rev. R. Grant, Vicar and the Rev. E.P. Grant, Curate, on the following subjects viz: a portion of the scriptures, the Prayer Book, dictation, geography, grammar, writing and arithmetic. The examination was conducted chiefly on paper. The first prize, a desk, was given to the best boy and girl for general good conduct. Two prizes 1st and 2nd were next presented to the two boys who had the greater number of marks in the first and second classes and a prize to one girl in the 1st and 2nd classes, besides another prize, first and second for needlework. These consisting of a writing desk, work box and books were delivered to the successful candidates with a short and impressive address to each by the Rev. R. Grant in the presence of a large number of parents of the children who appeared to take the liveliest interest in the proceedings. An address explaining the nature and objects of the prize scheme, containing as well a summary of the examination which was on the whole very favourable was delivered by the Rev. E.P. Grant (who we understand is one of the local secretaries in Dorset) and a subsequent one by the Rev. R. Grant. Cake and tea etc., was liberally provided by contributions from some parishioners and other friends for all the candidates who vied with each other as strenuously and as amicably in the gastronomical as they had previously in the intellectual contest. The business of the evening was enlivened by some pleasing music and singing. It is intended to hold this examination both at Midsummer and Christmas. We feel it both a duty and a pleasure to give publicity to the first attempt in the parish of Bradford Abbas, at least, of carrying out in a small and humble way the Diocesan Prize Scheme, in order that the Clergy and friends of education in other parishes, if they have not already done so may be induced to 'go and do likewise'. And for this special reason in order that they may prepare and send some candidates to any future occasion to compete for the prize in the larger Diocesan arena and who would necessarily labour under a disadvantage if they have never been accustomed to proper work.'

Under the 1879 Education Act each parish was bound to provide a proper school house and efficient teachers and the expenses of some were to be met out of what was referred to as a school rate. For Bradford Abbas the Rev. Grant remarked, 'this school is in a very efficient state as regards the boys but as regards the girls it is feared that it will not wholly satisfy the requirements of the new law.' Why the teaching of the girls was not satisfactory he did not record. At the time of the important change the total income of the school consisted of:

'Income from the two charities	33.00
Children's Pence	22.00
Mr Clayton	60.00
	£115.00'

Out of this had to be paid the salaries of the Schoolmaster and Schoolmistress and all the other expenses which were necessary for the successful running of the school. The Trustees, however, were anxious to avoid the imposition of a school rate which few of the villagers could have afforded, and would not have taken kindly to, as they had never been asked to contribute towards the upkeep of the school. It was thought that if the cost of providing sufficient school premises with competent teachers was wholly thrown upon the parish the annual charge would not have been less than £200, which would undoubtedly have been a heavy burden.

Mr Ring, however, 'of whose zeal and ability the parish have had ample proof', offered to take on himself the responsibility of carrying on the school both for boys and girls so as to satisfy the Government Inspector, on the following terms:

'That he be allowed

a) To occupy the present dwelling house with its garden free of rent, he paying the parochial rates in respect thereof and keeping the windows and roof in repair.

b) To use the present school house, the same being kept in repair as heretofore.

c) To receive for his use any grant that may be obtained from the Government, the income of the school Trust funds and the children's pence.

d) That he be paid in addition the annual sum of £35 by equal half yearly payment.'

Agreement was reached with Mr Ring on all these points and in order to make up the additional £35 to be paid to him, Mr Clayton offered to contribute £15 and Mr Bridge of Clifton Maubank £10. The balance in much smaller amounts was contributed by other leading villagers, after it was learned that neither the Great Western nor the London and South West Railway companies were prepared to make a contribution. I would mention that all of these arrangements with Mr Ring were with the agreement of the villagers as a parish meeting was held to explain the position and the efforts which had been successfully made to avoid a school rate being implemented.

Mr Ring had really set himself a formidable task for he had to get the children to attain a certain educational standard, as the amount of the Government grant depended on the results of the children's examination by the Government Inspector. One of his biggest enemies was the irregular attendance of the children, and it was very rare for there to be a full attendance for any length of time. The main cause of the irregular attendance was that although education was not compulsory until 1870, even those few parishioners who could see the advantages of their children attending school were not always able to afford the few pence they had to pay the Schoolmaster. It was not uncommon for a child who was sick on Monday and fit and well on Tuesday to be kept away from school all that week in order that the Schoolmaster would not expect payment for that particular week. This problem became even more common after the 1870 Education Act when it became compulsory for the children to attend school. In order to improve the situation Mr Ring devised a scheme where children who were absent for three consecutive days without leave of the

Master were considered 'out of school' and were to be charged double fees on readmission. This acted as a deterrent to absenteeism and secured a far greater regularity of attendance than was common in most country schools.

Just prior to the Government Inspector's first ever visit, the school was reorganised and whereas all the boys had previously been under the Master and the girls under a Mistress they were all placed under the Master, thus forming a mixed school.

In March 1871 Mr Ring was advised that the Government Inspector's visit could be looked for in the month of January each year, and shortly after receipt of this notice the Schoolmaster carried out his own examination of the children and recorded that he found things not exactly to his liking and resolved to rectify them at once. What the things were which were not to his liking he does not say but the following entries appear in the school log book giving some indication of the problems he was facing throughout 1871.

'1st May. The Headmaster kept the lowest class in until 1 o'clock as they did not get on well with their arithmetic as he had expected.

9th May. The home lessons were badly said, whereupon the Headmaster threatened the children with a double quantity next time if there was no improvement.

17th May. Home lessons were well said, which the Headmaster thought was as a result of his threat of 9th May.

30th May. Home lessons have been stopped for the next two or three months as the boys are required by their parents to assist them in their gardens during the evenings.

7th June. The Headmaster is experiencing difficulty in teaching the 4th class to read monosyllables and is endeavouring to devise a plan by which he can devote more time to the problem without neglecting the higher classes.

21st June. There had been a very small attendance due to the haymaking.

19th July. The Headmaster is finding it necessary to devote more time to reading throughout the school.

27th July. The Headmaster finds himself amply repaid by the progress the two lower classes have lately made in arithmetic.'

He was obviously being successful in improving the educational standards and as the first visit by the Government Inspector was scheduled for 1872 it was important that these standards be maintained, but in the last few months another very worrying matter arose as attendances fell off drastically, the reason being quite clearly shown in the school log book.

'10th December 1871. The Headmaster was obliged to close the school as the parents were afraid to send their children due to an outbreak of smallpox in the parish, one case being opposite the school.'

Fortunately the school was reopened on 1st January 1872 and the first ever visit by the Government Inspector was made on the 16th of that month. His report read as follows: 'The school passed a fair examination. New desks are required and measures should be taken for improving the ventilation of the schoolrooms.'

The improvements suggested were undoubtedly carried out as the Inspector did not see fit to comment on them in future years. Generally speaking the school obtained good reports:

1873 'The school is in a fair state of efficiency'.
1874 'This school is in an efficient state.'
1875 'The examination of the school was very satisfactory. Useless furniture should be removed from the school. The school would be better lighted if the present windows were removed and replaced with clear glass.'
1876 'The school is in order and has passed a creditable examination.'
1877 'The school is carefully taught and discipline is very fair. At times there is too much talking.'
1878 'The school continues to be taught with great care and most creditable results.'
1879 'It is a very pleasing school. The instruction is thoroughly sound and the children very orderly and well behaved. The weakest point, perhaps is the Geography of the 3rd standard, but taken as a whole the examination is very satisfactory.'
1880 'The elementary work is exceedingly well done, being neat, intelligent and accurate. The Geography and Grammar are fairly well known but specific subjects are defective. On the whole it is a very good country school.'

But in order to get satisfactory reports and results in the examinations each year a lot of hard work had to put in, for the better the results the better the grant. It meant that there was continuous pressure upon the children and as the examination day approached each year so the pressure increased in order that the children might reach the required standards and as, in accordance with the agreement that Mr Ring had with the Trustees, he was to pocket the grant it was obviously in his own interests to get the very best results he could.

The following entries in the school log book for 1885, made by Mr Ring show what the situation must have been like at the time:

'2nd June. Bessie Foster, after suffering severely for 10 days died this morning of brain fever. I believe her father has said that it was caused by over pressure at school, but I do not agree with him.

29th June. On Saturday last I went to see a little boy (Arthur Chainey) who was dangerously ill with inflamation of the brain. The Doctor says it is caused by over pressure at school. I think it very probable that such is the case. If ever pressure is telling on the children it certainly is telling on my health, but the parents cannot complain that the over pressure is reserved just before the exam. If over pressure does exist it is evenly spread over the whole year.

20th July. Mr Nutt, a "Medical Practitioner" of Sherborne has sent a certificate stating that he does not consider Arthur Chainey is capable of doing much mental work as he has recently suffered severe illness from over-pressure of the brain.

4th August. Henry Wadman is so exceedingly dull—in fact has very little intellect that it will be a gross case of over pressure if he were compelled to be examined in the 4th standard at the next examination.'

Even though there may have been these cases of over pressure there were very few complaints by the parents and, in fact, many parents from outside the parish seemed to like their children to come under Mr Ring's tutorship. It appears, at least according to Mr Ring, that many children who came to him from other schools were not as far advanced in their education as children of a comparable age in Bradford Abbas school and that the school, and Mr Ring, has an extremely good reputation. In 1878 the Rector of Thornford the Rev. W. Roxby, saw fit to write to Mr Ring stating that 'he hoped I would not take any children from his parish into the school without charging them much higher fees than the rest of the scholars'.

Mr Ring maintained strict discipline throughout the school and there are records to show that he did on occasions give certain children a flogging:

'4th January 1883. Gave a boy (Combs) a flogging for "playing truant"—four strikes on the hand. I am happy to say that this is a very rare offence at this school, and this is the only boy addicted to it. The last time he committed the offence—six months ago—I gave him a more severe flogging than I did today.'

It seems likely however, that Mr Ring did not like administering such punishment, for he saw fit, with the consent of the managers, to devise a system of good and bad marks, with the good marks to represent a money award at the end of the year; the bad marks to be deducted from the good marks as a substitute for corporal punishment. Whether the system he devised was successful or not I would not like to say, for the school log book contains many later references to corporal punishment. How today's parent would have reacted to the sort of 'flogging on the backs' of their children which Mr Ring inflicted I cannot imagine, but he certainly did have difficulties with certain parents as the following shows:

'9th August 1871. Uriah Lang, having stolen a book from another boy, the Headmaster sent him home for it. His father came to school and made a great disturbance; was abusive and would not leave the premises. The Headmaster felt that he should have sent for a policeman had there been one in the place. The boy being frightened by his father denied the theft, but before his father left he confessed that he had stolen the book and scratched out the name. The father then went off, but without expressing his sorrow for the disturbance or owning that he was wrong. The Headmaster remarked that this is the only parent in the parish who does not support his authority and he has determined to bring the case before the landowner as he feels he may be subject to a repetition of it.'

Whether or not Mr Lang was, at the time, the only parent not to accept the Headmaster's authority he certainly had more difficulties with parents in later years, including his former old adversary.

'19th November 1872. Uriah Lang again came to the school and abused me for slightly punishing one of his boys. He was very excited and called me a bad name. As this is the third time he has done so, I have no alternative but to report him to the Lord of the Manor, who I know will support my authority. I have refrained from doing so on the last occasion for I thought it might injure his prospects. 23rd January 1882. A man of the name of Foot has sent me a note stating that if I "will not allow his daughter Mary to pass the exam" he will "remove her from the school and send her somewhere else". He has done so. The fact is, the girl has not "made her times" during the past year and I told her I was unable to place her upon the exam schedule. I am however, anxious to have her present on the exam day. The parent cannot be aware that "passsing the exam" does not rest with the teacher but with H.M. Inspector and the Department.

29th May 1889. A man of the name of Kearly lately come to live in this neighbourhood came to me making a complaint that his child had been kicked on the leg while at school. First the man accused the Master, then one P.T. then the other. I have made enquires and find that the child was not kicked at school. The children who went home the same way as the child state that there was nothing the matter with the child when it left school, and that she ran along as usual, but that just as she arrived home Clifton) she complained of a pain in her leg. The man now says that the child is ill in bed, the man also said that his boy had been almost "flogged to death". The boy has never been punished since he has been here although he has more than once deserved a flogging for his deception.

31st May 1889. I find that the above is a perfect issue of falsehoods. The girl now confesses that she fell down and hurt her leg on the way home. Teachers ought to be protected from false accusations, and if the parent comes with the language of a blaggard proceedings should be taken against him.

24th June 1892. A man of the name William King, lately a dock labourer in London, had been bullying and blackguarding simply because I do not think it advisable to place his son in the 5th standard in all three subjects. His certificate shows that he had lately passed Standard 4 in a London Board School. He can read fairly, in arithmetic he is backward, while his writing is about equal to our Standard 3. I feel that he would not satisfy the requirements of H.M. Inspector. I have therefore declined to place his boy in standard 5 for the latter two subjects. The boy, I suppose acting under the direction of his father, is sulky and refuses to do any sums.'

But school was not all discipline and hard work and one of the days most looked forward to in the year was the annual school treat. The children would be given a half holiday and the normal procedure was for the children to assemble at the school at about 3 o'clock in order to attend church after which they would march to the grounds of the vicarage where they sat and enjoyed a picnic under the trees. After tea the younger children and girls would go into 'Hollies' for sports and games whilst the elder boys would play a game of cricket in 'Gollops' ground. The children really enjoyed these days, the cost of which was more often than not met by the wealthier villagers, including the Vicar and the Lord of the Manor. The children would also be given half days for specific village events, e.g. Club Day, as well as a full day's holiday the day following the Government Inspector's visit, and on Shrove Tuesday, Pack Monday Fair, Stoford Fair, Yeovil Fair and Guy Fawkes day. It was, however, very much at the discretion of the Headmaster whether or not they were let out on those days. If he considered that they were not at the standard required for the inspection he would not close the school which meant in any event that a number of children would be away whether or not it was an official holiday. One year he did not let the children have their customary half holiday on Guy Fawkes day as he felt 'they would get far more good at school than keeping Guy Fawkes in memory by running and letting off squibs'. The children also had Easter, Summer and Christmas holidays but they were much shorter than they are today—the Easter and Christmas holidays being one week only and the summer holiday only three or four weeks, although this holiday was often lengthened if the local farmers required the children to help them with the harvesting.

Throughout the period of Mr Ring's headmastership the number of children attending the school gradually increased so that by 1889 the average attendance was 133 which at that time was the highest on record. Early in January 1893 Mr Ring contracted a cold and only a fortnight later he died, aged 60, of inflamation of the kidney. He had been Headmaster for almost 39 years during which period there had been tremendous changes in the education system. He was buried in the churchyard at Bradford Abbas. The School Managers, who had by now replaced the Trustees of the two charities placed on record 'their high estimation of the services which the late Master J.J. Ring had rendered to the school since his appointment in 1854 and their sense of the great loss sustained by both the school and the parish by his death'. There can be little doubt that he was a great loss to the parish as well as the school for he had for many years been the organist and choirmaster at the church as well as being the assessor of taxes and at the time of his death he was the President of the South Somerset Association of the National Union of Teachers. The final Government Inspection for which Mr Ring was responsible was held while he was on his death bed and was very satisfactory, it being reported that the older children were in good order and systematically taught whilst the instruction of the infants was decidedly creditable.

Very soon a Mr Walter Walker, assistant of Reckleford School, Yeovil, was appointed Headmaster, but as he was unable to take up his appointment until 27th February 1893, a Master and a Mistress were temporarily brought in to fill the breach. On his first day at the school the Rev. Wickham and Mr A. Clayton attended to ensure that all was satisfactory and that Mr Walker got off to a good start. Apart from the Headmaster, there were three assistants—Ellen Helliker (Assistant Mistress) Charlotte Ring (3rd Year pupil Teacher) and John Phipps (Monitor). However, although the Inspector's report appeared to be satisfactory Mr Walker considered that there were several unsatisfactory aspects and within only a few days he had arranged a completely new timetable. He also noted that 'several parents make a practice of keeping their children at home on Friday afternoon while some send their children during the week to Yeovil and Sherborne with gloving work'. He followed these comments a few weeks later with the remark: 'Have now been master of this school 7 weeks but have not yet seen or heard of a school attendance officer for this district.' He comments that the spelling of Standard 2 is very weak as is the geography of Standard 3 and that Standard 1 was backward in arithmetic, but he was later to comment favourably on John Phipps's hard work in improving Standard 1. Mr Walker's methods were very different than those of his predecessor and it is greatly to his credit that he maintained and in many instances improved the education that the children were receiving. He started a system of conducting his own quarterly examinations of the children, which no doubt greatly assisted him in pinpointing weaknesses which he could strengthen in good time for the annual inspection. In the first inspection carried out during Mr Walker's headmastership, in early 1894, the Inspector reported: 'There is nothing really weak, though some of the arithmetic is only fair.' Of the infants he said that they were fairly well taught, and in 1898 he reported that the instruction is given in a very thorough manner and discipline is also quite satisfactory.'

No doubt Mr Walker's own quarterly examinations were of great benefit and a record still exists of the examination which he carried out in April 1898. It is interesting to see what the children were being taught and their own Headmaster's assessment of the standards the children were achieving.

SUBJECT	STANDARD 1	STANDARD 2	STANDARD 3	STANDARD 4
Arithmetic	Good	Good	Fair	Good
Reading	Fair	Fair	Good	Good
Writing	Good	-	-	-
Mental Arithmetic	Very Fair	Fair	Fair	Good
Tonic Sol Fa	Good	Very Good	Very Good	Good
Geography	Very Fair	Very Fair	Very Fair	Good
Object Lessons	Good	Good	Good	-
Dictation	-	Very Fair	Good	Very Fair
History	-	-	-	Good

SUBJECT	STANDARD 5	STANDARD 6	STANDARD 7
Arithmetic	Very Good	Good	Very Good
Reading	Very Good	Good	Excellent
Composition	-	Very Good	Very Good
Mental Arithmetic	Good	Good	Good

It is quite obvious from the above that those children who had spent a few years under Mr Walker's tutelage were reaching a satisfactory, if not high, level of education and were being well prepared, educationally speaking, for their life after their school days were over.

The Object Lessons which Standard 1, 2 and 3 were being taught covered a whole variety of subjects, many of which the children must have found extremely interesting. Those for the year in which the above examination was held were as follows:

STANDARD 1 Horse and foal. A barn. Donkey. Other buildings on a farm. Cow and calf. Haymaking. Sheep and lamb. Harvest time. Pigs. Implements used on a farm. Shepherd's dog. Garden produce and how to grow it. Rabbits and hares. Garden flowers. Garden tools. Ducks and geese. Turkeys and pigeons. Rats—the good and harm they do. A blacksmith's shop. The harvest mouse. A post office. The fox. Hunting. Game birds. Fishing. Wild birds. Brickmaking.
STANDARDS 2 & 3. The cat. Knives. The duck. Bread. The spider. Salt. The cow. Milk and butter. The sheep. Cheese. The mole. Cows. Tea. The railway train. Coffee. The union jack. The sugar cane. The diver. Cotton. Lighthouses. Rice. A lifeboat. Football and cricket. Corn. Birds. Coal. Earthenware. Candles. Glass.

With all the good work that Mr Walker was doing it is sad to have to record that the most tragic event in the history of the school occurred while Mr Walker was at the helm. It was the custom during the winter months for some of the children who lived a distance from the school to bring their dinners with them and to remain on the school premises during the dinner hour, when they would be supervised, not by teachers, but by older pupils. On fine days they would play outside but on wet days they would stay in a classroom where there was a stove. On Monday, 21st November 1898,

'A sad accident happened to a child named Alice Smith, aged 7 years. It appeared that during school dinner hour she threw a piece of paper on the stove in the classroom and standing too near the lighted paper fell out onto her dress, which was quickly enveloped in flames. Fortunately Mr John Lang was at work in the school yard, and seeing the child, had the presence of mind to cover her with his coat. The headmaster, Mr Walker, who was passing by rendered the same assistance, thereby it is hoped saved the child's life. Mr Lang was severely burnt on both hands. Prompt help was given in dressing the child's burns, which covered the body from the waist upwards, by Mrs Uriah Lang, and then she was taken to Mrs Dawes home to await the Doctor's arrival. Dr Ingram was most prompt in attendance, and after a careful dressing of the wounds, the child was conveyed to the Yeovil Hospital.

Through all her terrible suffering the child remained perfectly conscious and was wonderfully brave and patient; her thought was for her mother ("Mother don't cry") and in answer to the Vicar whose voice she recognised she tried to be still while, now and again, the pain seemed unbearable. None of those who ministered to the little sufferer but felt that they were "taught by a little child". The little sufferer succumbed to her injuries on Wednesday.'

Two days after Alice Smith's death the school log records that a large guard had been placed around the stove in the infants' room and the following day at an inquest held at the White Lion Inn, Kingston, Yeovil, the foreman of the jury expressed great concern at the absence of a guard. and the lack of proper supervision during the dinner hours. Nevertheless no blame was attached to anyone and a verdict of accidental death was returned.

On 25th August 1900 Mr Walter Walker resigned as a Headmaster as he had obtained a new position and said that he would leave when a new

Headmaster had been appointed. In fact he took lessons for the last time on 24 September 1900.

The new Headmaster was Mr Harry 'Bomber' Warr, who is still remembered with a certain reverence amongst the older villagers. He was born and educated in Sherborne but he came to Bradford Abbas from Freemantle National Boys School, Southampton. During his 33 years' residence he was to earn himself a reputation which will probably never be surpassed in the village. He was undoubtedly a brilliant teacher—one of the best it was said—and under his leadership the school reached higher levels than it had ever achieved before. It got to the stage where an Inspector saw fit to say, 'This school is one of the few that it is a real pleasure to inspect. The discipline is so good and the children so keen and intelligent that it is a pleasure to examine them.' It seemed that nothing was too much trouble for Mr Warr when it came to the welfare of the children and those who spent their entire school life under him always speak of him with great respect. It seems that he was a fair-minded man and was not slow in giving credit where credit was due. On the other hand he was not slow to administer punishment as and when he thought it necessary. A lot of his popularity probably emanated from the fact that it

School gardening class, 1909. The gentleman wearing the boater is the Headmaster, Mr Harry Warr.

was not only his scholastic duties which attracted his attention but all other activities in the village.

At the time of Mr Warr's arrival there were three other teachers—Miss I. Roddell, Miss Lovering and George Webb. The first two were fully qualified but George Webb was only a pupil teacher, and was not very efficient. The number of staff employed at the school had been more or less the same for a number of years and was to continue at the same level, but although there was stability as far as the Headmaster was concerned, there was a constant turnover of other teachers, which did not help the smooth running of the school. At one stage in Mr Warr's early years, the school was short-staffed for a considerable length of time, despite constant advertising, so it was rather surprising to find that within seven years of his arrival Mr Warr was able to bring one lad (Willie Lang) up to such an educational standard that he won a County Council Scholarship which was tenable at Foster's School, Sherborne. This was the first time that any child from Bradford Abbas School had reached such heights but it was only the first of Mr Warr's many successes.

One innovation which Mr Warr introduced was the formation of a school gardening class for the boys. It is surprising that in a village such as Bradford Abbas at that time that gardening was not already part of the school curriculum. But it was not and Mr Warr arranged for the lads to work in part of the garden of St Mary's House (then known as the Old Vicarage). Mr Warr took full responsibility for the lads' tuition and their work was regularly inspected by the County Council Instructor in Horticulture. Such was the success of the class that in its second year Wilfred John Chaffey won the first County Prize and within six years the school class had reached an extremely high standard when the County Council Instructor's report read:

'This is a most excellent class. The plots are always well kept and the most made of the work, both master and pupils taking a very keen interest in the gardens. This class and Buckhorn Weston are the best in the county and about equal merit.'

Another innovation of Mr Warr's was the idea of the children giving an entertainment to their parents each Christmas, a custom which continues to this day. The first such entertainment was held on 19th December 1901 and was such a success that one villager described it as 'the best thing I've seen in Bradford'. The local newspaper reported that looking through the programme it was impossible to say which was the best rendered of the 23 acts. With the proceeds of these entertainments the children were to be given an entertainment of their own which at Mr Warr's suggestion developed into a Christmas party each year. More often than not, with the help of some of the wealthier villagers, these parties were often thrown open to all the children in both Clifton Maubank and Bradford Abbas, whether or not they were attending the school. These parties were eagerly awaited and enjoyed as the following report of the 1902 event by the Rev. C.F. Medcalf, who was acting for the Rev. Wickham while he was in Italy, shows.

'Some time before 3.00 p.m. all the juvenile population of the United Parishes of Bradford Abbas and Clifton Maubank might have been seen gathered before the school doors. They had come to see the Christmas Tree kindly given by Mrs Clayton for their benefit, and eagerly and anxiously they awaited the moment when they would be permitted to gaze upon it. The minutes passed slowly by, but at last the church clock struck the hour of 3.00 p.m. and the doors were opened and in rushed the eager throng to the expected treat. Soon they were tightly packed, like so many sardines on the benches, their eyes turned towards the folding doors beyond which they knew was the wonderful tree, which bore something better than mere fir cones and resin. Another moment and the doors flew back, and a sigh of satisfaction went through the assembled throng as they beheld the brilliant spectacle. The tree was indeed a very fine one, prettily decorated and beautifully lighted, its branches weighed down with all sorts of toys. For a little while the children were allowed to gaze upon it before it was despoiled of the treasures. And then, they were marshalled up by standards by Mr Warr, to receive their presents from Mrs Clayton's hands. Not only once, nor twice but three times did they leave their seats to return with some new possession. Books, toys, marbles and sweets were seen on every side. Many of the older girls, past or present members of Mrs Clayton's Bible Class also received presents. But all good things have to come to an end, and at last all the presents had been given away and it was time to disperse. The Rev. C.F. Medcalf thanked Mrs Clayton on behalf of the children for her kindness in giving the tree and Mr Warr led hearty cheers for Mr, Mrs and Miss Clayton, and all who assisted them, and then the party broke up, each child receiving an orange and a bun at the schoolroom door.'

There were two other celebrations in the school year which also created much interest amongst the children and their parents—the awarding of the medals and certificates for regular attendance and the Empire Day Celebrations. For a number of years the County Council awarded special medals to children who had an unbroken attendance record during a whole year and lesser awards for others with a good but not complete record. Some children achieved remarkable records, and two lads, Robert Wadman and Joseph Higgins, attended school for eight years without missing a lesson, whilst Desmond Higgins managed 7 years, Lionel Higgins 6, and Frank Garrett 5. These medals were most coveted awards and they were instrumental in almost guaranteeing a better attendance record among the children, relieving Mr Warr of a problem which had plagued his predecessors. The day the medals were awarded was also eagerly anticipated and parents were invited to watch the ceremony. A report of the ceremony held on 9th May 1918 survives and reads:

Bradford Abbas school, c.1924.

'The medals and certificates for regular attendance for the year ended 31st July 1917 were presented by Canon Wickham on the following children:

UNBROKEN ATTENDANCES	INFANTS	Bessie Garrett
	STANDARD I – IV	Horace Garrett, Ivy Garrett
	STANDARD V & UPWARDS	Hubert Rodber, Frederick Coombs, Frank Garrett, Alfred Boucher, Olive Templeman

'The school was open 411 times and the following were present more than 398 times; 97 per cent, obtained the medal with red and white ribbons and a certificate. Cecil Smith 408, Neville Burrough 407, Leonard Coombs 406, Leslie Cox 406, Edith Walbridge 405, Stanley Coombs 404, May Templeman 404, Dorothy Bartlett 403, Nina Stevens 402, Hilda Gillham 401, Matilda Upshall 401, Harold Coombs 401, Mildred Borough 401, Thomas Weller 401, William Weller 399, Bertram Gill 398, Ena Ring 398, and Mildred Ring 398.

'The vicar expressed a hope, in which the headmaster Mr Warr joined, that this year a higher percentage of attendances would be reached, and that a large number would win the red and blue ribbon for unbroken attendances. The percentages of attendances for the whole year was 90.31.'

The Empire Day celebrations were usually held in the school yard and many parents would turn up to watch their children pay homage 'to a great and glorious empire' every year. With the passage of time and the changes which have now taken place throughout the world the British Empire no longer exists, but in the early years of the present century all were very conscious that Britain's influence covered vast areas of the earth's surface and patriotism was the 'in thing'. And so, each year Empire Day was a great opportunity to instil this patriotism into the children, as the following report of the ceremony held on 24th May 1909 shows.

'A pleasing ceremony took place in the school playground on Monday when Empire Day was observed. A flag has been presented to the school by Mrs Duff and this gift has been generously supplemented by a fine flagstaff, the gift of Mr A. Clayton. The children assembled in the playground at 11.30 a.m. Each child wore a bunch of daisies and in addition many wore their attendance medals. Among a large number present were Mr, Mrs and Miss Clayton, Col C.E. Duff, C.B., and Mrs Duff, the Rev. G. Wickham and Mrs Wickham, Mr W.C. Whittle, the Misses May and Kathleen Cooper and the majority of the parents of the children. The ceremony of saluting the flag was performed, the flag being hoisted by Mrs Duff. Patriotic songs were sung and a stirring address was given by Col Duff.

'The children gave an exhibition of flag drill and figure marching, two of the evolutions forming the initals "E" and "A".[1] The accompaniments were admirably played by Miss M. Bendall. At the call of Mr Warr rousing cheers were given for the King, Queen and Royal Family and the children in their characteristic manner also expressed their thanks to the generous donors of the flag and staff. The proceedings throughout were most successful'.

Mention of the Royal Family brings to mind the good offices of the Rev and Mrs Wickham who, following their visit to Germany in 1905 where they stayed with Princess Louise of Battenburg, they returned with a present from the Princess for the children of Bradford Abbas School. The gift consisted of two illuminated texts painted by H.R.H. Princess Alice for her mother, Queen Victoria, on her birthday. Mr Harry Warr had the texts suitably framed and hung in the school.

On 22nd January 1907 the school were honoured by a visit from Princess Louise of Battenburg, who was staying with the Rev. and Mrs Wickham, and after being introduced to the Headmaster, Mr Warr, 'she inspected some of the work and she also heard the children sing some of their songs. The children were delighted with the honour paid to them and gave rousing cheers for the Princess.'

It was a pity that on the very day of the Princess's visit the attendance was low, not due to any disrespect to the royal family, but simply because of the very wet weather which meant that the children from Wyke and Clifton Maubank were unable to attend. To date, no other member of the royal family has visited the school.

Mr Warr continued as headmaster until 1933 when at a meeting of the School Managers held on 8th February 'a letter from Mr Warr, resigning the headmastership of the school was read with regret'. It came as a terrific shock to the village, for everyone realised that the school and the village were to lose a remarkable man. His record of scholarship successes, the consistently good reports of H.M. Inspector of Schools and the Class I of the school clearly indicated how successful his work had been. But not only had he been successful at the school but he had been a good servant to

---

1 Edward VII and his Queen, Alexandra.

Woodwork class in the village hall, c.1924.

the village, so much so that one leading villager recorded that 'few men can have been more intimately the confidant of those in trouble and difficulty and more sacrificing in their leisure time to those common interests which mean so much to the life of the community.' During his life in the village he was captain of both the Cricket and Football Clubs, the chief mover in the formation of the Tennis Club, Honorary Secretary of the Men's Club, Parochial Church Council, Parish Council, and Clifton Maubank Parish Meeting as well as being a Trustee of the Village Hall, local Assessor and Collector of Income Tax, Overseer and Rate Collector, Churchwarden and Choirmaster. On top of all these activities he also found time to be the *Western Gazette* correspondent, bellringer, to conduct the Women's Institute Choir at the Dorset Choral Competition and to compile an excellent little book *A Short History of Bradford Abbas*.

The villagers felt that they were losing a true friend and they were not slow in expressing their feelings:

'18th April 1933. The warmth of affection which exists between the parishioners and Mr Harry Warr who leaves the village tomorrow on his resignation of the headmastership of the school was strikingly shown by the gathering which assembled in the Village Hall this evening to say farewell to him and Mrs Warr, and to present them with a token of gratitude, goodwill and best wishes of the whole village and of Clifton Maubank and Wyke.

The Village Hall was filled with young and old, so many of whom had been taught by Mr Warr during his 32 years' association with the school, while others who had not that qualification were equally desirous of their appreciation of the character of one who had been their friend and fellow worker over so long a period. It was peculiar that so much of the entertainment of the social should be provided by Mr Warr's own pupils, Mr Leonard Purchase, the Misses Burroughes, Mrs W. Patch, Mr and Mrs Woolacott, and Miss Lumbard; while others who assisted were Miss Cooper of Wyke (one of whose recitations was a 'lament' at Mr Warr's departure), Miss Joyce, a colleague and Mr Jimmy Frizzell and friends from Yeovil. The Vicar, Rev. J.G. Vassall, presided over the gathering and for the presentation ceremony was supported by Col C.E. Duff, Mrs Cooper, Mrs E.T. Mellish, and Mr G. Good (Members of the Managing Body of the School). Among others present were Mr A.W. Turnbull of Clifton Maubank and Mrs Forder etc., Col C.E. Duff, who made the presentation to Mr and Mrs Warr, said, as one who had the pleasure of knowing Mr Warr for 25 years he did not wish to meet a better man anywhere. Having attended to the many honorary positions which Mr Warr had filled in the Parish Col Duff said he had always found Mr Warr a real friend, always cheery, ever ready to do anything that wanted to be done, and carrying out whatever he undertook in an excellent manner. His resignation was a tremendous blow to the School Managers. Continuing Col. Duff said that it was thought best not that all the organisations with which Mr Warr had been connected should each give him a separate parting gift but that all the parish should combine in one gift. The response had been extraordinarily good and he had the pleasure in asking Mr Warr to accept a cheque for £40. He believed Mr Warr had thoughts of buying a wireless set, but in whatever way he used the money he hoped he would put on it the following inscription.

"'Presented to Mr Harry Warr by his friends at Bradford Abbas, Clifton Maubank and Wyke as a token of their esteem and gratitude for his life and many good works among them during his 32 years' residence, especially as headmaster of Bradford Abbas School.'"

'With that gift went their good wishes for good luck and long life in retirement. Col Duff asked Mrs Warr to accept a gift of books from the subscribers.

'The Vicar said one person he would like to have been present that night was the late Canon Wickham for he believed a great deal of the fine character and life which Mr Warr had shown and which had helped them all so much was due to his association with Canon Wickham when he came first as headmaster of the school. Continuing Mr Vassall said that when he first came to Bradford Abbas 12 years ago a Yeovil tradesman told him that he had no fear of going to Bradford Abbas because the "Bradford Lawyer" would see him through. Mr Vassall spoke of all that he personally owed to Mr Warr for his help and guidance. With reference to Mr Warr's school work the Managers became almost tired of receiving report after report on the school from the authorities "Worthy of the highest commendation". They were repeatedly reminded of what a wonderful man they had at the head of the school, and it was true that Mr Warr had brought that school from the bottom grade to the highest. They regarded Mr Warr as one of the leading teachers in the County and were proud of his capabilities. It was a wonderful thing to be able to say that he had never heard one child leaving that school say he or she was sorry that Mr Warr had been his or her headmaster, and

Mr Harry Warr, Headmaster of
Bradford Abbas School 1900–33.

during that time over a 1000 pupils had passed through his hands. They were all exceedingly sorry that the time had come for Mr Warr to give up his work among them, his work, his friendship would be remembered in that place for many years to come. Mr Vassall intimated to the gathering that Mr Warr was leaving the village on the anniversary of his wedding and that they wished him many happy returns of the day. Mr Vassall spoke of Mr Warr's kindness to the children in providing free, year after year, cocoa for those who remained at the school for dinner and concluding wished both Mr and Mrs Warr many years of happiness and assured them of the gratefulness of everyone in that village for all that they had done during their residence there.

'Mr Warr in expressing on behalf of his wife and himself the warmest thanks for the kindness shown toward them said that he never regretted the day he came to Bradford Abbas, where he had spent so many years of happiness. He hoped that the 1000 or more children who had passed through his hands had received some benefit from his influence and teaching. During the past 79 years there had been three headmasters of that school, so that either the Managers had been fortunate in their choice of headmasters or those who had been appointed had been so contented and comfortable that they had remained there as long as they could. He had been singularly fortunate in having two such splendid men as Canon Wickham and Mr Vassall who had given him such a free example and been such good friends. Although he was leaving Bradford Abbas his thoughts would often be with them, he would be seeing them sometimes and he hoped that they would call and see them in their new home. He had loved the children and would always be interested in their welfare and thinking about them. The gathering sang "For He's a Jolly Good Fellow" and cheers were raised for both Mr and Mrs Warr.

'The Vicar warmly thanked the Committee which had arranged the presentation; Mrs Turnbull and Mrs Cooper for the part they played in collecting subscriptions in their respective hamlets; Mr T. Patch and Mr Mears for arranging the hall, and to Miss Mead and Miss Joyce for collecting in Bradford Abbas.

'Refreshments were served and an enjoyable evening was spent.'

No such gathering to say farewell to a good friend had ever been held in the village before, nor in fact since, and so the man who could be said to have truly earned the name 'Mr Bradford Abbas' left for West Moors and passed from the village scene into what was to be a long and happy retirement until he died in 1965. It is ironic that not one person from Bradford Abbas attended his funeral.

It was not until 30th October 1933 that the School Managers appointed another headmaster, Mr R.C. Day, who took up his duties on 20th November 1933, when the Rev. E.C. Douglas and Col Duff also attended to introduce the new Headmaster to the children. During the period between Mr Warr's departure and Mr Day's arrival the school had been provided with teachers from the county supply staff but standards and discipline had deteriorated rapidly to such an extent that it appeared that the school was nearing a state of anarchy, so when Mr Day commenced his teaching at the school he had many problems to face. However, after only three months the Managers reported that he was 'already making his influence for good felt'. More often than not, however, it is the case with a new Headmaster that he introduces new systems and methods which do not always meet the the approval of the existing staff.

When Mr Day became Headmaster, there were already two mistresses at the school—Miss Joyce and Miss Barrett—neither of whom appeared to be as co-operative as they might have been with the new Master. As early as March 1935 the School Managers were clearly unhappy with the situation and at their meeting of 19th March 1935 in a report on the teachers the following is recorded:

The school, c.1938. The gentleman in the middle of the second row is the Headmaster, Mr R.C. Day.

'Mr Day has worked really hard and there is a noticeable improvement in the school in every way. He has interested himself in the village as well as in the school life, but as regards the school his work has been somewhat hampered by his junior teachers, who, the Managers feel, do not show unqualified loyalty to him and to his methods. In his own class however, one is conscious of a very happy atmosphere and we feel that we are fortunate to have him as our headmaster.'

With regards to the two mistresses they said that they were compelled to endorse what Mr Day had written but went on to say with regard to Miss Joyce that they further felt that she had been so long at the school that she was in danger of 'getting into a groove'. They considered that she might do better starting afresh in another school. As for Miss Barrett, they said that they had already expressed dissatisfaction both with her disciplinary powers and some of her methods and that she should be given a fresh start in another school.

Whether pressure was brought to bear on the two mistresses, I know not, but Miss Joyce resigned in April 1935 to be followed by Miss Barrett only a few weeks later. They were to be replaced by Miss Payne and Mrs Watkins, with both of whom the School Managers were to express their satisfaction.

One of the first tasks that Mr Day set himself on becoming Headmaster was to revive the entertainment which the children put on each year for their parents and which was originated by Mr Warr but had been allowed to lapse. At the beginning of the 1934 spring term the Headmaster started rehearsals and by 13th February the children entertained their parents thus:

'To give a good two hours' entertainment after only three weeks in which to train the children, make the costumes and prepare all the front and back stage paraphernalia is no mean achievement. It was done by the Headmaster, Mr R.C. Day and the staff, Miss Joyce and Miss Barrett, and the result of all their work was seen in the hall. The building was filled with appreciative parents and other parishioners, who thoroughly enjoyed the entertainment, acting and singing of the children. The help of Mr W. Patch and Miss Lombard in the dressing of the children was appreciated. Messrs Long and Jeffreys did service at the door and Arthur Courtney and Walter Hendley sold the programmes. The songs by boys and girls led up to a fairy play "Snow White and the Seven Dwarfs" which was interesting for a delightful naive and confident performance by Hazel Patch as

Snow White and competent acting by Fred Gale as the Prince, Norah Hallett as the Queen and Ruby Cox as the maid. The dwarfs who so amused the audience were Victor Chant, Raymond Davies, Desmond Gosney, Teddy Mear, Albert Parker, John Paulley and Tom Rand.

"The Kingdom of Arcades" was a play in 3 acts, showing the revolt of the children from the restrictions of parents and school life, the setting up of a kingdom of their own, and how their troubles made them glad to return to a warm bed, parental attention and scholastic duties. The many costumes, particularly the soldiers, were colourful and effective and there was some pretty dancing by Mary Sheard, Joyce Purchase, Joyce Cleal, Ruby Cox, Yvonne Myles, Nancy Sheard, Betty Blackmore and Norah Hallett. The characters were taken as follows:

King—Cyril Gosney; Lord Mayor—Stanley Bagwell; Physician—Gordon Puckett; Field Marshall—Walter Cleal; Admiral—Ronald Forse; Royal Recanter—Fred Gale; Confectioner—Christopher Chaffey; Headsman—John Gill; Herald—Bernard Patch; A nuisance—Raymond Davies; Queen—Joan Forse; Princess—Florence Bayliss; Lady in waiting—Sybil Purchase; Court Ladies—Elsie Chant, Betty Gosney, Marion Gillham, Sophia Wilding and Minnie Wilding; Nursemaids—Ruth Fowler and Phillis Fowler, Soldiers— Phillip Bagwell, James Chant, Edward Cleal, Austin Coombs, Desmond Gosney, Leonard Gosney, Denis Puckett and Bruce Puckett; Guards—Gilbert Burrough and Sammy Puckett; Court Jester—Robert Hallett.

The concluding item which proved very popular was the "Wedding of Mr Mickey Mouse". Its success was contributed to by the quaint and amusing expressions on the animal masks. The characters were: Mickey Mouse—Fred Gale; Mistress Mouse—Elsie Chant; Preacher Man—John Gill; Guests—Billy Gosney, Sophia Wilding, Minnie Wilding, Phillip Bagwell, Ronald Force and Ronald Hallett. There was a warm demonstration of appreciation of the children's performance by the audience at the close, and the Headmaster and his colleagues were congratulated on an enjoyable entertainment and their success in presenting bright and amusing little productions from meagre resources of scenery and stage effects.'

Mr Day continued these entertainments (which were on a much more lavish scale than any such entertainments previously seen in the village) each year but he also encouraged the sporting life of the school, an activity which was surprisingly lacking under his predecessor. Mr Day was responsible for what is now the annual school sports and the first of these was held on 24th July 1934 in a field adjoining the school which had been kindly lent by the Vicar, Rev. E.C. Douglas. The children had been divided into four houses—Assyrians, Athenians, Romans and Spartans—and a shield was given by Mr and Mrs Forder for competition amongst the boys and a silver cup given by Mrs Maxwell of the Grange was competed for by the girls. The shield was won by the Assyrians and the cup by the Spartans.

The school could also now boast of netball and football teams, the latter being particulary successful in maintaining good results. In fact, only one year after Mr Day's arrival the team lost in the final of the Ismay Cup by only one goal to nil and it was said that the team played particularly well, with Teddy Cleal, Gordon Puckett and Cyril Gosney outstanding.

Another very successful innovation by Mr Day was the introduction of a school magazine very simply headed 'Bradford Abbas School Magazine' in which the children were to be responsible for the editorials, articles and publishing, and what a success they made of it. I have in my possession a copy of the second issue of the magazine dated 1938. It makes most interesting reading and is a mine of information particularly with regard to the beekeeping (a swarm was given by Mr W. Gale) and poultrykeeping, both of which were part of their school activities. The article by Desmond Gosney on 'The School Poultry' gives in great detail the way in which they incubated the eggs and the type of food given to the chicken and why. There is also an interesting article on wild flowers by Rita Fowler who also wrote a riddle-me-ree which throws up the answer 'primrose'. It is a pity that there is no longer such a magazine. Apart from the concern over Vincents Angina, of which I have written in an earlier chapter, when the school had to be closed for over two months, the life of the school was most satisfactory and was to continue to be so under the energetic Mr Day. However world events were soon to affect the school for with the outbreak of the Second World War on 3rd September 1939 it was only a matter of a couple of days before about 100 boys and girls from St George's Roman Catholic School, Southwark, had to be provided for as they had been evacuated from London. Four of their teachers had come with them. There was no way in which the school could absorb such an influx and it therefore became necessary to commandeer the Village Hall for use as a classroom. It was decided to fuse the two schools into one and this was done with the result that all classes contained children from both schools. That the two schools operated fully was largely due to the efforts of Mr Day and it was said that it was a very happy school, but in 1940 and 1941 there was a constant changing of teachers, which added greatly to the Headmaster's worries. He worked extremely hard, but successfully, to keep the school operating efficiently.

In early 1942 Mr Day suffered an extremely painful illness which it was believed was brought about by the extra work imposed upon him by the wartime conditions, and he was absent from the school for two months during which time the school was efficiently run by the other teachers. By now the London children were drifting homewards and the work imposed on Mr Day was getting a little easier but on 1st September 1942 he tendered his resignation. A week later he accepted the post of Headmaster of Bovington Camp School with the result that the School managers agreed to release him early and so he left the school on 25th September 1942, with in his own words 'mixed feelings'. So the problem of appointing a new Headmaster arose and the School Managers were very quickly left in no doubt that the new Headmaster would have to be a Mistress. There were few applications for the position and the Managers appointed a Miss Edith Flowers who indicated her acceptance of the position but surprisingly wrote a fortnight later to say that she was withdrawing her acceptance. The Managers decided that they would appoint Mrs Kathleen Mary Whitten of Bournemouth as Headmistress and she took up her duties on 6th January 1943, this becoming the first Headmistress in the history of the school. Her reign was to be short for at the end of February, after barely seven weeks in charge, she tendered her resignation. Why Mrs Whitten should resign after so short a period is far from clear, but it could be for one of two reasons. The first reason was that there was no accommodation in the village for her. The house which had been used by successive Headmasters was no longer available and had not been since 1933, when Mr Warr retired. It was now occupied by a family, and although one of the Managers accommodated her in his own house with her furniture stored at another, it was obviously not a very satisfactory arrangement. In her final entry on 31st May 1943 in the log book she wrote, 'my period of duty here has been of short duration owing to the lack of accommodation in the village of a suitable house'.

There was another problem which may have accounted for her resignation, for at the Managers' meeting on 26th March 1943 there is recorded a most interesting minute:

'At her own request Mrs Whitten met the managers and reported a very recent visit of Mr W.E. Wright, His Majesty's Inspector to the school. She said that he had noted a general deterioration in the school, which had been in decline for some time. She also stated that he had given her verbal reports on each of the assistant teachers, one favourable and the other unfavourable. He had given it as his opinion that the school was overstaffed and that one teacher might properly be removed.'

I feel that the problem of providing accommodation could have been overcome without too much difficulty and that Mrs Whitten could have remained at the school as she was not responsible for the deterioration of the school's standards. It could well have been that she saw many problems ahead and the accommodation issue was merely used as a reason for moving on. It was very disappointing to the Managers that she decided to leave as it was recorded that 'in a very short time that Mrs Whitton has been here she has given good promise of bringing the school to a high state of efficiency and discipline'.

The School Managers were left, therefore, with the problem of appointing a new Head Teacher and out of three applications that they received, the position was offered to Miss Emily Couch, who was Headmistress of Leigh School. She readily accepted the position, taking up her duties on 3rd August 1943. All went well with the school until the summer holidays of 1945 when Messrs King of Sherborne reported that there was no water in the school well. The Managers were anxious to keep the school open as at this time the county education authorities were making far-reaching proposals for uniting various schools, and Bradford Abbas, it was suggested, should be amalgamated with Thornford. The problems with the water supply were only aggravating, if not hastening, a possible unification. The children were not allowed to assemble in the playground due to the well having been opened and all children were to come into and go out of the school by the north door. The boys' lavatories could not be used and the girls had to use their own lavatories first, followed by the boys. The children were also anxious to keep the school open and several of the elder children volunteered to bring water to the school from a pump in Mill Lane. They did so with large containers from the school canteen which at the time was in the Village Hall. Mr Underdown, one of the School Managers and a local farmer also gave considerable assistance by bringing churns of water daily. Unfortunately

May 1st 1953.

all their efforts were in vain as they found it impossible to cope with the school sanitation and with great reluctance the Managers decided, on 17th September 1945, that the school had to be closed. The younger children were sent to Nether Compton School under Mrs Coleclough and the senior to the Abbey School, Sherborne under the Headmistress Miss Couch. And so after some 200 years, the children of the village were no longer able to spend their whole school life within the confines of the village school. When the school was finally reopened in 1947, it was not the same, for at the age of 11 they had to continue their education elsewhere. At the same time as all of these changes were taking place, Miss Couch, the Headmistress, tendered her resignation. The School Managers were asked by the County Education Officer if they could persuade her to continue and after meeting with her she agreed to withdraw her resignation. This was good news for the school because in the three years that she had been Headmistress the Managers were able to report that her work was showing good results in discipline and in class work.

In early 1951 the School Managers had to decide on the future status of the school, whether it was to be an aided or a controlled school. The managers, in their wisdom, felt that the school should be treated as an aided school which meant that it would carry on much as it had before, except that the Ministry of Education would bear half of the cost of what had previously been the Managers' costs. It would still remain a church school. It was not until 1963 that it became a voluntary controlled school, taking its present name St Mary's Voluntary Controlled School. The name 'St Marys' was suggested by the Headmaster Mr Leslie Gardner at the time that the changes were being considered.

In 1952 Miss Couch resigned and was succeeded by Mr R.F. Edwards, a bachelor, who took up his duties on 12th January 1953. It had again not been possible to consider a married teacher due to the lack of accommodation in the village.

Mr Edwards had only been in charge of the school a few months when he began to have differences with the School Managers. The main problem seemed to be with regard to the Headmaster's attitude to the life of the church in the village for after expressing satisfaction with his teaching ability a minute of 14th May 1953 goes on to say:

'In view of the assurances given at the time of his appointment that he would have the spiritual welfare of the children at heart the managers were bound to express their disappointment at Mr Edwards's evident disinterest in the spiritual life of the parish. As headmaster of the school the managers liked him to set an example.'

Mr Edwards promised to do what he could to rectify this state of affairs, but in the school log book he recorded that he 'felt bound to place on record that apart from the Vicar's weekly visit for Scripture no Manager has called at the school since he became headmaster'. This is rather ironic as he also says that some of the Managers asked that the children should stand when they entered the classroom, which Mr Edwards refused to make them do. He also stopped the old practice of the children having to salute the Managers. The question of Mr Edwards entering into the church life of the parish continued to cause concern to the Managers and the question of Mr Edwards's dismissal was considered. However, a more crucial meeting of the School Managers was held on 25th September 1953 which is amply covered by the entry in the school log book for that day.

'A meeting of the managers, Mr Easton (Education Officer) and Canon Bailey (Diocesan Representative) was held at Manor Farm, Wyke. The headmaster, Mr R.F. Edwards was invited to attend and he took with him Mr Ball, the National Union of Teachers Area Representative. Charges that the children had no spiritual guidance and influence from the headmaster had been made by the managers. The Local Education Authority representative Mr Easton, Canon Bailey and Mr Ball all informed the managers there was 'no case' and that they had no grounds upon which they could dismiss the headmaster. The parents of the children of the school had been interested enough to hold a protest meeting regarding the matter and a letter was sent to the correspondent (Rev. J.N.D. Perkins) of the managers expressing their complete confidence in the headmaster and a vote of no confidence in the managers.'

All present at this meeting agreed to treat the discussions with the greatest confidence as the outcome of the meeting was that 'the Managers expressed their appreciation of Mr Edwards's work for the school and looked forward to a time of happy co-operation together'. But this confidence was broken and caused considerable embarrassment to the Headmaster, with the result that the Managers issued a written statement to stop all rumours. By the end of 1953 there was a much more amicable relationship between the Managers and the Headmaster and he was congratulated on his continued improvements in school life. However, Mr Edwards's troubles were not over, as in early 1955 he began to experience difficulties with the behaviour of one of the mistresses' classes. He found it necessary to rebuke her and only two months later he 'had to go into the infants' room several times to keep order as the Assistant Mistress seems unable to do so'. At this time she complained that she was feeling ill so he sent her home, but two days later a more serious incident occurred.

'During the Religious Instruction lesson the headmaster had occasion to go into the infants' room, because the terrific din made it impossible for Classes I and II to work. He found the room in chaos. When asked what the children were doing the Assistant Mistress stated that she refused to answer. The headmaster pressed for a reply but she insisted she would not say as he had told her when she first started that he would not interfere with the Religious Instruction work. He explained that as headmaster he was responsible for work being done in both departments. As her attitude persisted he said he would take her class into his room and that it would stay there until she had prepared her day's work since much of the trouble in the infants' class was due to her non-prepared work. He told the children to stand and lead into his room. Miss Bennett stood in front of them and said that he was not to take her class away. Rather than create a scene in front of the children he asked her very quietly not to make a fuss and to be sensible. She still refused to allow the children to pass so he left the room and sent for Captain Bevan, the Vice Chairman of the Managers. Captain Bevan came across and in front of the Assistant Mistress the headmaster explained the situation. Speaking to Captain Bevan, the Assistant Mistress said she "reserved the right to say what she was doing during her religious instruction lesson". The headmaster took the infants into his room and kept them there until dinner time.'

The Assistant Mistress left the school during the dinner break and she never returned.

On 29th April 1956 a centenary service was held in St Mary's Church in the presence of a large congregation. The Vicar, the Rev. C.G. Kerslake, officiated and was assisted by the lay reader, Mr Leslie Gardner, who was soon to become Headmaster, and the sermon, tracing the history of church schools, was given by the Rev. J.S. Maples, the Diocesan Director of Education. Lessons were read by Mr Edgar Patch, representing the old pupils and by Mr Edwards, representing past and present members of the teaching staff, whilst two children carried bouquets of flowers from the altar to the font, where they were received by the Vicar. It was a pleasurable service which as it happened turned out to be the last conducted in St Mary's Church by the Rev. C.G. Kerslake as he died very suddenly only three days later.

In June 1956 Mr Edwards advised the Managers that he would be leaving as the Air Ministry advised him that he was to be appointed Headmaster of a Royal Air Force Association Children's school in Cyprus and following a very pleasant ceremony in the school on 27th July 1956 Mr Edwards left to take up his new post. He left behind him a happy school and he described the children as 'the nicest set I have ever come across'.

He was succeeded by Mr Leslie Gardner, who was known to many villagers, as he was already a lay reader at the church. It was during his term as headmaster that the proposal to build a swimming pool and a new school was seriously considered, although Mr Gardner was not to see either come to fruition.

In 1963 Mr Gardner became a Minister at Bampton, Devon, but continued with his school duties until he resigned in 1964, to be succeeded by Mr Leslie Russell, who took up his duties early in 1965.

Mr Russell had spent all his teaching career in Dorset, commencing at Blandford Boys School in 1949 and as well as teaching at other schools in the county he had also served as Head Warden to the Dorset school camps from 1962 to 1964. He came to live in Manor Close with his wife and young family and he proved to be most energetic. It was during his term of office that both the new school and the swimming pool were built.

Since 1947, when the school had reopened after its long closure due to the inadequate water supply, the number of pupils had steadily risen year by year until in January 1984 the number of children attending the school was over 100, and the trend was for the numbers to continue to increase due to the considerable amount of new building that had taken place in the village in the previous three years. And so, by 1963 the question of a new school at Bradford Abbas had reached the top of the County Council's priority list. The new school was therefore built and the official opening ceremony was held on 14th July 1966, when the school was dedicated by Archbishop Lord Fisher of Lambeth, before a good attendance of parents and friends.

But the new school was found inadequate to accommodate all the children and the old buildings continued to be used, as they are today. The numbers on the register had, by 1967, made it the third largest school of its kind in Dorset. In addition the school had obtained a new playing field alongside the River Yeo and a teachers' centre had been opened at the school which was the first in Dorset and probably the only one in a primary school anywhere in the country. It was said at the time, at a prize-giving ceremony that 'these are great days to be young in Bradford Abbas' and how true these words were, for a few years at least. With the new school buildings, sporting activities increased with the boys winning the North Dorset Small Schools Football League by not dropping a point out of their 12 fixtures. On the athletic track the school gained 3rd place in the North Dorset Schools Primary Championship. With all the enthusiasm that there was in the village at this time it was not surprising that a swimming pool was built. Ably led by the Headmaster, funds were soon raised and after much hard work by many parents who physically assisted with the labouring work the new pool was opened officially on 15th July 1967 by Mr Hayfield at a fête which had been organised to raise the balance of the money required. The swimming pool was a major effort by the villagers and the total cost amounted to £957 19s 8d, but this would have

The Managers and Headmaster

of

St Mary's V. C. School, Bradford Abbas

Request the Pleasure of the Company of

M. E. M. Garrett.

At the Official Opening and Dedication of the New School Building
by The Most Reverend Archbishop Lord Fisher of Lambeth, P.C., G.C.V.O., D.D.

on Thursday, 14th July at 2·30 p.m., to be

followed by afternoon tea.

R.S.V.P.
The Headmaster,
St Mary's V.C. School,
Bradford Abbas,
Sherborne,
Dorset.

*Invitation to the
official opening of
the new school.*

*Part of the new
school which was
officially opened in
1966.*

been considerably larger had not so many parishioners given their time and services freely. The pool, for those interested in statistics, measures 40ft x 20ft, is 2ft 6in. to 3ft 6in deep and has a capacity of 15,000 gallons.

After five years Mr Russell left to become Headmaster of the new County Primary School at Ringwood and he was succeeded by Mr K. Roach. It was during his term as Headmaster that the St Mary's School suffered its first teachers' strike, with the school closed for the morning of 9th December 1969. I would add that this was not a local dispute but part of a campaign by the teachers' unions nationally. In 1971 Mr Roach was awarded a Walter Hines Page scholarship which entailed four weeks' travel to the United States during which period the school was run by Mrs Norfolk, the Deputy Head.

Mr Roach left the school in 1972 to be succeeded by Mr R.A. Lincoln who himself left in March 1975 to be succeeded by Mr John Arscott. He left at the end of the summer term in 1982, to be succeeded by the present Headmaster Mr David Penny.

Probably the greatest problem facing the school at the present time is the number of children attending, for the numbers are falling and it would seem that they will continue to do so. It is to be hoped that the school has greater days yet to come but the skies look cloudier by the year as more elderly people move into the village as a retirement base. The school has had its problems before, however, and no doubt will again and I am sure that it will continue for many years to come. It is now a happy school and long may it continue to be so.

CHAPTER VII
The Village and the Villagers

If it were possible to cast oneself back through 200 years of history the visitor to Bradford Abbas would have found a village which consisted of North Street (including the Cross), Bakehouse Lane, Grope Lane, Churchwell Street, Church Road, Mill Lane, Westbury, Higher Westbury and a few scattered houses lying outside the main pattern. The roads themselves were no more than dirt tracks but there were cobbled pavements in North Street, Westbury and Church Road. The church was the dominant building. Most of the houses were built of stone taken from the village's own quarry together with some Ham Hill stone. If the same visitor was to return to the village today he would still see many of the buildings he saw 200 years ago but he would find them very much in the minority compared with the numbers of houses less than 30 years old. There is, however, little doubt that he would find the village just as interesting as even the new estates are rapidly taking their place in the story of Bradford Abbas.

This chapter will provide a tour of the village, hopefully providing an insight into what can be seen and brief glimpses of the lives of villagers in the past.

Ambrose Close lies immediately to the east of Bishop's Lane and adjoins the western side of Emlet. It consists of a residential estate, almost all bungalows with just two semi-detached houses. It was built in the early 1960s by Mr M.P. Osmond of Gillingham, who originally intended to name the estate 'Bishop's Close', presumably because of its proximity to Bishop's Lane, but as the then Vicar, Rev. G.R. Buchanan, pointed out, the enclosure had always been known as Ambrose Close, and he requested that the new estate should bear the same name—a request which was readily acceded to.

For generations it was part of the Bradford Abbas estate, being let in conjunction with Westbury House, and it was not until 1954 that it came into private ownership. When Wyatt Paul was the owner the Football Club played their home matches here and other village activities took place in the field from time to time. However, the club had to find a new pitch in 1954 as the new owner needed the field for his cattle. At the time considerable thought was given by the Parish Council to how they could obtain the field and turn it into a recreational area.

Thirteen of the bungalows on the estate were built by Sherborne Rural District Council for elderly people but these properties passed into the hands of West Dorset District Council upon the reorganisation of local government in 1974.

When *Babylon Hill* is mentioned today it usually refers to the route by which the dual carriageway runs down the hill. However, this was not always the case for according to maps of 1821 and 1828 Babylon Hill consisted of only one small field to the east of Underdown Hollow and the fields on either side of the present highway all had their own individual name, Hambreys, Underdown, Underdown Mead, New Close and Middle Spear.

It is of course the main A30 London–Exeter road which now runs down the hill and many people can still recall when it was just a narrow road, parts of which still survive in two laybys on the south side of the highway. The present road was completed and opened to traffic on 4th January 1968, two months ahead of schedule, the whole section of the road from Loscombe's Cross to Yeovil Bridge costing £80,000. This part of the dual carriageway took sixteen months to complete.

At the bottom of Babylon Hill can be seen Snell's Printing Works, the site of what was the Tollhouse Garden Centre and on the opposite side of the road is a filling station and a scrapyard. The first garage on Babylon Hill was on the site of the Tollhouse Garden Centre. When an application was made to build a garage on this site the Sherborne Rural District Council decided against the proposal as they were strongly against petrol stations being built on beauty spots in their area. However, after much debate the matter was finally resolved and a garage and later a workshop were built. The filling station on the other side of the road came after the Second World War as did Snell's Printing Works. By 1970, the garage had been demolished and was replaced by the Tollhouse Garden Centre which was advertised as being designed to cater for modern demands, and where 'enthusiasts can buy anything from a packet of seeds to a motor mower, ham stone etc.'

In October 1970 a 2-ton scale replica of a Dutch windmill was erected outside the Tollhouse Garden Centre's main premises. The model, which was 24 feet high with 24-foot span open sails had been obtained through Dutch bulb suppliers. It was in fact one of the only two in the world, the other being in America. Unfortunately it has now been taken away.

There have been many fatal accidents on Babylon Hill and these have increased considerably since the advent of the motor car. I will only relate one here which is of some interest as it involves a villager and on his tombstone the words 'In the midst of life there is death' can be read. It was only too true in this particular case.

'24th July 1891. Mr Walden, dairyman of Bradford Abbas met with an accident which terminated fatally. He was returning from Yeovil in his trap when on going up Babylon Hill the trap got too near to the bank with the result that Mr Walden, who was sitting on a barrel was thrown upon the road. The horse continued his journey, eventually reaching home, when Mrs Walden was surprised to see the trap without her husband. She and her son went back to search for Mr Walden and found him about a mile and a half from the house. He was conveyed home and Dr Flower attended from Yeovil. It was discovered that a serious injury was sustained to the spine and the whole of the body from the shoulders was paralysed. At an inquest held in Sherborne (four days later) Mr Walden, the deceased's son, was the first witness examined. He said his father's horse arrived home on Friday night about 12 o'clock but his father was not in the trap to which the horse was attached; witness went to look for him and found him lying on his face at the corner of the hill leading to Bradford from Babylon Hill. His father was sensible. With assistance, witness was asked by a juryman what kind of seat his father had in the trap and he replied that it was a barrel he had borrowed in Yeovil. His father was a heavy man and witness conjectured that the barrel swayed, owing to the trap striking the bank, his father must have lost his balance and been thrown out from the trap. William Glover of Yeovil said deceased was drinking with him at the Globe and Crown on Friday evening and he left there to go home at about five minutes to eleven. He got into the trap and drove off all right. Witness did not consider him the worse for drink and thought him capable of driving home. Dr Flower of Yeovil said he was summoned at 10.30 pm on Saturday to Bradford and went immediately. He saw deceased in a sitting room where he was lying. His body from the shoulders downwards was paralysed owing to the spinal cord being injured. He continued to attend deceased until death ensued. The jury returned a verdict of "accidental death" and added a rider to the effect that they were of the opinion that the turn in the road to Bradford Abbas from Babylon Hill was dangerous to anyone driving there at night and asking that it should be immediately altered.'

Needless to say the corner was not improved.

Finally it would seem that the original name for the hill was probably Raborn from whence it was changed to Badell and then to the present Babylon.

Back Lane lies at the eastern end of the parish and is extremely narrow in places. I would imagine that in the past it was of little significance except possibly for local farmers wishing to move cattle without having to take them through the buillt-up area of the village. In maps of 1821 and 1838 no buildings are shown on either side of the lane, and it is only during the last 40 years or so that any houses have been erected in this area.

At the southern end of the lane are the allotments and these have been situated here since 1962. At the extreme southern tip can be seen the remains of steps used by the cricketers as they made their way to play matches in the field opposite the Old Rectory.

Bakehouse Lane runs from the southern end of North Street, more familiarly known as the Cross, eastwards until it meets up with Back Lane, thus forming a crossroads with Fanny Brooks Lane. The name obviously derives from the fact that many years ago the communal bakehouse was situated here before it became part of the village poorhouse which I have described earlier. The Old Bakehouse was situated at the western corner of the lane adjoining the Cross and opposite it stood an old farmhouse, which in 1841 was a public house (The Hare & Hounds) but it was demolished many years ago and is now an empty space where heavy equipment is parked.

Baker's Piece is, or was, a field which lies directly to the south of Corville Auto Engineers and the Old Police House. In fact these establishments were built on what was in 1838 part of the field, as was the house which is slightly to the south-east of Corville Auto Engineers.

Beggar's Bush Lane runs northwards from the Sherborne–Yeovil road just to the east of the junction with Quarry Lane. The lane, which is nothing more than a cart track, is now blocked by a massive tree stump, but it stretches for some 200 yards until it runs into a field known as Beggar's Bush. On the right hand side of the lane is a small cluster of trees planted, I understand, by Mr Wyatt Paul when he decided to fill in the old quarry from which stone had been extracted for use in building the older houses in Bradford Abbas. In fact the last major load of stone to come from this quarry was that which was required to build the new organ chamber in St Mary's Church. Contrary to popular belief Beggar's Bush Lane is not a public footpath and never has been.

Bishop's Lane runs from the railway bridge in Westbury westwards for a few yards before turning northwards and eventually meeting up with the Manor Farm road. How the name 'Bishop's Lane' arose is not known but for many years there were no buildings on either side of this road. The first building to be erected in Bishop's Lane was the bungalow now known as Mon Repos which was erected by the village blacksmith, Mr Wyndham Pomeroy, who had it built just before the outbreak of the Second World War. It is now an extremely busy stretch of road which carries much of the traffic heading for Yeovil. The entrances to Queen's Road, Ambrose Close, and Manor Close are in this lane.

As you enter Bishop's Lane from the southern end of Westbury there is an extremely acute corner which is very dangerous to pedestrians. It was apparently considered to be very dangerous in 1860 for the Vestry meeting attempted to get Bishop's Lane rerouted in order that there would be no dangerous corner and so that Bishop's Lane would run directly into the bridge, going through what is now the garden of Westbury House. But neither the Railway Company nor the local landowner allowed this rerouting to take place so the position at the corner of Westbury and Bishop's Lane is still exactly as it was when the railway was built in 1860. There are in fact now two bungalows in Bishop's Lane. It was in Mon Repos that Mrs Ena Fowler, who was later to lay the foundation stone for the new Village Hall, lived most of her married life, her father of course being Mr Wyndham Pomeroy, the village blacksmith who had the property built.

Bradford Hollow is the narrow track which runs down from the Bradford Abbas–Sherborne road until it emerges at Yeovil bridge just to the rear of Snell's Printing Works. It is today more often referred to by the locals as 'Little Hollow'. In his book *Description of Sherborne* Joseph Fowler describes it thus:

'Some of the old tracks down the escarpment have developed into deep, sandy hollow ways, whose sides are sometimes so high and close together that very little sunlight penetrates their depths. Bradford Hollow, leading down to North Farm, between Bradford Abbas and Yeovil, is the most striking example in the neighbourhood. It is more like a tunnel than a lane, and it was only as our eyes became accustomed to the darkness that Rupert Jones was able to see the detail for his drawings. These hollow ways were formed and deepened solely by traffic, though there are some (covered ways as they are called) which may have purposely been sunken in very early times to enable people to get down the hill face unseen.'

There is no doubt that Roundhead troops advanced unseen up through the hollow when challenging the Cavaliers at the Battle of Babylon Hill and even today it is possible to travel unseen along this route. The hollow is little used these days and although still classified as a second class county road it would be virtually impossible to drive a vehicle throughout its entire length. It certainly is a very quiet place which no doubt attracted many young lovers in the past and many tokens of love can be seen scratched into the sandstone walls. Unfortunately many of these scratchings are rapidly disappearing as is a rather magnificent scratching of a nude which adorned one side of a small cave entrance. There are two small caves in the sandstone cliffs, one of which is easily accessible and the other which is not—although many of the younger folk of the village do make their way to this second cave even though the access is hazardous.

It was in the days of horses an extremely important route and there were many requests made by the Parish Council to the higher authority for the route to be kept open. In 1904 the locals were complaining that it was virtually impassable for foot passengers and that 'this was disgraceful as it was used considerably by the villagers'.

With a place such as Bradford Hollow, which can be very frightening at nights, it is inevitable that legends should arise. I have been told in the past that a ghostly coach and horses can be seen passing this way from time to time and also that a murder was committed here. It was talk of the supposed murder which intrigued Professor James Buckman, who in 1882 was living at Coombe House, and he decided to investigate the matter further. In doing so he called in the assistance of a scientific friend, Professor E. Lees, F.L.S. F.G.S., who wrote as follows:

'Some years ago a murder was perpetrated at this spot and as tales of horror never die out, so as to keep up the memory of a crime that renders the place too dismal to be trodden after nightfall, stains of blood, so the rustics say, still remain upon the sides of what bears the name 'The Bloody Cave'. When visiting my friend Professor Buckman he told me of the tradition appertaining to this cave, which exciting my curiosity I asked him to take me to the direful spot. There I saw, certainly, on the sides of the excavation and on the sand rock around numerous sanguine patches, but not believing in their being actual bloodmarks formed by guilty hands, I carried away several specimens for examination at home. I found, as I expected, that these sanguine marks, on subjecting them to the test of the microscope were in reality a kind of cryptomatic vegetation belonging to the tribe of Algae. In fact this substance bears the botanic name of Palmella Cruenta and has the English name Gory Dew. In damp places it occasionally appears upon the ground and looks as if port wine has been spilt there; and has suggested bloody ideas to superstitious minds.'

And so a legend is disproved.

Bradford Leaze lies in the north west extremity of the parish, banked on three sides by the River Yeo. It is now part of the Yeovil Golf Club and has been since the first nine holes were laid out in 1919. It was in fact the common land of the parish and in 1838 the Tithe Commissioners recorded:

'The whole quantity of common land subject to tithes within the said parish is seventy eight acres, three roads and thirty eight perches, statute measure, being a close of pasture called Bradford Leaze, which is annually stocked in common by the respective owners of leazes thereon from the 14th day of May to the 14th day of December with black cattle and from the 14th day of December to the 14th day of February with sheep and is hained or laid up from the 14th day of February to the 14th day of May.

The total number of leazes is eighty two which fifty four belong to the said Marquess [of Anglesey] in possession and twenty six lessees for life. The remaining two leazes belong to the Vicar. Each leaze entitles the owner of it to pasturage of one head of black cattle and two sheep during the respective periods above mentioned.'

By 1849 the acreage had dropped by some eight acres due, no doubt, to the ground having been bisected by the Wilts, Somerset and Weymouth railway. Eventually all the leases came into the hands of the Lord of the Manor and the area can no longer be classified as common land. In very early records of the parish the field is referred to as New Leaze Common.

Broadway Lane no longer exists. It went from a point just south of Westbury railway bridge across the fields to the west before finally meeting up with Castle Lake Lane which runs southwards from the present Manor Farm. In fact it ran more or less parallel to the Sherborne–Yeovil railway track. The lane was closed in 1860 but not without some strong opposition from the inhabitants. Mr Clayton was challenged by the Vestry as to what right he had to close the lane as it had from time immemorial been considered a parish road and had always been kept in repair by the parish. Nevertheless Mr Clayton was adamant and the lane remains closed.

According to the 1838 Tithe Apportionment *Butcher's Bar* lies just to the south of Manor Farm road. A Vestry Minute of 30th January 1849 advises that a resolution was passed that a quarry be opened here for the supply of stone for the roads. Whether this resolution was ever implemented is not recorded and certainly no trace of any quarry remains. In this field is a small well-house which provides water for Clifton Maubank House through lead pipes.

Castle Lake Lane runs southwards from Manor Farm before losing itself shortly after passing under the railway. Up to 1860 it met up with Broadway Lane. Contrary to popular belief it is not a public footpath and never has been.

Church Road is one of the most interesting roads in the parish. In fact it could be considered to be the main road. With the church of St Mary the Virgin lying at its western extremity it is quite obvious how the road got its name, although I have often heard it referred to as High Street by some of the older villagers.

I have in my possession a photograph of Church Road which I would date at about 1870 and which shows clearly the cobbled pavement which used to run along the south side whilst the church steps, which are now inset into the cemetery wall are shown protruding well out into the dirt road.

With a road such as Church Road it is difficult to know where to start as there are so many interesting buildings. The church and the old school have already been covered in earlier chapters but in close proximity to these two buildings is the Village Hall which was completed in 1982. The present hall is the third to have stood on this site. The first hall was erected in 1911 but it only lasted 8 years as it was destroyed by fire. This original hall was built of wood on a brick foundation at a cost of about £400 and the money had been raised by public subscription and with considerable financial help from Col Duff. It had rapidly become the centre of the village social life and at one end of it, which Col Duff personally owned, was housed the Men's Club.

It is not known for certain what caused the disastrous fire but the building was completely destroyed, including the equipment within it, in an incredibly short time. Nevertheless despite the disaster and even despite the fact that all was not covered by insurance, the village, with a great deal of help from the Men's Club who were insured, raised sufficient funds to enable a new hall to be officially opened on 4th May 1920. This new hall, which was to last for over 50 years, was a former YMCA hut and contained a main room measuring 42 feet x 30 feet with a Men's Club room at its east end. By about 1970 it had become quite obvious that the building was

The Village Hall which was built in 1911 on the site of the present village hall.

rapidly falling into disrepair, despite valiant efforts to keep it functional, and that a new hall was desperately required. And so a Committee was formed, charged with the task of fund raising. This was done very effectively and aided by grants the new hall was built. It is not of timber like the previous two but is of stone with a tiled roof and contains a main hall, committee room, storage room and a stage. The land upon which it stands is owned by the parish having been donated by Mr Wyatt Paul in 1938. The hall is under the ultimate control of the Charity Commissioners (a trust deed was drawn up in 1938) but is managed by a Committee which consists of representatives of the various village organisations. The Committee won a competition in 1988 for the best-run Village Hall in West Dorset, coming second in the whole county.

Immediately to the east of the Village Hall is St Mary's House. It is probably of the seventeenth century and may well have been built specifically as a Vicarage but one cannot be too certain about this. Writing of the vicarage during the Rev. Matthew West's incumbency, 1777–1812,

St Mary's House formerly the vicarage but now a private dwelling.

Hutchins recorded that 'the Vicarage House which stood a few yards south of the church was much repaired and improved by the Vicar, Mr West, and was said to be a convenient and comfortable residence'.

However, an Act of Parliament of 1824 was to change its status as it was decreed that a new vicarage house be built to replace it and when the Rev. Robert Grant came to take up his duties in 1829 St Mary's House became a farmhouse. A farmhouse it was to remain until the Rev. Gordon Wickham moved from the Vicarage into St Mary's House on 1st June 1904. In fact it was the Rev. Wickham who named it St Mary's House in order to avoid any confusion with the vicarage from which he had just departed. However, St Mary's House did not become the official vicarage again until 1923 when Walter Wyatt Paul sold the house to the Governors of Queen Anne's Bounty and the Rev. J.G. Vassall for £1250. St Mary's House continued to be the official vicarage for the period until the parish was in plurality with Thornford from 1952 to 1962, when it was sold. When the village again had its own Vicar in 1963 it was repurchased. Once again, however, St Mary's House is a private residence, having been sold for the second time as the parish has for the second time gone into plurality. During the period in which St Mary's House was a farmhouse there was to the rear a brewhouse and a weaver's shop as well as the site of the old pound, but when it became the vicarage again in 1904 good use was made of the garden for tennis and bowls. There has recently been a double garage erected in the garden and an outhouse to the rear has been converted into a rather pleasant dwelling. The garden of St Mary's House stretches as far as the River Yeo, to the bend in that river which is locally known as 'Vicars Bend'.

In 1962 St Mary's House was almost destroyed by a fire which started in the linen cupboard on the first floor. The occupants, Capt. & Mrs Bevan were awakened by the barking of their Norwich terrier to find the house filling with smoke, and only prompt action by the local fire services saved a major disaster from occurring. Even so there was severe damage to a dressing room and the whole of the roof.

Just to the east of St Mary's House is an open space which is immediately opposite the Rose & Crown Inn. This field, which is owned by the Dorchester Brewery, Messrs Eldridge Pope & Co., was the subject of a planning application some 3 years ago which was resisted very strongly by many, but not all, of the local population. The application

Field opposite the Rose & Crown Inn, Church Road.

went to appeal and the Inspector dismissed the proposals, so it is still an open space today. However, this was not always the case as in earlier years at the north-east corner of the field stood the Fox Inn and alongside that was a tenement of three dwellings. None of these cottages or the inn now survive but adjoining the field to the east is Tudor Cottage. This building is extremely old. Its name may give some indication of its age but of this there is no degree of certainty. It is a substantial building of local stone and has a fine thatched roof. On its north-east gable it has a stone with the initials RL and date 1641 cut into it. It is undoubtedly one of the oldest houses in the parish.

Slightly farther to the east stands the Grange, a very substantial building. It was probably built between 1860 and 1870 by Albert Clayton Esq., when he came to reside in the village to manage the estate for his father. There had been previously on this site a tenement of three dwellings which was directly alongside Church Road and not set back as far as the Grange. Over the front doorway in stained glass can be seen in monogram form the initials 'A.C.' Albert Clayton lived at the Grange from the date it was built until he died in 1914. His daughter Violet was born there and his wife continued to reside there until she left the village in 1926. She went to live at Upwey only to return to the village in 1930 upon her death to be buried alongside her husband and daughter in St Mary's Churchyard. It was upon the death of Albert Clayton that the estate passed to Walter Wyatt Paul.

The Grange is another building in the parish which has suffered from fire. In the early hours of a summer morning in 1932, villagers and servants in their night attire fought the blaze. Surprisingly little damage was done to the building but there was considerable damage to a large quantity of valuable silverware.

Old Downs, formerly the Seven Bells Inn.

Almost adjoining the Grange is the house now known as Old Downs. It is of the seventeenth century and retains its original windows on the

northern side of four and three lights with moulded oak frames. The doorway has a moulded frame and four-centred head and is hung with a battened and nail-studded door with panels. Inside the building there is an original moulded beam and the staircase has a newel with an ornamental finial. It was, in the early years of the nineteenth century, the Seven Bells Inn before it was used as a farmhouse, but it is best remembered by the older villagers as the old bakery. It is still more often than not referred to as the Old Bakehouse despite its present name. Here the Patch family plied their trade as master bakers for well over 100 years until 1957 when Thomas Patch died, and the family ceased trading. This meant that there was no longer a bakery in the village. A word, however, about this Thomas Patch before we move along. He was a native of the village and started work in the bakery when he was 14 years old, spending all of his working life (51 years) baking bread in Bradford Abbas. However, he always found time to take an active part in the affairs of the community and he served as a churchwarden for 25 years as well as being a member of the Parish Council, The Village Hall Committee, the Horticultural Society and the School Management Committee, and at the time of his death he was the oldest member of the Men's Club.

When his widow sold the premises it became a licensed restaurant and was renamed Old Downs. It is now, however, a private residence.

The last house on this side of Church Road is Greystones which is a substantial stone house.

On the opposite side of the road and immediately facing Greystones are two modern detached bungalows. These are No's 1 and 2 Church Road and it was in 1969 that No.1 which was occupied by Mr Bob Underdown was the subject of an article on the front page of the Daily Telegraph. When the bungalow was built there was no front gate and it was necessary to walk 50 yards up a drive to the rear of the dwelling and another 30 yards around to the front door. Mr Underdown knocked a hole in his front wall and erected a gate only 6 yards from his front door. He had not obtained planning permission and in their wisdom the Sherborne Rural District Council decided that this gate would encourage callers to leave their cars in Church Road and so an enforcement order was issued. Mr Underdown appealed, and a public enquiry was held and it was decided that he could not use the gate. This was the decision of the Inspector who was also concerned that it might be a traffic hazard despite the fact that he parked his own car in Church Road during the whole of his visit to the site. Mrs Underdown was infuriated by this decision with the result that she placed a notice on the gate simply stating, 'According to the government this is not a gate.' The gate remained there for several years and was in constant use but no further action was ever taken by the authorities. The present owner, however, has now closed the gap.

Moving westwards the next dwelling is Cherries, a modern bungalow which has been built in the garden of Ruskin House, a large stone-built house, where at one time a veterinary surgeon resided and what were dog kennels can still be seen. Immediately to the west of Ruskin House are two stone and partly rendered semi-detached cottages, Rose Cottage and the Laurels. Next door to the Laurels is the village Post Office and Stores, currently occupied by Mr & Mrs Keith Watkins. As far as I have been able to trace the Post Office has always been on its present site. It was originally

The village Post Office.

no more than a thatched cottage, single-storeyed, but it was enlarged and improved in 1889 into the building which we can see today.

In 1851 the Keeper of the Post Office was a Mr George Ridout and letters arrived at 8.45 am and were despatched to all parts via Sherborne at 2.00 pm. Mr Ridout was succeeded by a Mrs Ann Ashdown, who herself was succeeded by a Mr Jacob Wills. The Wills family were to run the Post Office or be connected with it for almost sixty years and although William Patch is described as postmaster in 1935, it must be pointed out that he married a Miss Gladys Wills, whose mother was a former postmistress and a direct descendant of Jacob Wills.

Up until 1954 the premises were part of the Bradford Abbas estate for which the tenant, Mr Frank Smith, was paying a rent of £55 per annum exclusive and it was at the sale during that year that the tenant became the freeholder. During Mr Smith's period at the Post Office petrol was also sold from one pump alongside the premises. Although this petrol pump has long since disappeared, it was not until 1987 that the tank itself was unearthed in order to allow development to take place.

Just to the west of the Post Office stands the village War Memorial, which stands on a site which, in 1838, was occupied by a blacksmiths's shop with a cottage alongside. It is a small stone structure with a tiled roof and was erected in 1917 by Mr Bartlett of Yeovil with Mr C.E. Benson as architect, at a total cost of £120 19s 6d. Within, on a central panel are the names of those who fell in two wars, whilst the side panels contain the names of all those who served in the same wars. An inscription reads:

'Be of good comfort, O my children
For ye shall be remembered.'

Like so many other things in the village at the time the War Memorial was the inspiration of the Rev. Gordon Wickham and the cost of the structure was met by public subscription, to which almost every house in the village contributed. It was dedicated on 18th November 1917 by Bishop Wallis, Archdeacon of Sherborne, following a short but solemn service in the Church. The iron gates were added later out of excess funds for the whole project.

Only a few yards westward is the Rose & Crown Inn. It has been suggested that it might have been built as early as 1460 as a resthouse by

The account for the War Memorial.

The War Memorial, 1917, without the iron gates which were added later.

The Rose & Crown Inn, 1905.

monks but if this is the case, and there are very good reasons for believing it to be true, it has been much altered and contains many more characteristics of the seventeenth century. It retains a doorway at the rear with a four-centred head whilst another doorway in the front retains its original moulded jambs. Old hitching rings still hang from the front walls.

How long it has been a public house is not easy to ascertain but from my recent researches it appears that it became an Inn between 1851 and 1861. Certainly in 1851 the Rose & Crown stood at the southern end of Westbury facing the old school but according to the census returns ten years later the inn was at its present site. It has previously been a farmhouse, but at the same time there was also a brewhouse on the site. Until more recent times there were farm buildings at the rear.

On the outside wall facing Churchwell Street is an old Sun Insurance plaque and above it a peculiar carved head. I can give no explanation for the latter but a copy of the original insurance policy, dated 17th September 1770 survives and reads as follows:

288953	ELIZABETH HAGGARD of the Parish of Bradford Abbas in the county of Dorset, widow, on her new dwelling house, brewhouse and cellar adjoining each	
15/-	other as aforesaid not exceeding fifty pounds	£50
March 1771	Household goods therein not exceeding fifty pounds	£50
	Barn and stable adjoining rear not exceeding fifteen pounds	£15
	Utensils and stock therein only not exceeding thirty pounds	£30
	Barn called Higher Barn with Waggon house not exceeding twenty pounds	£20
Sundry	Utensils and Stock therein only not exceeding thirty pounds	£30
	Corn and Hay in a Barton adjoining not exceeding one hundred pounds	£100
	House only near the Horse Pool in Bradford Abbas aforesaid in the tenure of John and Saml Garratt labourers not exceeding five pounds	£5
	All stone, timber cob and thatched	
		£300

The earliest landlord of whom I have a record is Samuel Hall (1851) and I believe that it was during his tenancy that the Inn was opened in its present building.

In 1879 the licence was transferred from Samuel Hall to Wyndham Garrett, who in applying for the transfer stated that he required only a six-day licence which was a situation which was to continue until 1963 when a licence for opening on Sundays was applied for and obtained. It is believed that Wyndham Garrett was asked to apply for a six-day licence by the Lord of the Manor who, on returning from church one Sunday morning was confronted by a drunken villager brandishing a pint of ale. This so annoyed the squire that he was no longer in favour of Sunday opening.

But not opening on Sundays did not meet with everyone's approval for on 28th September 1882 Mr Joseph Jacob, shopkeeper of Bradford Abbas applied for a licence to sell beer from his premises on Sundays when the Inn was closed and to support his application he handed in a petition containing 114 signatures. The application was nevertheless refused and an entry in the school log book written by the Headmaster Mr John James Ring gives as good a reason as any for the refusal: 'The principal inhabitants requested me to oppose the application and present a petition from them against it. I am happy to say my opposition was successful'.

In 1881 a certain Charles Rawlins was caught in the act of stealing from the till, the amount involved being 13s 3³/4d. Following a prosecution by Wyndham Garrett the culprit was sentenced to one month's imprisonment with hard labour. As a result of this case, and only ten days later, none other than Mrs Rawlins was also in court.

'Ellen Rawlins of Bradford Abbas was summoned for assaulting Wyndham Garrett, landlord of the Rose & Crown Inn. The prosecutor said that on 10th October defendant came into the Rose & Crown and said "What have you been doing to Charley? You have locked him up." She then gave him a smack on the face with the flat hand. He ordered her out of the house and she again struck him. As he was putting her out she gave him another; she also broke a pane of glass in the bar window. Defendant pleaded guilty and was fined 5s and 8s costs.'

In 1882, the licence was transferred from Wyndham Garrett to Abel Marsh who died tragically at the inn in November 1889 when he fell down the stairs when he was on his way to bed. As a result of this accident the licence was then transferred to Mr Marsh's daughter Rosina who only held it for a few months when a Mr Joseph Dawe became the new landlord in late 1890.

In 1899 the inn was leased by Woolmington Brothers of Sherborne at £18 per annum. In 1923 they sold various of their properties to Messrs Eldridge Pope & Co Ltd., which included an assignment of the lease on the Rose & Crown, by which time the rent had risen to £100 per annum. Messrs Eldridge Pope & Co Ltd., continued to lease the inn until 1954 when as a result of the death of Wyatt Paul they purchased the freehold at the subsequent sale of the estate. At the time of the sale the rent was £90 per annum with a further £40 per annum being paid in respect of the paddock at the back. This paddock was later to be sold and is where Churchwell Close now stands. According to the 1954 sale catalogue the inn consisted of an entrance passage, smoke room, public bar, private sitting room, scullery, kitchen, wash-house, closet and 5 bedrooms, which had two staircases leading to them. Water was obtained from a well in Churchwell Street.

The modern Rose & Crown Inn consists of one long carpeted bar with a thatched canopy over the serving area and the walls adorned with pictures of the lads of the village together with various pieces of harness and ancient agricultural tools. In the bar there is a magnificent stone fireplace which was only discovered in 1966 when the then landlord, Mr Frank Whitemore and his wife Gladys were troubled by a smoking chimney. Workmen were called in and

'Soon after piercing through the plaster they encountered something hard and came across what appeared to be some decorative carved stonework. Further careful investigation disclosed even more. Workmen removed the old grate and uncovered a large original fireplace. Above it were four attractive panels.

The Rose & Crown Inn as it is today.

Unfortunately one of the panels was found to be damaged. A mason contracted by a Yeovil firm set to work and fashioned another so that the panels are now complete once more.'

The stone fireplace in the Rose & Crown Inn which was discovered in 1966.

It would appear that this fireplace is not a part of the original building and has come from some other magnificent edifice such as Sherborne Abbey or more likely, in the writer's opinion, from Clifton House, with which the tudor rose patterns would seem more likely to be associated.

Churchwell Close is a small cul-de-sac which is entered from Churchwell Street. Its western end adjoins the churchyard. In this close are four substantial stone-built and tiled houses. The close stands on the site of what was a small farmyard or paddock which contained an implement shed, stables and cowstalls. When planning permission was applied for to develop the close there was considerable opposition from the inhabitants of Churchwell Street who went so far as to organise a petition and submit it to the local planning authority. However, the petitioners did not have the support of the Parish Council and the application was approved. When the houses were eventually built a small Fiat car was offered to the purchasers, no doubt as an added incentive to buy what at the time were considered to be expensive properties.

Churchwell Street runs northwards from Church Road until it meets up with the western end of Grope Lane. Officially, the street runs as far as the southern end of North Street but I am treating the section which was Grope Lane separately as it was always a lane in its own right and to many of the locals still is.

At the southern end of Churchwell Street stood the old village pump or churchwell, from which the street quite obviously derives its name. The site was, until 1972, clearly indicated by a concrete square standing above the normal level of the road. Unfortunately it was considered to be a hazard to traffic and pedestrians alike and so it was levelled and only a rainwater drain now marks the spot where the old pump stood. There are

Farm buildings which originally stood to the rear of the Rose & Crown Inn and which were demolished to enable Churchwell Close to be built.

Church Well St, Bradford Abbas.

several references to the old church well in the parish records. In 1780 Thomas White and Samuel Giles were paid 16s 3d for work done about the church well and three years later the former was paid 1s for 'riting the churchwell'.

In 1817 the inhabitants of Churchwell Street agreed 'to keep the road in good repair from the Church to churchwell to the house at the hithermost part of Grope Lane and that the same shall be done exclusive of any charge whatsoever on the surveyor of the highways.' This was agreed to by John Custard, Thomas Reed, Charles Hebditch, Richard Ridout and John Garrett who indicated his agreement with a cross. In 1847 Mr Vincent offered to put a pump at the churchwell for £2 and in 1858 the Vestry resolved 'that the chairman be requested to write a letter to Mr Clayton detailing the circumstances of the churchwell being dry whereby his tenants and others were deprived of the convenience which they have for a length of time enjoyed, and that he be requested to put it in a state of repair.'

Churchwell Street, 1905. The old village pump can be seen to the right of the picture as well as the open ditch.

The first house on the right as you go northwards up Churchwell Street is a substantial stone and thatched detached cottage. The remains of what may at one time have been a window can be seen in the wall and it was here, in the early years of the century that Mrs Higgins used to sell the children her homemade sweets. Immediately to the north of this property is a modern detached house, Quantocks. Upon this site until recent years stood another substantial but low-roofed thatched cottage often referred to as the Garrett house, due to that family having lived there for generation after generation. The last occupant of the house before it was demolished was Mrs Kate Osborne (née Garrett). Immediately to the north lies the Old Schoolhouse where prior to 1856 the village school was held and until 1933 it was the house of successive headmasters before becoming a private house. It was in fact burnt down and rebuilt in 1834. The last house on this side of the road is Little Orchard. It may well have been a butcher's shop in the last century but it appears that there is something of a local legend pertaining to this dwelling. I have been told by previous occupiers that there was a door in the building which bore the mark of an upraised hand, very similar to the crest of the Harvey family who used to reside at Clifton Maubank. Apparently, all efforts at painting, scraping, varnishing etc. failed to extinguish the hand and even after work had been done on it and it seemed to have gone, it would return again after only a few days.

Directly opposite to Little Orchard is a large modern detached house, which stands on what was formerly the site of two stone and thatched semi-detached cottages end on to the road. They were in a state of considerable decay and the low wall which runs alongside the modern dwelling is all that remains of the two original buildings on this site. Even the well and pump seem to have disappeared, being covered by a modern garage.

Coombe Ditch Lane runs southward from Coombe House until it meets up with Westbury at the junction with Cross Roads. In 1838 the village pound where stray cattle were placed stood at the most southerly point of this lane. The trees on the eastern side of the lane were planted to hide Queen's Road from Coombe House.

Coombe House lies apart from the rest of the built-up area of the village. It is a substantial stone house with outbuildings and was built about 1863 as a farmhouse by William Clayton Clayton Esq., when, as Lord of the Manor,

Coombe House, the most impressive of the new farmhouses built by William Clayton Clayton, c. 1860.

he adopted the policy of erecting larger farmsteads, thus reducing the number of small holders.

The first occupier of Coombe House was Professor James Buckman, F.G.S., F.L.S., F.S.A., who in many respects was a remarkable man. He was born in 1814 at Cheltenham, and was educated at a private school. He went to London with every intention of studying medicine but he later returned to Cheltenham where he became honorary secretary and lecturer to the local Library and Philosophical Institute. In 1846 he accepted the Chair of Geology and Botany at Cirencester Agricultural College—a position he held until he and three other Professors resigned over difficulties with a new Principal. It was as a result of this resignation that he came to Bradford Abbas 'where he took a large farm, which he conducted on modern principles'.

He spent much of his leisure time studying the geology of the area in which he had come to live and work, with the result that he gathered a large and varied collection of ammonites, belemnites, brackiopods and other couchifers, including several which were new, from the highly fossiliferous beds at Bradford Abbas. He wrote several learned articles about his discoveries.

In 1876 he was largely responsible for the founding of the Dorset Natural History and Antiquarian Field Club and he was elected Secretary at its first meeting—a position he was to hold until his death in 1884. He was the author of a number of works including *The Ancient Straits of Malvern or an account of the marine conditions which separated England and Wales, History of British Grasses,* and *The Site of Ancient Corinium,* as well as being a regular contributor to agricultural and scientific journals. He was also responsible for excavating the ancient remains on East Hill, Bradford Abbas and the Roman Villa at Thornford.

His farming methods were the most modern of his day and he was particularly successful with his root crops. In 1865 he was awarded a trophy for the best crop of swedes, won by using a special type of artificial fertilizer. He achieved 41$^1/_2$ tons per acre. He was also responsible for breeding out of the parsnip its habit of growing multiple roots, eventually producing the now-familiar single main root. The trophy which he won for his output of swedes is now in the County Museum at Dorchester.

It was while he was at Coombe House, which he himself called the Villa, that his wife died and his son, Sydney Buckman, came of age. It was on the occasion of the latter's birthday that he invited his labourers and a few friends to a birthday party at which a set of valuable books was presented to the young man by Professor Buckman's bailiff, Mr Emmanuel Sherring.

On 22nd November 1884, surrounded by his five children, he died suddenly and unexpectedly and at a private funeral (largely attended by freemasons) he was buried in St Mary's Churchyard three days later, alongside his wife at the eastern end of the cemetery where his tombstone can still be seen.

Upon the death of Professor Buckman the house was occupied by Mr Walter Paul, father of Wyatt Paul, who later moved to Manor Farm, with Wyatt Paul occupying Coombe House. Upon the death of his father Wyatt Paul moved to Manor Farm and Coombe House was taken by Capt. the Honorable Wilfred Cairns (later Earl Cairns) and his wife. Wilfred Cairns promptly left for South Africa to take part in the Boer War and upon his return to the village he was given a rousing welcome.

'The village was *en fête* owing to the return of Major the Hon. W. Cairns from service in South Africa. A meeting hastily called by Mr Warr was attended by nearly every man in the village and it was determined to give Major and Mrs Cairns a hearty reception. The village was gaily decorated. The carriage was intercepted by a voluntary team numbering about 35 at the head of Quarry Lane and drawn through the village to the vicarage and back to Coombe. A salute was fired at the forge. The bells rang out a welcome and the schoolchildren lining the road between the church and the School House cheered as only children can. A small band of musicians played a welcome at Coombe and after a few words of thanks from the Major, the villagers dispersed.'

Wilfred Cairns was born on 28th November 1865 and was educated at Wellington. By the time of the outbreak of the Boer War in 1899 he was a Captain in the Prince Consort's Own Rifle Brigade. He was the heir to Earl Cairns. In 1905 Earl Cairns died in the South of France and Wilfred Cairns succeeded to the title, but he continued to live at Coombe House. When he became Earl he was the father of three daughters which caused him some concern as two of his predecessors had left no male heir. So it was 'a great satisfaction' to the new Earl when his wife gave birth to a son, Lord Garmoyle, in 1907. To celebrate the event Earl and Lady Cairns paid for members of the mixed department of the school, together with their teachers, Sunday School teachers, choir and the Vicar's Sunday School class to go on an outing to Weymouth. In all 74 adults and children went, ending the day by giving 'three cheers for Lord Garmoyle'.

Earl and Lady Cairns left Coombe House in early 1908. During their comparatively short stay in the village they had taken an active part in the various activities, the Earl being a member of the Parish Council, a School Manager and captain of the Cricket Club, whilst Lady Cairns was instrumental in organising functions for the ladies of the village and was always a willing helper at village feasts etc.

Colonel Charles Edward Duff came into Coombe House on the departure of Earl and Lady Cairns. He was born in Ceylon (now Sri Lanka) and was educated at Cheltenham College and Sandhurst. He served in the second Afghan War 1879–80 and in the Boer War (1899–1902) and for some time during the latter he commanded the 1st Scottish Horse. He was a Lieutenant Colonel of the 8th Hussars from 1901 to 1905 and Brevet Colonel in 1904. He retired from the Army in 1906. It was said that during his army career he was a very fine shot and a brilliant polo player, being twice in the winning team of the inter-regimental polo tournament in India.

As was to be expected of a man with his background, he very soon became involved with just about every organisation in the village. He served on the Parish Council, being Chairman for the last 22 years of his life as well as representing the village on the Sherborne Rural District Council for 25 years, a position he held until his death. It is longer than any other villager has served on a council other than the Parish Council. He was particularly generous to the Men's Club and the school but his first love was probably the church where he worshipped each Sunday and where he served as Churchwarden for over 20 years. His death, in 1936, came as a shock to all who knew him, even though he was 77 years of age and had been suffering ill health for some time. His funeral at St Mary's Church was the largest the village had seen for many years and prompted the Vicar, the Rev. E.C. Douglas, to write,

'So he passed over and all the trumpets sounded for him on the other side. There seems but one thing I can write about this month and that is the irreparable loss to Bradford Abbas through the loss of Colonel Duff. It was not only because of its tragic suddenness (for sudden it was to us because it was so unexpected) it was not only that a man whom all honoured and were proud of had been taken, but because each of us felt he had lost a friend. The loss is a personal one. 'The Colonel' has passed on, but his wonderful personality, his deep sense of duty, his unfailing cheerfulness, his keen sympathy, his devotion to his church will live in the memories of us so long as we have memories to employ.

'We knew him as a man of great natural ability, an indefatigable worker with wide interests and social charm. He was seen at his best with children whom he loved and who responded to his affection. His whole life was given up completely to the happiness of others.'

Colonel Duff's widow left Coombe House a short while after her husband's death and Colonel Daubney became the new owner. Colonel Daubney left Bradford Abbas in 1940 for military service and in 1945 Mr & Mrs Frederick Richardson moved into Coombe House, where Mrs Richardson continued to reside long after her husband's death, until the property was sold to Mr John Haynes, a successful publisher of car manuals and general books, who has recently opened a car museum at Sparkford.

It surprises many newcomers to the parish to learn that *Compton Road* which goes eastwards from Yeovil Bridge towards Over Compton lies in the parish of Bradford Abbas. Until 1954 it was within both the civil and ecclesiastical boundaries but in 1954 the spiritual needs of the residents were transferred to Over and Nether Compton.

Sixteen houses were built along this road in 1938 by Mr Wyatt Paul and were described as:

'Nos 1–8 being brick built with upper storey rendered and asbestos tiled roofs whilst the remainder (Nos 9–16) are built of rustic bricks with asbestos tiled roofs.'

These houses were rented until 1954, the lowest rent being £39 per annum and the highest £44 per annum but upon the break-up of the estate in 1954 many of the tenants took the opportunity of purchasing their houses.

Early in the 1980s a further 11 dwellings were built and they are contained in a separate section named 'Underdown', which is the name of the old field in which they stand.

Compton Road is sometimes referred to as 'Old Showground Road' due to the fact that the Yeovil Agricultural Show was, for many years, held in an adjoining field.

There is a second *Compton Road* which runs from the crossroads at Coombe until it meets up with the main A30 London–Exeter Road at Loscombe's Cross. For part of the way it is the parish boundary and is sometimes referred to as Compton Lane, East Lane or East Farm Road. In 1889 the Sherborne Rural District Council decided that it should not be used for locomotive traffic as the road was too narrow for vehicles to pass. Vehicles do still use the route however and although it is still far too narrow for vehicles to pass, passing bays have now been made in a couple of places. A few years ago the Parish Council requested that this road be renamed 'Loscombe's Lane' but their efforts met with no response from the County Council.

The Cross lies at the southern end of North Street and was, during the latter part of the seventeenth and early part of the eighteenth century considered to be the centre of the village. The name derives from the fact that at one time a market cross stood here which was said to be similar to, but smaller than the conduit on the Parade in Sherborne. From this cross tradesmen displayed their wares, proclamations were made, market tolls collected and fairs held. It was pulled down at the end of the eighteenth century, for no apparent reason, by the Overseer, without any advantage to the parish, and to the disgust of many villagers. No trace of this cross now remains, and it is important to note, contrary to what many people believe, that the cross that stood at this site had no connection whatsoever with the preaching cross that stands in the churchyard. The old market cross was completely destroyed.

The Cross. It was here that the original village market cross stood until it was destroyed by the Overseers, c.1800.

It was at the Cross that the horse pond was situated and this is shown very clearly on the 1838 Tithe Apportionment map as lying between the two stone cottages on the west, and the three cottages standing on the east. In fact if the pond was still there today it would have been necessary to walk around it in order to pass under the railway bridge. It was at this horse pond that the ducking stool was positioned. However, in 1852 the Vestry decided that the horse pond should be filled in without further

Cross Cottage.

delay and that a proper place should be provided for the horses to drink. There is now an old stone trough alongside Cross Cottage which, with its constant supply of running water, was provided to replace the pond.

Cross Cottage itself is of interest, being at the southern end of a block of three stone and thatched tenements which were probably built in the sixteenth century but have been much altered, at least internally, since. In the south wall, high up, is a window completely blocked up whilst in the wall between Wisteria Cottage and Glyn Cottage there is another smaller window, which until recent years was also blocked up, which immediately brings to mind the window tax of years ago. Inside the building are some original moulded ceiling beams. Yew Tree Cottages directly opposite are three seventeenth-century stone and thatched tenements which retain some original windows with moulded oak frames and mullions. Inside is an original plank partition. The cottages nearer to the railway are of the seventeenth century but have been much altered and it was in one of these cottages that the village laundry was at one time situated. The three cottages on the eastern side, now very neatly thatched, had galvanised roofs, no doubt to protect them from the sparks from the railway engines which passed along the railway line alongside. The two cottages on the western side are slated.

Cross Roads runs from Back Lane until it meets up with the northern end of Westbury and the southern tip of Coombe Ditch Lane. Cross Roads is most certainly a modern name. The small stretch of the road from Back Lane to the top of North Street was known as Dole Lane, and I rather suspect that the whole length of this road was in fact so named. The field now adjoining the northern side of the road (now part of Coombe House and referred to quite incorrectly as Lower Coombe) was formerly called Dole.

The residential estate which is named Cross Roads, but in fact leads off it and was built where there was previously an orchard. It was erected in the early 1960s and consists of two semi-detached houses and several detached bungalows, all built in reconstructed stone with tiled roofs. Two of the detached bungalows are unusual in that they have flat roofs. They are in fact the only flat-roofed dwellings in the parish.

East Farm can be approached in two directions—either via Greenway Lane or from Compton Road. There is nothing very interesting about the buildings, all of which are comparatively modern, but at one time when the farm was owned by Cow & Gate Ltd., it was by far the largest pig farm for miles around—it was said that there were as many as five thousand pigs on the property at any one time. Cow & Gate Ltd. subsequently sold the farm.

East Hill's name aptly describes its position in the parish. According to old maps East Hill ran from Red Lane Hill southwards until it joined with the northern side of the field now known as Crats.

Fanny Brooks Lane goes eastwards from Back Lane for approximately half a mile before meeting up with the Sherborne Road. About 50 yards from the Back Lane end and on the right hand side can be seen the remains of steps leading to a cottage, which as local folklore would have it was the residence of Fanny Brooks. There are a variety of stories about this lady and in one respect they all seem to agree that she was a witch. Certainly there was a Fanny Brooks living in the village and certainly she lived in the cottage. She is also recorded as having children out of wedlock. But whether or not she was a witch, who can tell. I believe that the locals became suspicious of her because her cottage was isolated from the main body of the village and because she kept herself to herself and this led to the belief that she practised witchcraft. She was certainly treated as an outcast and despite her efforts to disprove any accusations laid against her she was so persecuted by the villagers that in the end she took her own life by hanging herself. The lane has borne her name ever since.

Owing to its somewhat isolated position, it was, until recent years, a favourite camping site for gypsies, particularly in early October each year at the time of Pack Monday Fair in Sherborne. One well known Dorset personality who visited the lane in the early years of this century was the well-known Mary Ann Bull. She used to travel throughout the county selling 'reddle' (a red chalk used by shepherds for marking sheep), silver sand and peat and when she stopped in the lane with her pony and 'ancient vehicle' the village children were very frightened and would go nowhere near her as they were convinced that she had evil powers.

In 1908 some excitement was created when some children, playing in the lane, found a complete set of clothes including a pair of boots. There were suspicions of a terrible tragedy and all sorts of rumours were rife but as is so often the case, a perfectly logical reason was found when a traveller confessed to having taken advantage of the quietness of the lane to change his attire.

I have heard tales of a ghost at the junction of this lane with Back Lane. As far as I know the two persons who related the tale to me are unknown to each other but their stories were precisely the same—both said they heard heavy footsteps and a person brushing past them after placing a hand on their shoulders, but saying nothing. One of the persons, I knew from his wife, arrived home in a terrified state.

Farm Road, sometimes referred to as Manor Farm Road, leads westwards from Bishop's Lane to Manor Farm. The section of the road from Bishop's Lane to the junction with Quarry Lane was not laid until at least 1858 when Manor Farm house and outbuildings were being built and it was made up to meet with an already existing trackway then known as Butcher's Bar Lane. Once the buildings at Manor Farm had been

The Old Rectory, 1905. This was built 1824–8.

completed and the new route via Farm Road was being used the expense of maintenance began to cause concern to the Vestry:

'1859 It was resolved that in consequence of the road being much more used than it was before the buildings were erected, Mr Clayton had applied to defray one half of the expenses, the parish engaging to pay the other half.'

It is, of course, now maintained by Dorset County Council.

Grant's Hill is the very short section of road which goes from the junction of Church Road and Back Lane to the junction where it is necessary to turn right to go to Thornford.

The largest house on Grant's Hill is now what is known as the Old Rectory, and previously as Yeoleas and even earlier as the Vicarage. It was built in 1828 and the Rev. Robert Grant became the first Vicar to take up residence there, hence the name Grant's Hill. This house, which was built in a field called Limekiln Close, was the only house in this small part of the village until York Cottage and Goodlands were built in 1921.

The Old Rectory was built in accordance with an Act of Parliament of 1824, which united, ecclesiastically, the parishes of Bradford Abbas and Clifton Maubank, and in this Act is clearly stated:

'That it shall be lawful for the said Edward Smedley[1] and his successors, Incumbents of the said United Rectory and Vicarage, to cause the cottage, formerly the Rectory House of Clifton Maubank to be taken down, and the materials thereof, or so much of such materials as shall be fit and proper to be applied in building a new vicarage house and offices in the parish of Bradford Abbas or in or towards repairing or rebuilding the wall or fences of the churchyard of the parish of Clifton Maubank.'

Whether or not the materials of which the new vicarage was built came from the old rectory at Clifton Maubank I cannot be certain, but quite definitely there would not have been sufficient for the substantial new edifice. The house was to remain as the vicarage for almost 100 years. Except for the last few years, the Rev. Grant lived in the new vicarage for the whole of his ministry, but in the latter years it was occupied by the various curates whom the Rev. Grant employed to carry out his duties. When, in 1886, he finally resigned as Vicar his successor, the Rev. Gordon Wickham, was unable to move into his new home immediately owing to some necessary repairs being carried out, and so for a short period he went to reside at Manor Farm to await the completion of the work.

When the Rev. Gordon Wickham did move into the building it became the centre of village activities and one of his first acts in 1886 was to have a parish room built over the coach house. It was built by Messrs Andrews of Thornford and Lang of Bradford Abbas under the supervision of the architect, Mr C.B. Benson. The room was capable of holding over 200 people and the entire cost was met by the Vicar. It continued to be used as the parish room until 1911 when the first Village Hall was built, but even after that it was used until quite recently for communal activities. During the last five years it has been converted into a dwelling house.

In 1904 the Rev. Gordon Wickham moved to St Mary's House but the building continued to be the official vicarage until 1923 when it was sold to General Sir G.M. Harper.

Greenway Lane is the narrow surfaced lane which goes northwards from the Sherborne–Yeovil Road just to the west of Coombe House. East (or Higher) Farm can be approached via this lane, but if one continues to walk further north, coming off the surfaced section, there are magnificent views of the surrounding countryside.

---

[1] Vicar 1812–25.

Grope Lane is now officially part of Churchwell Street, and is a narrow stretch of road which meets up with the cross at the railway bridge. All the dwellings along here are modern, but at one time in the early nineteenth century there were two houses on the northern side and eight on the southern side. None of these dwellings can now be seen, the majority of them having been destroyed by fire. On 22nd June 1891 sparks landed on the thatched roof of one cottage and within an hour four houses had been burnt to the ground. The Vicar, some few days later, applied to the London & South West Railway Company for compensation for the four families who had lost their homes, receiving eventually the sum of £30.15.0.

Higher Westbury is a short stretch of road which goes from Westbury to the Cross. In 1838 there was a carpenter's shop at the west end and on the southern side were four thatched cottages, known as Snook's Row. There are no longer any old dwellings in this road for the four thatched cottages were burnt down in a disastrous fire on the afternoon of 15th September 1938. They were reputed to be 400 years old and had only recently been redecorated by the owner, Mr Wyatt Paul. They were estimated to be worth £1000. Mr James Higgins one of the 'lads of the village' was a tenant of one of the cottages and only eight years earlier had celebrated his 60th wedding anniversary. At the time of the disaster he was a widower and was living with his granddaughter, and he was most reluctant to be removed from the burning cottage. The press report of the occurrence goes on to say:

'Mr Higgins who was brought downstairs by his granddaughter, in his pyjamas, was in bed at the time. He had been bedridden for the last two years. After he was got out of the house, he sat, well wrapped up, in a shed a few yards from the house where he had lived for 55 years, and watched the flames destroy it. Many villagers, as soon as they heard of the fire, rushed to the scene and their first thought was for old Jimmy Higgins who sat there watching and refused to be moved. He was still there three hours after the blaze had started.

' "It is a fire and there tis," said Mr Higgins. "I am safe and that's all that matters. I have lived 92 years and this is not going to upset me now and I won't be moved." '

The area where these cottages were destroyed became known familiarly as 'the ruins' and each summer the children were brought up from the school to pick the plums which were still growing there. In 1960, however, a planning application was submitted to erect bungalows not only on this site but also a little further to the east and closer to the railway line. The locals were not too happy about new buildings being erected, but the antagonism was considerably increased when one bungalow was built across the public footpath which went from Higher Westbury under the culvert to Churchwell Street, before a diversion order had been obtained. There were meetings with representatives of the Sherborne Rural District Council but despite all the furore and unease the footpath under the culvert was diverted to where it is today.

Before leaving Higher Westbury it might be as well to mention that before the culvert was built there was a ramp on either side of the railway track over which pedestrians had to pass if they were using the footpath. However, as there were a number of accidents at this crossing (including two deaths), the Railway Company decided to get rid of the ramps and to build the culvert which we have today.

Lease Lane runs from the southern end of Underdown Hollow onto what is now the Yeovil Golf Course and what was formerly the common land of the parish, known as Bradford Leaze.

Loscombe Cross lies at the extreme north-east of the parish where it borders Over Compton on the London–Exeter road. Hloscumb or Luscumb as it was earlier recorded literally means dry valley and sure enough away to the south-west is a deep dry valley which eventually meets up with the Sherborne–Bradford Abbas road at Wyke Firs.

Manor Close is one of the new residential estates built during the early 1960s and was so named by the developers as the field was presumed to have been part of Manor Farm. In fact it never was, for until 1947 it was church land and was let by the Churchwardens to a local smallholder who eventually became its owner. The land was known as Post or Post Four Acres.

When Manor Close was originally built there was a shop at the entrance to the estate but this has now been converted into a dwelling.

Manor Farm house and outbuildings were built about 1858 by Mr William Clayton Clayton as part of his policy of creating larger farming units. The farmhouse, which commanded extensive views to the south, was built of dressed stone with a slate roof. It was of medium size and had its own private drive, and it consisted of an entrance hall, dining room,

Manor Farm buildings—part of one of the farms erected by William Clayton Clayton, c.1860.

drawing room, back hall and office, kitchen, pantry and six bedrooms with some good dry cellars.

The first occupant of the property was Mr John Smith Caddy, who was for several years a churchwarden at Bradford Abbas Church. He originated from Biddiscombe, Dorset, and according to the 1861 census returns he farmed 450 acres and employed 23 men, 7 boys and 7 girls. At this time he was 46 years of age and had eight children, two of whom were born at Manor Farm. When he left Manor Farm Walter Paul became the occupier and was later succeeded by his son, Wyatt Paul who continued to farm here until his death in 1954, at which time the premises were acquired by the present owner Mr Ronnie Loxton. Mr Loxton carried out extensive alterations to the farmhouse and it is now an attractive one-storey dwelling. The original farmhouse is unrecognisable.

There are four cottages and a substantial house (known as Rock Cottage) all of mid-nineteenth century date, and all within close proximity of the farmhouse itself whilst across the road are extensive farm buildings which, in 1954, were said to consist of cowstalls (for 73 cows), bull house, hay and root stores, cart horse stables, harness room, range of piggeries etc., a corn store and estate sawmills. It is of interest to note that since 1824 the owner of Manor Farm has had a liability to meet the cost of repairs to the chancel of Bradford Abbas Church, and it is a liability which on occasions has had to be faced up to, but I believe that this responsibility is likely to be removed in the near future.

Mill Farm, sometimes referred to as Limekiln Farm, lies astride the Bradford Abbas–Thornford footpath. I am of the opinion that this farm may well have been the site of the mill mentioned in the Domesday Book under Bradford Abbas. There is no mill there now but there was for the greater part of the nineteenth century, and in 1825 the property was described as 'A Farmhouse, Grist Mills and Flax Plot'.

There are also the remains of some limekilns (hence the alternative name) and leading towards Thornford, very much in the direction of the Roman Villa in that parish, are the very distinct remains of what would seem to be an ancient trackway. The only water meadows in the parish are between the farmhouse and the River Yeo.

In 1845 the tenant of Mill Farm was a certain William Chancellor who took a fancy to the parish funds as the following minute indicates:

'7th July 1845. The Overseers' Accounts were inspected, when it appeared that Wm. Chancellor, one of the Overseers, who has absconded, had collected £29.3s.4¹/₂d. part of a rate due together with £12.2s.5d. in hand and arrears of £1.1s.3¹/₂d. amounting altogether to £42 7s 1d and of which he paid £20 to the Treasurer of the Union, leaving a deficiency of £22 7s 1d to account for. It was resolved that the following advertisement be sent to the Hue and Cry Gazette.
'£5 Reward.
Whereas William Chancellor, who occupied a mill in the Parish of Bradford Abbas, Dorset, absconded on or about the 15th May leaving his children chargeable to the Parish. The above reward will be paid by the Parish Officers to any person who will cause the said Wm. Chancellor to be delivered to them to be dealt with according to law. The said Wm. Chancellor is about 50 years of age, 5 feet 9in length, slender made, darkish hair, rather weak and winking eyes, pale complexion, has a stooping and awkward gait. He generally wore leathern small clothes and gaiters and had the appearance of a miller.'

There is no record that the 'criminal' was ever caught and two years later the Auditors recommended that the missing money be written out of the records. For many years in the late nineteenth and early twentieth century the King family farmed here. They were described as farmers and lime burners and they were a family who always took an active part in the life of the village. Thomas King, the last of the family to live here, was a leading light in the Men's Club and for three years represented the village on the Rural District Council. A copy of his 1908 election address still survives and shows clearly that 'politicians' do not change very much.

'Ladies and Gentlemen.
Three years ago you did me the honour to elect me unopposed as your representative on the Rural District Council. During my three years of office, I have served the Parish to the best of my ability, and I believe have given general satisfaction to the parishioners. Every question which has come before the Rural District Council affecting the welfare of the Parish has received my careful consideration and I have at all times acted in a manner which I considered would be conducive to the best interests of the Parish as a whole.
'It is well known that my family and I have been connected with the Parish for generations, that we have been considerable employers of labour and that my interests are deeply bound up with the Parish.
'I have been again nominated and if you do me the honour to re-elect me on Monday April 6th you may rest assured that I shall, as I have done in the past, look after the best interests of the whole of the Parish irrespective of creed or party.
'I have the honour to be, Ladies and Gentlemen
'Your obedient Servant,
Thomas King.'

This election address was of little avail, however, for he was heavily defeated by the Rev. Gordon Wickham.

Thomas King left Mill Farm in 1914, one of his last acts before leaving being to make 'financially possible' a hot supper for members of the Men's Club.

Mill Lane's name derives from the old flax mill which was formerly worked at the southern end of the lane. The buildings still stand and the actual site of the water-wheel can clearly be seen including marks made on the walls by the rotating wheel. The buildings are of the seventeenth century but the upper part was partly restored early in the eighteenth century and the interior has exposed timber framing. The garden is most attractive and many fossils, particularly ammonites can be found there. During the First World War the premises were occupied by German prisoners of war who were put to work on Wyatt Paul's farm as well as at Clifton Maubank where it was said that they were giving satisfaction. It was, in fact, one of the prisoners of war at Mill House who carved the very attractive little crucifix that can be seen near the west tower in St Mary's Church.

At the extreme end of the lane where it meets with the River Yeo is what is called locally 'the iron bridge'. The present bridge was built in 1894 by the Sherborne Rural District Council, replacing an older but narrower bridge. The surveyor had reported that in order to prevent cattle straying

The iron bridge, Mill Lane. It was from this bridge that young Reggie Tuck was swept away by the river and drowned.

across the bridge he had erected posts at each end and that some people were requesting that these posts be removed in order that they might ride their horses across the bridge. But to their credit councillors would have none of this and although they ordered the posts to be removed they replaced them with the kissing gates which are there today.

For many years there was wire netting over the side rails of the bridge which was placed there after an unfortunate accident occurred. On 27th October 1916 seven-year-old Reggie Tuck was playing with other children on the bridge and upon reaching for a stick he fell through the rails into the water and disappeared. There was a strong current running at the time and the water was above the banks, flooding fields thereabouts, and although a boat was quickly requisitioned no trace could be found of the lad. His body was eventually found well down the river near Clifton House over a month later. A small circular plaque marks his final resting place in St Mary's Churchyard. Facing Mill House is an attractive thatched cottage which could also be considered to be one of the oldest in the village. It is now named Little Thatch and was for many years the home of Thomas Coombs who was to find fame in his later years as one of the 'lads of the village'.

A little farther to the north and beyond Mill Cottage is another medium-sized dwelling, Milworth. This was previously two cottages but was converted into the pleasant house it is today by Mr 'Pinkie' White who for many years had a windmill generating electricity in his garden. An ancient pump can still be seen in the front of the building.

In the middle of the nineteenth century there were several other cottages situated in Mill Lane and at the entrance to the lane stood the village stocks where there is now an attractive rockery.

Narrow Path is not a highway but the name of a field, part of which is now a section of Yeovil Golf Course. It is however, of considerable interest for in this field are the remains of a Roman building which to this day has not been properly excavated. However, a brief excavation was carried out in 1958:

'Diagonally laid wall foundation stones running approximately north and south were uncovered, just below the surface. These were some 2 feet 6 ins in width and extended for some 20 feet north and south, burnt on the west face; then occurred a gap of 13 inches, a short length of stone again followed by a flat $2^1/2$ inch local stone, some 6 feet long and 2 feet wide. Probing further south in the Mudford Sands with a trial trench at the end of the apparent foundations would give a building some 70 feet in length. A cross trench east and west revealed a rough stone floor ending about 21 feet eastwards which would give an overall width of say 23 feet. At the north east corner, however, a considerable amount of large stones had been inserted into the Mudford sands, more or less in the form of a buttress. No pottery was found inside the north end of the building nor any habitation dirt. This existed, however, all round the building and probing gives the impression of an area of some 200 feet square having some 10 inches below the present surface a layer of pottery, bones and usual occupation small stones, but only 6 inches thick. Probing suggests another possible building 65 feet by 28 feet roughly parallel to this one and some 108 feet west. The only coins were on the surface (Lucilla c. 164, and Gratlian c. 378–383)'

As far as I am aware no further work has been carried out on this site.

In this field during the late summer can be seen bright yellow flowers—Flea banes. It is well known that these flowers were very popular with the Romans and although it has been described as 'an ill looking weed' the Romans held it in greater esteem for they used it to make wreaths. This appears to be the only field in the parish where these flowers grow.

North Farm, also known locally as Yeovil Bridge Farm, is now the home of Express Dairies, and was another of the farms built by William Clayton Clayton Esq. in the middle of the last century. The farmhouse itself was built of local stone with a slate roof and faces south overlooking what is now part of the Yeovil Golf Course. There were two workers' cottages close to the farmhouse and later the old tollhouse on Yeovil Bridge also came to be used as a worker's cottage for North Farm. The total acreage was 147 and was described as being 'of highly productive pasture and fertile, arable, and a most valuable block of rich grazing land adjoining the River Yeo'.

Very little is known of the tenants of North Farm but when the Good family were farming there in the early years of this century one observer said, 'The land in its present state bears testament to the diligent labour of both father and son.' Today the buildings are used as offices and a modern bottle cleaning plant and dairy have been built.

The late Harry Warr in his interesting little book *A Short Account of Bradford Abbas* wrote of *North Street* as it was in 1880:

*Thatched cottages,
North Street.*

'There were then no gaps in North Street, but houses closely packed on each side of the road, miserable hovels many of them, vastly different to the cottages now existing. Halfway down North Street on the right hand side stood a large chapel, for the dissenters were at that time numerically strong. This building has now disappeared, a room in a cottage now sufficing.'

North Street is one of the principal streets of the village and in an area of such interest it is difficult to know where to start. I will, however, start with the semi detached stone and slated cottages which lie immediately to the south of Chantry Cottage. They were, according to a date upon the wall, built in 1885, but prior to that time there were two smaller cottages and a carpenter's shop on this site. It could well be that the two dwellings that stood there contain parts of the original buildings. These cottages were always part of the old Bradford Abbas estate but are now council houses, as they were acquired by the Sherborne Rural District Council in 1954. They are, therefore, the oldest council houses in Bradford Abbas, in age of building, but they were not the first.

As one walks northwards the next building is Chantry Cottage—one of the most attractive and, apart from the church, probably the most photographed building in the village. It is of the seventeenth century or earlier, though it has, of course, been much altered over the years. In 1912 when some alterations were being carried out a curious find was made.

Chantry Cottage.

'Whilst repairing the ceiling of the kitchen in the house of Mr John Lang, a miscellaneous collection of articles was discovered in the space between the ceiling and the floor above. They consisted of several cows' horns used no doubt for drenching purposes, a quaint little earthenware jar, an iron two-pronged toasting fork and several wooden articles, the last named being almost reduced to powder. How long these articles have been in their curious hiding place is difficult to surmise, as the house, an old thatched one, is evidently a great age.'

On the east wall of the building is an unusual hitching ring depicting the head of a lion, and some crown glass as well as a rather unusual letter box can be seen.

Some forty yards north is another pleasant stone and thatched cottage of the early seventeenth century whilst to the rear of this are four modern semi-detached houses. These were built on what in 1962 was an open space but on earlier maps cottages stood there.

Heartsease Cottage is the next house immediately to the north. It is built of local stone and slated and was formerly two cottages. The building itself is of no great interest but the present occupier, Miss Evelyn Dainty, made a magnificent contribution to the Bradford Abbas Women's Institute Scrap Book in 1965 with an article entitled 'Nature Notes—by a Nurse on night duty' which I would recommend. Miss Dainty has also laid claim to local fame in recent years due to her family, which consists of children from all over the world with whom she corresponds and also as the leader of a local pressure group, Loners Lib, which meets regularly in Heartsease Cottage.

The two cottages immediately to the north of Heartsease Cottage, Kandala and Squirrel Cottage are again of the seventeenth century and are most attractive in appearance with an abundance of flowers in due season covering their east walls. These two cottages have changed very little, if at all, externally since the day they were built but internally they have been considerably altered and there is a magnificent open fireplace in Kandala. Kandala was previously named Hi-Lou, due to the fact that the outhouse containing the earth closet was on a higher level than the rest of the house. Just a few yards further north is a terraced house now known as Apple Tree Thatch and previously known as Virginia Cottage. There is also a fine open fireplace in this building which was discovered by Mr and Mrs Keith Watkins the present Postmaster and his wife, when they were the residents. It is also the house in which Mr Stanley Blackmore lived with his family for many years. Mr Blackmore was a taxi driver and when he was reported missing in the summer of 1963 he became national news. Despite an extensive police search it was several days before his body was found, in a ditch near Yetminster, and it became a case of murder. The village became a centre of intense police activity with every house being visited but at the time of writing the killer has never been found and as the years roll by the chances of the culprit being brought to justice seems to get more remote.

Adjoining Virginia Cottage is Chapel House, again of the seventeenth century, where many of the older villagers can remember attending Sunday School—the lessons were held in the sitting room with the very large window in the east wall. There is little doubt that this house was the meeting place for dissenters and there is strong evidence that Mr Robert Bartlett and Mr Benjamin Walters, two Congregationalist Ministers preached here in the late years of the seventeenth century. Immediately adjoining Chapel House is another terraced cottage, Hill View. The present owner, Mr David Ash, whilst carrying out improvements at this cottage found very definite evidence of a fire that had occurred here, a fire which I believe happened in August 1909 and which was very quickly discovered and put out, avoiding damage to the thatched cottages on either side. But Hill View is of interest in a very different way for in January 1975 a series of letters appeared in the Western Gazette, the correspondence being started by a Rev. Fred Gardener who wrote:

'The ghost I saw was in the thatched cottage where I now dwell, in Bradford Abbas. It appeared to be a benign entity attired in Tudor period costume. Since this cottage is 300 years old, the appearance of the Tudor period ghost is quite in keeping with the character and age of this old thatched dwelling house. I have seen other entities elsewhere.'

This letter brought a response from Mr Walter Cleal, who after giving a brief description of his family background went on to say:

'Altogether five generations of my family lived there until we moved to our present address in 1962.
'While I do not dispute Mr Gardener and his ghost, I can honestly say no one of the family heard tell of the said ghost in all the years we lived there.'

The Rev. Gardener was not to be outdone, however, and in response he wrote:

'All I can say, with sincerity, I am not a child, nor a fool, and I endeavour in all good faith to give the truth as I see it. All I know I saw a ghost or entity or apparition in the inglenook of the living room of the cottage call it what you will.'

And there the matter rests.

There is only one more cottage on this side of the road, Thatch End, which is in fact an end-of-terrace cottage. This whole line of cottages is probably the most attractive in the village.

If we now cross the road there are facing us two old stone and tiled cottages, with modern extensions, but they bear on their west wall the initials and date 'M W 1696' as well as the remnants of what appears to have been a large window, possibly for a shop. It was while alterations were being carried out here in 1954 that the carved wooden head of a man together with a newspaper dated 22nd June 1749 were found. The carved wooden head appears to be a wigmaker's block and was given to the Dorset County Museum.

About 60 yards to the south and standing back a little from the road is a terrace of four houses which were erected in 1936 by the Sherborne Rural District Council. This was the second batch of council houses to be built in the village and probably the last for which the Parish Council selected the tenants—which they did by drawing the names from a hat.

Just below the council houses are two stone and slated dwellings known as Coombe Cottages. An old hitching ring can be seen on the west wall. The last house on the eastern side of the road of any significance is Orchard Close, which stands immediately opposite to Chantry Cottage. Like so many other houses, it was originally two dwellings, but it later became one and was known as Brickyard House. It was for many years the home of the Jeffery family, one of whom was described by himself as an 'Animal Doctor'. They were well-known village characters in the earlier years of the century.

Just below Orchard Close lies Wesley Cottage which is modern. It was so named, no doubt, due to the fact that it stands on what was the site of an old galvanise Wesleyan Chapel which was demolished in about 1970.

Finally, I should mention that the remains of the old cobbled pavement which was formerly on both sides of North Street can clearly be seen in various places.

Orchard Close, North Street, as it was in 1954.

Potters Leaze is a small wood on a steep slope adjoining the southern end of Yeovil Golf Course, and was known many years ago as a famous fox culvert. In September 1875 Professor Buckman's youngest son found here a rare fungus which was sent away for analysis.

'It proved on examination to be a specimen of the very rare *Sparrisis Crispa* which has only recently been observed in England and Dr Cook in his *Handbook of British Fungus* has only named two places where it has been found. A specimen was, however, exhibited at Hereford in 1874, gathered near the Wrekin in Shropshire. The *Sparrisis Crispa* may be described as forming a roundish mass of crisp, pale, yellowish, intricate, fleshy, but brittle branches rather broader and

The old Wesleyan Chapel in North Street which was destroyed in 1971. Wesley cottage now stands on this site.

serrate at the extremities, curled and folded, variously tubed, the whole springing from a thick rooted stem, the greater part of which is concealed in the soil. From 4 to about 12 metres in diameter. The fungus becomes first yellowish then brown and though persistent for a fortnight or three weeks resolves itself finally in a liquid loathsome mass.

'There is only one species of the genus *Sparrasis* that has hitherto been found in Britain, and this is of very rare occurrence so that it has been a fortunate find for the Cryptogaimic Flora of Dorset.'

Queen's Road consists of 53 dwellings varying in size from small semidetached bungalows to 4 bedroomed semidetached houses. They were built by Sherborne Rural District Council following a long campaign by the Parish Council who consistently fought to have the houses built to satisfy a pressing demand for accommodation for local families. The original name proposed for the road was Emlet, this being the name of the field in which it was built, whilst another name suggested was Coronation Avenue as the coronation of Queen Elizabeth II was imminent when the buildings were being erected. Finally, it was decided that the present name would be the most suitable.

A great deal of the credit for the houses finally being built can be given to one man, the late Mr Percy Pettitt. When he came to the village just after the Second World War he immediately took an active part in village life, with a particular interest in the field of local government. In 1950 he stood as a candidate for the Sherborne Rural District Council and he scored a convincing victory over the sitting candidate. It could truly be said that he was the first councillor from Bradford Abbas to sit on the District Council who had a truly working class background. He said quite simply, 'My policy is for improvement and betterment of conditions for this parish. My chief concern is that an adequate water supply shall be installed as soon as possible and the facts of the case are that until this is achieved, sanitation and housing cannot be considered.'

He was to see all of these things happen within his first five years in office. On 31st March 1954 the Parish Council recognised his efforts.

'A vote of thanks was proposed by Mr F. Mear, seconded by Mr T. Patch to Mr P. Pettitt for the hard work he had done for the village and they all agreed that he worked hard.'

In recent years many of the tenants have acquired their own homes.

Sands is a short stretch of road from the top of Quarry Lane to where it meets Manor Farm Road, just before the entrance to Underdown Hollow. It was previously known as Hulkham Bottom Lane, and was frequently unusable due to flooding. During the early years of this century, the Rev. Gordon Wickham raised £60 by public subscription as the parish's contribution to having the road raised to the position it is today.

South View is one of the new estates in the village, having been built during the years 1961–63. There are six semidetached houses, four detached bungalows and 26 semidetached bungalows. The estate was really built in two stages, the northern end being built first and a little later the southern section. The southern part of the estate was built upon what were the village allotments and the Parish Council had to find an alternative site. New allotments were created on their present site in Back Lane.

Smith's Bridge, which is of the sixteenth century and referred to by the locals as 'Smear's Bridge'.

Thornford Road runs from the junction at Grant's Hill to the village of Thornford but the Bradford Abbas section of the road stops at Smith's Bridge as the River Yeo is the boundary between the two parishes. It is interesting to note that whilst the name Smith's Bridge appears on the official maps many of the older inhabitants refer to it as Smears Bridge.

The bridge itself is scheduled as an ancient monument, as it is of the sixteenth century. It passes over the River Yeo on two arches, the central pier having sharp cutwaters. The voussoirs are chamfered, but instead of the usual string course at road level there is an oversailing course surmounted by the parapet. This produces the desired appearance and at the same time allows the bridge to be a few inches wider. The coping stones are held together by wrought iron cramps set in lead and it will be noticed that the old wrought iron does not rust like steel. The whole of the south-west parapet was demolished by an accident in 1972 and was rebuilt with the original stones and cramps and rails were set. Rails were not actually placed upon the parapets until September 1853.

Underdown Hollow is a name which is very rarely used these days except in official correspondence for it is more familiarly, but incorrectly, referred to as Bradford Hollow. It is now the most regularly used route for traffic going from Bradford Abbas to Yeovil but it is quite narrow in places and largely unsuitable for heavy lorries and the like. Repeated attempts to have the road widened have proved unsuccessful. It has high sandstone banks and now that the trees have grown again after being severely lopped a few years ago it is an extremely pretty stretch of road when the sun is shining, but very dangerous in the autumn when the leaves are on the road. Before it was metalled as it is today it was not the easiest road to travel along, due to its steepness, and for other reasons. Earl Cairns pointed out in 1903 that 'if good gravel was laid down instead of the greasy local stone it would be a great improvement but in any case unless the hedges at each side of the cutting are cut very close the roadway never has a chance of drying. It is often positively dangerous for horses either going up or down, and is very hard on animals drawing heavy loads.'

Vicarage Oak is a field which lies at the northern side of Red Lane Hill adjacent to the Coombe crossroads. It was in this field that Celtic remains were found by Professor Buckman in 1878. A further excavation was carried out in 1958, the report of which reads:

'Ploughing and robbery had taken away all the southern end of the building uncovered apart from the herringbone foundations. However, at the north end, dressed stone walls, 2 ft. 2 ins. in width had remained in part. Sufficient excavation was carried out to ascertain the size of the building which appeared to be some 82 ft by 24 ft. Inside the building, close to the south-east corner, a flue 15 inches wide had been built against and parallel with the east wall foundations but not bonded in. The flue, the east wall of which was 1 foot 10 inches away from their foundations, survived for 8 feet and was filled with ash but its northern end was destroyed possibly by previous excavation.

'At the north-west corner the Keinton stone paving of the floor was still in position though broken by agricultural operations and the stone rubble which appeared to have been packed in it during levelling operations. The slabs originally carefully squared and dressed and to be 1¹/₂ to 1³/₄ inches in thickness, 19 coins (14 of 3rd century, 5 of 4th century) were found. I am indebted to Mr. R.A.G. Carson for the identification. The pottery adjacent to the walls also seemed of this date.

'Inside the building, some 12 feet from the north-west corner an earlier trench had been filled in to carry the later wall, and in the fill and ash of this trench was found practically a complete pedestalled bead rim bowl (Brailsford Type 2), also pieces of types 3 and 12.

'Small finds were in parts of Kimmeridge Shale and bronze bracelets, a bronze broach with a spiral spring, a leaf-shaped and a barbed and tanged flint arrow head. The site is on the edge of the inferior volite at its junction with the Mudford Sands.'

Wessex Drive lies in the south-east corner of the village with its main access into Back Lane. It was built in the early 1960s on the site of an orchard.

Westbury runs snakelike from its junction with Church Road northwards until it meets up with Cross Roads at the southern end of Coombe Ditch Lane. It is one of the oldest streets in the village and there are several interesting buildings to be seen, but regretfully there are many that have been destroyed, not the least being the old Rose & Crown Inn which stood where the bungalow Mayflowers now stands. This old inn was a substantial stone and thatched building and was burnt down in the middle of the last century. The old entrance to the grounds of the inn can still be seen in the wall immediately facing the churchyard.

The two blocks of semidetached houses immediately to the north of Mayflowers were built about 1830 (at least they do not appear on a map of 1825 but do appear on one dated 1838). They are substantial, stone-built and slated with handsome stone mullioned windows. Until 1954 they were part of the Bradford Abbas estate. No. 1. has been the home of the Gill family, I believe, almost from the time it was built and the present occupier is Mrs 'Midge' Gill, the widow of Freddie Gill who was clerk to the Parish Council for 30 years whilst for many years in the adjoining house lived his brother Tommy and sister Rosa Gill. Tommy Gill was secretary of the Sick Benefit Club for over 40 years. At No. 4. lived Lily Ann Chainey who lived in the same house for 72 years and at the time of her death was the oldest person in the village.

Just above No. 4, Westbury is the the railway bridge, over which the main London–Exeter trains pass and just beyond this is the junction with Bishop's Lane. This road junction has always been considered dangerous and it is interesting to note that when the railway was being built in 1859 efforts were made to get Bishop's Lane diverted so as to enter Westbury between what is now the Forge and Westbury House. A Vestry minute reads:

'1st February 1859. Resolved that the Waywardens be directed to write to Mr Gibson respecting the new approach to the village on the Yeovil road which has been made by the Railway authorities pointing out the extremely sharp and dangerous turning by the corner adjoining the B'smiths shop and enquiring whether Mr Clayton contemplates, as has been reported, making a more direct approach to the bridge avoiding the sharp turnings and coming in between Mr

Cottages in Westbury, built about 1825. In the mid-nineteenth century, a husband, wife and eleven children lived in the cottage on the left, with room for a lodger.

The Forge, c.1905. ▲

Westbury House, ▶
with the door of the
carpenter's shop
open opposite. It
was in this
carpenter's shop that
the fine oak lectern
in the church was
carved.

Hockey's house and the cottages—also to enquire whether he will take any steps with the Railway authorities to effect these improvements. The Waywarden is also directed to point out the lowness of the bridge on that part of the line, which instead of being 16 ft in the clear between the arch and the road is only 13 feet.'

A further minute of 28th April 1859 reads:

'A proposition was made by Mr Clayton to the effect that if the Parish would consent to have Emletts Lane and the paths across Emlett stopped he in conjunction with the Railway company would engage to make a new line of road from Yeovil to come in between Mr Hockey's and Mr Thorne's houses in a line with the roadway under the railway bridge. In which case Broadway Lane and the angular part of the road would be stopped. The consent of the Vestry to the above proposition was unanimously given.'

'However, although all parties were in agreement regarding the dangers of the road junction, no agreement could be reached as to who would bear the cost and so the proposals were simply dropped.

Just beyond the road junction with Bishop's Lane is the house now known as The Forge. It was formerly two cottages which have now been converted into one dwelling. In one of these cottages lived the village blacksmith with the forge alongside. The old forge still, in fact, stands and although the sound of the blacksmith's hammer on the anvil can no longer be heard, a well-worn mounting stone can still be seen. The old forge is really only recognisable to those who knew where the blacksmith worked as it is now used as a garage. It is also interesting to note that when Bradford Abbas Parish Council was formed in December 1894, the then village blacksmith, William Lush, topped the poll which was held by a show of hands, and not on a secret ballot as it is today. The present occupant Mr Badger Goss was, in his prime, a nationally known figure, a leading motor cycle scrambler.

The next building is Westbury House, but years ago there were cottages between the old blacksmith's shop and Westbury House, and where these cottages formerly stood is now part of the extensive gardens attached to the latter dwelling. Westbury House is a large building, facing to the south, and is built of local stone and is thatched.

I was fortunate enough to be given the opportunity by the present owner, Mr Gordon Warren, to look over the house, when he was carrying out extensive improvements, and at the time I was there it was only the four walls and roof which were intact. Having seen the gutted house it was quite obvious that it had formerly been two dwellings, with the eastern end being by far the oldest. At the western end, however, there is a massive open fireplace with what appears to be an oven on the north side. There is also an open fireplace at the eastern end but not so large, and Mr Warren informed me that when he was demolishing the inner walls he found several dead birds in the plaster where it was quite impossible for them to have got on their own. One can only surmise that they were placed in the walls in such a manner quite deliberately by the builders, for some purpose known only to themselves. The stones which make up the four outer walls are only held together by mud and what would appear to be one of the original stout wooden beams was uncovered, although it is now, unfortunately, much damaged. In stripping the interior, Mr Warren found windows which he never knew existed and had obviously been blocked up generations ago. He also found another door in the southern wall just to the east of the present front door. The eastern end of the house would appear to be early seventeenth century with the western end probably added a century later.

For many years it was the home of the Lang family, whose carpenter's shop was on the opposite side of the road in the house that is now known as Kenlea. Here Uriah Lang and his wife Mary brought up their twelve children, with some of the sons eventually going into partnership with their father in the carpenter's shop, and upon his death continuing the business as Lang Brothers. The business finally closed in either 1931 or 1932 upon the retirement of Mr William Lang, who with his brother in 1905 made a gift to the church of the wooden lectern which they had carved themselves and which is still being used. An interesting point regarding William Lang is that he was given a free education as he was the tenth or 'tithe' child.

The three houses on the opposite side of the road are also built of local stone and are probably of the late seventeenth or early eighteenth century. To the east of Westbury House and on the opposite side of the road stood two substantial semidetached thatched cottages, where the modern bungalow Ledras now stands. In the first of these cottages lived Samuel Ring, one of the 'lads of the village'.

Just a little further to the north lie Westbury council houses and opposite them is a building which in recent years has been converted into small flats. It was built originally as a shop, and was first occupied by Yeovil Co-Operative Society but they closed in January 1968, probably due to the competition from two other shops in the village at the time. It was then used as a retail outlet for an electrical firm and then as a wholesale warehouse for motor cycles before being converted.

A little further to the north, and on higher ground, are a row of 8 houses, 4 blocks of semidetached which were the first council houses to be built in Bradford Abbas by the Sherborne Rural District Council. They were erected in 1931 but during 1986 extensive improvements were carried out. They are usually referred to as Emlet which was the name of the field in which they stand.

On the corner of Emlet where it faces South View and on the opposite side of the road was a fine horse chestnut tree which was something of a village landmark. It was chopped down quite unnecessarily although it was showing some signs of dying by a newcomer to the village much to the disgust of many villagers.

There are only two further houses actually situated in Westbury and although their access is from that street, their address is surprisingly Queen's Road.

Worth is a field which lies to the rear of No.'s 1–4 Westbury and is of some interest in that it is the only Saxon name left in the parish—worth meaning an enclosure.

As well as being the name of the bridge over the River Yeo, *Yeovil Bridge* was also the name of a field alongside. Situated almost on the bridge is a toll house, part of the Sherborne turnpike. It is a substantial Ham stone-built and tiled dwelling.

CHAPTER VIII
Social Life

Bradford Abbas, it must be said, leads an extremely active social life. In fact there are organisations in the village which cater for the tastes of most people and in that respect the village is much more fortunate than most other villages in the county of Dorset. At one time in certain quarters, Bradford Abbas had the reputation for being a quarrelsome village and no doubt with the advantage of hindsight this can be considered fair comment. Certainly in the political field candidates at parliamentary elections were not always given a fair hearing and on the social front several organisations had serious rifts, which tended to show themselves when major village events such as Coronation or Jubilee celebrations were being organised. In more recent years there was trouble over the building of a new Village Hall when there were several different committees set up which were in opposition to one another.

However, it is not the purpose of this chapter to enter into the rights and wrongs of any particular matter but to give a brief history of the organisations that exist in the village and of organisations that have long since disappeared from the village scene.

In 1886, when the Rev. Gordon Wickham became Vicar, there was no parish room or Village Hall and only two village organisations—the Temperance Society and the Friendly Society, more commonly known as the Sick Benefit Club. Whilst the Temperance Society held regular meetings and the occasional concert it could not be said that its activities suited everybody's taste whilst the Friendly Society only held its annual club day. There were also, at very irregular intervals, concerts organised by the church but these were normally of a highbrow nature, and not all to the liking of the villagers who were nevertheless often 'recommended' to attend by their employers or other influential villagers. It was therefore with a great deal of anticipation and enjoyment that the parishioners would look forward to any village event but the only events in which all could participate were celebrations of a general nature—e.g. Jubilee or

June 22. 1911

Bradford Abbas, Clifton Maubank & Wyke

Coronation Festivities.

Programme of Events.

6 a.m. **A Peal on the Bells,** the Bells will be rung at intervals during the day

12 a.m. **Special Coronation Service in the Church.**

2 p.m. **Sports in the Cricket Field,** by kind permission of Mrs. Wills and [the Cricket Club.

4.30 p.m. **Presentation of Commemorative Coronation Mugs by Mrs. Daniell,** of Clifton Maubank.   **Tea for all under 16.**

6.30 p.m. **Supper,** consisting of Roast Beef, Boiled Beef, Ham, Boiled Mutton, Pickles, Salad, Cheese, Bread.—Beer and Minerals.—In a Field adjoining S. Mary House, by kind permission of the Rev. Gordon Wickham, **for all over 16,** each Person to bring a Knife, Fork, Plate and Glass.   After the Meal these can be Stored in Schoolroom.

8. p.m. Concert or Dance.

9.30 p.m. Display of Fireworks.

"GOD SAVE THE KING."

Pianos Supplied by Messrs. E. PRICE & SONS, Ltd., Yeovil.

SPORTS.

1. **Sack Race,** over 16	3s.	2s.	1s.
2. ,, ,, under 16	2s.	1s.	6d.
3. **Three-legged Race,** over 16 Blindfolded.	3s.	2s.	1s.
4. ,, ,, ,, under 16 ,, ...	2s.	1s.	6d.
5. **Egg & Spoon Race,** for Women	3s.	2s.	1s.
6. ,, ,, ,, ,, Girls.	2s.	1s.	6d.
7. **Bicycle Race**	5s.	3s.	2s.
8. **Stone Picking Race,** Boys	2s.	1s.	6d.
9. ,, ,, ,, Girls	2s.	1s.	6d.
10. **Wheel-barrow Race,** over 16, Blindfolded.	3s.	2s.	1s.
11. **Flat Race, 200 Yards,** under 16.	2s.	1s.	6d.
12. ,, ½ **Mile,** over 16	3s.	2s.	1s.
13. **Throwing the Weight,** over 16.	3s.	2s.	1s.
14. ,, ,, ,, under 16.	2s.	1s.	6d.
15. **Kicking the Football,** Women	3s.	2s.	1s.
16. ,, ,, Girls	2s.	1s.	6d.
17. **Bucket and Orange Race,** (Boys)	2s.	1s.	6d.
18. **Pick-a-Back Race,** Men	3s.	2s.	1s.
19. **Skipping Race,** Girls	2s.	1s.	6d.
20. ,, ,, Women.	3s.	2s.	1s.

No Competitor to take more than One First Prize ~~and~~ or two Second Prizes.

☞ All are asked to do their part in making the Village bright with Decorations.

O. Chaffin, Printer, Sherborne.

Coronation Poster, 1911.

Coronation celebrations—and these were by their nature few and far between.

However, the Rev. Gordon Wickham on arriving at Bradford Abbas was obviously alarmed at the lack of social life and he personally paid for a parish hall to be built and encouraged village gatherings. It is really from 1886 onwards that the social life began to take shape much along the lines that we see today. The Rev. Wickham, on the very first Christmas in which he was resident at Bradford Abbas, invited the old people of the village for a dinner. There were 15 in attendance with a combined age of 1097 years, the eldest John Pitt being 86 and the youngest Tom Bishop a mere 53. A note tells that Lucy Napper aged 90 was unable to attend. When he married the following year the Rev. & Mrs Wickham regularly held parish teas year after year and they were much enjoyed. At the first of them there were 90 persons present and after dining those present would be entertained by lantern slides and sing-songs whilst some of the ladies present dispensed 'the cup that cheers but does not inebriate'.

One of the biggest social events in the history of the village was held in the grounds of the Old Rectory to celebrate Queen Victoria's Diamond Jubilee in 1897:

'Favoured by perfect weather Bradford Abbas kept the festival in honour of the Diamond Jubilee. All arrangements were left to a Committee (appointed at a village meeting) consisting of the Vicar (as Chairman) Messrs Jeffrey, Leeding, Wills, W. Lang, T. Hitchcock, J. Patch, Mrs James Higgins and Mrs John Bragg. The chief burden fell upon the tea committee, Messrs Leeding, W. Lang, and Mrs James Higgins who catered successfully for over 600 guests. The ringers gave their services and ringing commenced at 2.15 pm, vying with the salutes at Mr Pomeroy's forge in suitably opening the afternoon's festivity. At 2.30 pm, the children assembled in the school, bearing their flower trophies, for which the Vicar had offered prizes, and whilst there, a jubilee medal was presented to each by Mr W. Walker, the Headmaster. At 3.00 pm the Town Band arrived from Yeovil and played the children to the Vicarage. The procession of children, headed by the choir in their white dresses and carrying flags and the two large flower trophies, which they had made themselves, was one of the prettiest sights the village has seen, especially when they reached the lawn and displayed in the letter S on reaching their appointed station. A hymn 'All the mountain heights adoring', each verse ending with the refrain 'God save the Queen' was then sung, and the prize for the flower trophies were adjudged by Mrs Albert Clayton. Teas were served in the drive for the children at 4.00 pm and for adults from 5.00 pm to 7.00 pm, ham sandwiches being added to the latter, who sat down in relays of about 180. The cake and bread were provided by Mr J. Patch, W. Whittle and Mr Walden supplying milk and butter. The tables were served by Mrs Wickham, Mrs Cooper, Misses Whittle, Collis, Kent, Cooper, and Patch. In addition to village friends Mrs Wickham had a garden party. In a field adjoining "Jaspers Close" kindly lent by Mr Jacob Wills the children were provided with swings by Mr W. Lang and the maypole by Mr George Leeding and Mr W. Lang, while the sports were energetically managed by Messrs. J. Escomb and Basil Kerr, Wills and Treverhard, present and past pupils of the Vicar, Messrs Wills, W. Lang, Misses Whittle and Collis, cricket being superintended by Mr W. Walker. Prizes were provided by the Committee and some of Mrs Wickham's guests. Dancing on the lawn commenced early and continued vigorously, the Yeovil Town Band in this, and throughout the afternoon and evening, playing excellent music. The Bishop of Wakefield's hymn was sung with effect at 9.00 pm and a display of fireworks by the Vicar's pupils, Mr Jeffrey, P.C. Miller, Mr E. Higgins and the Vicar with salutes from the wilderness preceded the finale of the National Anthem—sung with the utmost enthusiasm at 10.00 pm.

'Needless to say the Vicar's call for three cheers for the Queen and Royal Family was heartily responded to and the band played its guests, now numbered about 1000 out of the grounds at 10.15 pm. The villagers felt no doubt that favoured by glorious weather and excellent organisation they had worthily celebrated the 60th Year of the Queen's reign.

'A word must be added to the decoration. Never has the village been so gay. Churchwell Street, Church Street and Mr James Higgins's house were bright with flags of all colours. Mr Albert Clayton's, the Post Office, Mr G. Leeding's and Mr E. Higgin's houses and the Vicarage were all illuminated at night and the Vicarage grounds were bright with fairy lights, and coloured fires among the trees.

Mrs Clayton displayed a crown over her front gate and a large 'V.R.' adorned the Vicarage porch.

Thus ended a day that will never be forgotten by these privileged to take part in it.'

I doubt very much whether the village has ever had such a day before or since.

There have been other successful events such as the 1937 Coronation festivities, but generally speaking what other big events have occurred have been of a moneymaking nature. Of course, individual organisations have had events and it is to these village organisations that I now turn.

Cricketers, c. 1920.

It seems that the first ever *Cricket Club* in the village was formed in 1887 when at a meeting held in the school a committee was elected— J. Sherring, J. Patch, G. Leeding, W. Lang and J. Lang—and one of its main objects was to enrol new members.

By 1900 the club was thriving and weekly matches were being played against teams from Yeovil and neighbouring villages, but the opening match of each season was an internal affair, as it had become something of a tradition for the married men to play the single men, the latter more often being the winners. The club members were expected to pay a subscription of 2/- per season with the under 16s being asked to contribute only 1/-. The income from this was really insufficient to keep the club solvent, but each year when the annual deficiency was announced, for that is what it became, some kind benefactor was always on hand to balance the books and keep the club alive.

It appears that the Vicar, Rev. Gordon Wickham, was the club Captain for the first 15 years but in 1902 he found that he was unable to play regularly and he resigned the captaincy, to be replaced by Mr Harry Warr, who was already Vice-Captain as well as club Secretary. It was in this same year that the club began to run into difficulties in raising a team and it became necessary for outsiders to be brought in to make up numbers.

However, interest in the club soon revived and the next season proved to be the best in terms of results. Although the club had a disastrous start, being bowled out for only 15 runs in their first match, against Hardington, they went the rest of the season unbeaten, which included dismissing Stoford for 10 runs and Yetminster for 19. The Captain, Harry Warr was the star player that year, twice scoring 73 runs and taking most wickets.

In 1911 the Cricket Club was responsible for organising a concert which marked the opening of the first of Bradford Abbas's village halls on the present site. The money raised that evening was put towards the purchase of chairs and providing an outside lamp.

The club was at this time playing its home matches in the field adjoining Grant's Hill. In 1913, due to the late harvest, the members decided that it was not worth running a team that season, but the Vicar promised that the field would be available the following year. But often a break such as that can have a disastrous effect, with members' interest being lost, even if only for a season, and so it proved for the village team. At the Annual General Meeting held in the Village Hall in February 1914, there was such a lack of enthusiasm that the meeting had to be adjourned. At the new meeting a month later the view was expressed that the young men of the village should take advantage of the facilities provided for them, as the club had been given additional equipment and could also be proud of an asphalt practice pitch. At a further meeting held in May it was reported that the Rev. Wickham had paid the membership fees of 10 of the upper schoolboys and that the team was showing much promise. It was considered that the generous gesture of the Vicar should be supported as in the past too much dependence had been placed upon the veterans of the club, and within a few weeks there were more than enough lads willing to play.

Nevertheless, 1914 was to be the last season, for with the outbreak of the First World War the club closed down. It was not to be revived until 1925 under the captaincy of Sir Edward Anson, who was largely responsible for the club's revival. This second club lasted only a few years, largely due to the untimely death of Sir Edward Anson. Then in 1938 it was decided to form yet another club. And so, on 1st March 1938, a meeting of all interested villagers was held, at which it was reported that Mr Wyatt Paul would make a field available (where Ambrose Close is now built) and Mr Paul's gesture was greatly appreciated. Mr E.R. Underdown was asked to be President, Mr R.C. Day becoming Captain, Secretary and Fixtures Secretary, Mr W. Patch was Hon. Treasurer and a committee was chosen consisting of Messrs F. Smith, N. Garrett, G. Cox, C. Smith, H. Gillham and C. Ring. Mr F. Smith undertook to be responsible for the wicket. This club, the last of the three, proved to be the most successful and survived, except for a break during the Second World War, until 1957, when it was dissolved. There is at present a cricket club in the village who play their matches on the sports club ground but they are very much under the control of the Sports & Recreational Club.

Mainly through the efforts of the Vicar, the Rev. Gordon Wickham, and the Schoolmaster, Mr W. Walker, an *Evening Continuation School* was opened in 1895. It was hoped that those in the village, who, through no fault of their own, had not been fortunate enough to enjoy the benefits of a proper education would take the opportunity to improve their knowledge by attending evening classes. The subjects to be taught were geography, arithmetic, mensuration, vocal music and gymnastics with the classes being held on Mondays, Thursdays and Fridays in the parish room during the winter months. The school was placed under the jurisdiction of the Education Department which meant, as with the children's school, that the classes were visited each year and that a grant could be obtained. For the first year four teachers were appointed, Rev. Wickham, Messrs W. Walker, G. Giles and J. Lang, and 40 villagers, whose ages ranged from 56 to 14, enrolled. The school was quite obviously an outstanding success and when the Government Inspector examined it only four months after its inception he was able to report:

'The school here has made a splendid start. The attendance was good throughout and the work was well done in all respects. A word of special praise must be bestowed upon the physical exercises.'

The school continued to operate successfully year after year with consistently good reports and regular attendances by the students, who undoubtedly realised the advantages to be gained by increasing their knowledge. However, as things turned out in the end the school had a comparatively short life as it closed in 1913, when it seemed that attendances were falling away, never to open its doors again. Only two years earlier the Government Inspector had seen fit to comment:

'It would be a great advantage, and add materially to the usefulness of the school, if employers of labour could be induced to take an interest in the school and encourage their employees to attend'.

The first ever *Football Club* in Bradford Abbas was formed on 28th December 1900 with the Rev. G. Wickham as President, Mr Harry Warr as Secretary and Mr Reg Jeanes as team Captain. The headquarters of the club was a room at the Old Mill, which had kindly been made available by Mr T. Whittle, and had been fitted up as a recreation room by the club President. Those over 15 years old had to pay a subscription of 2/- per season with the younger members contributing 1/-. A series of friendly matches, both home and away, were arranged, and for the first year of its existence the club's overall playing record was: played 12, won 5, drawn 4, lost 3. This was not at all bad for the first season with the most convincing victory against Milborne Port Night School by 5–0. On the other hand the defeats included a disastrous drubbing of 6–1 by the visiting team from the Nautilus Works in Yeovil.

For the opening match of the second season, on 21st September 1901, the opponents were again the Nautilus Works but this time the match was played in Yeovil and Bradford Abbas were on the receiving end of a 5–1 defeat. This was a remarkable result when you consider that Bradford Abbas were only able to muster seven men. The team struggled throughout the early part of the season and although results began to show a slight improvement towards the end, one leading villager saw fit to comment that 'when they have learnt to keep their places and play for side not self, they will give a good account of themselves'. The overall results for the second season (this time under Mr Harry Warr's captaincy) were: played 19, won 5, drawn 5, lost 9. It cannot be said that the season's results were good, so it is not surprising that as the time approached for the opening of its third season there was considerable doubt as to whether it could raise sufficient players. This prompted the Vicar to rent a field for the use only of the few who wished to have a game of football, and he formed a junior club. The Vicar was obviously disappointed that there was no senior eleven for he wrote in the Parish Magazine that it was a shame, 'more especially as the village produces many young men who could play if they had sufficient energy'. It seems, however, that the young men 'got the message' because the senior eleven was revived just in time for the opening

Bradford Abbas Football Club, c.1947.

of the season, which proved to be only moderately successful from a playing point of view.

The problem of getting sufficient players again reared its head the following season and there were again a number of people who promised to play but once their names were on the team sheet they either made some excuse not to appear or did not turn up at all, with the result that the team was invariably under strength. The Vicar was very much aware of the situation and wrote in the Parish Magazine:

'If the club is to obtain credit for its successes, it must be by never playing short and not being forced to rely on outsiders. Nothing should interfere with a member's attendance once he has given his promise to play.'

The Club continued to survive, although getting sufficient players from the parish itself without having to call on outsiders was a perennial problem. It gained no honours in the league but completed every season until, as far as I can ascertain, it closed down in the late 1920s.

The club was re-formed in June 1934 and was officially known as Bradford Abbas, Clifton and Wyke Football Club but I have never heard it referred to as anything other than Bradford Abbas Football Club amongst the locals. This club proved to be very successful in providing the local lads with a game of football even though season after season they failed to get amongst the honours list. The mainspring of the club at this time was Mr Harry Gillham, who devoted a great many years to fostering the club through its difficulties until in the late 1960s he decided the time had come when he could no longer be a leading participant. His work did not go unrecognised, however, for he has now been elected Life President. He had what he would probably consider his just reward when at the end of the 1963–4 season the club very nearly did the double by winning the Division III Knockout Cup and being runners up in Division III of the Yeovil and District Football League. In the cup final, Bradford Abbas defeated Somerton (who were the Division III champions) 3–1, Eddie Garrett, Tom Farrow and Mike Dewberry scoring the goals. This match also brought some reward to another faithful servant of the club, Ron Gosney, who turned out regularly for more seasons than I care to remember and who never let the team down.

Perhaps the proudest moment in the history of the Football Club came in 1975 when it won the Dorset Minor Cup for the first time in its history when they defeated Poole Yachtsmen 2–0 at Dorchester. About 100 people from the village travelled to see the match but it was not a good game until Maurice Beard scored a spectacular goal for Bradford Abbas and a goal direct from a corner by Kevin Gosney sealed a well-deserved victory. Team captain Bill French proudly collected the trophy and a jolly good evening was enjoyed by all. The Football Club is now part of the Sports and Recreational Club consortium and continues to be reasonably successful. There is also another team which play in the Yeovil Sunday League under the name of Bradford Sports. They are managed by Maurice Beard who seems to be making as much of a name for himself in the annals of the Football Club as some of his illustrious predecessors. It was a great day for Maurice when the team to which he devotes so much time were also successful, in 1987, in winning the Dorset Minor Cup for Sunday teams.

At a simple ceremony held in the Rose & Crown Inn on the 11th January 1964 the President of the Bradford Abbas Sick Benefit Club (as the *Friendly Society* came to be known), Mr A. Franke, presented an inscribed watch to Mr Tommy Gill, the long-serving Secretary. This ceremony

The Sick Benefit Club, 1926.

marked the end of an era in the history of the society and of the village, for when Tommy, after over 40 years in office, decided that the time had come when he could no longer carry out his duties, no replacement could be found and it was reluctantly decided that the society would have to finally close its doors. At one time or another nearly all the men who lived in the village between the two World Wars, and to a lesser extent after the Second World War, had been members of the society, which had the admirable object of assisting its members in time of sickness and providing a sum of money at death. It is to the great credit of the society in its later years that no member abused the advantages which were to be gained from membership.

The story of the Friendly Society in Bradford Abbas goes back to the early years of the nineteenth century when Club Day and the fancy dress dances were annual events which were much anticipated by villagers. Abuse there certainly was in the early years but as happens so frequently, good often arises from a bad beginning.

A copy of the rules of the society established in 1858 still survives and makes interesting reading. It is not possible here to print these rules in full, but what follows are, I think, probably the most interesting extracts.

'RULE X

That if any member of this Society who shall have been admitted six calendar months, shall be rendered unable to work by sickness or any other malady (unless such sickness proceed from a loose and wicked life, or any species thereof, or be brought on by drinking, wrestling, fighting, or any improper conduct, or who hath any distemper, whereof he hath been afflicted from his infancy, or any distemper, or wound, or disorder, which he might have happened to have had at the time of his being admitted into this Society, and not made known to the Committee which cases are not relievable by the Society) and shall give seven days' notice to one of the stewards, such stewards shall visit him as stated in Article 6 and at the expiration of one week after the seven days' notice (if entitled) the stewards shall pay the sick member seven shillings per week, for four weeks, and four shillings per week for the four next following weeks, if his illness so long continue, and after receiving the aforesaid sick pay, no member shall receive any more for the same illness for the space of six calendar months, but after the expiration of that period he shall be entitled to sick pay as before stated: and if a sick member should have been able to follow his occupation, and any sickness or accident should again happen to him he shall be entitled to receive the same pay as if no former sickness had occurred; and any member residing in the parish of Bradford Abbas, who shall make a claim on the funds of this Society, shall produce a certificate from a Surgeon, signed by the Clergyman of the parish in which the member resides.

RULE XIII

That if any member of this Society whilst receiving sick pay be seen in a public house, or beer house, or visiting at any other public place, or intoxicated, or in any measure what ever shall be engaged in his own business, or that of others, he shall, for the first offence, forfeit all such sick pay from the date of such misconduct to which he would have been entitled during such illness, and be fined at the discretion of the Committee; and for the second offence he shall be expelled from the Society. If any member witnessing such misconduct shall, within twenty-four hours fail to give information of same, either to the Secretary or Stewards of the Society, he shall be fined the sum of two shillings.

RULE XVI

That if any member bring an accusation against a brother member or members and cannot prove the same he shall be fined two shillings and sixpence for every such offence, and any member defrauding or attempting to defraud the Society in any manner whatever, or attempting to pass bad money to the Stewards, shall forfeit five shillings or be expelled. That all fines and forfeits be paid immediately on being incurred, or the next time a member incurring a forfeit pay his monthly contribution, and if a member, so liable, refuses to pay such fines and forfeits, he shall be excluded.

RULE XVII

That if any member during the time of a general meeting or the annual feast shall interrupt the president, vice-president or stewards or refuse to keep silent at the command of either presidents or stewards he shall forfeit threepence for each and every offence, or if he shall curse, swear, challenge, insult, disturb, or abuse any one or more of the members present, either by foul language or wanton behaviour or shall utter any seditions, obscene or profane expressions, he shall for the first offence, forfeit sixpence, and for every subsequent offence on the same day or evening, the sum of one shilling, and every distinct oath, wanton act, abusive expression, or repetition of any affront shall be deemed a separate offence, and in case of fighting at any time of the day when the club is assembled, or at any time of the night after it has assembled (that is to say, before day-light, the following morning) the member who strikes the first blow shall forfeit five shillings, and the member who returns the blow being so struck, shall forfeit one shilling, and any member attending any meeting of the Society intoxicated shall forfeit one shilling; any committee man attending the business of this Society in a state of intoxication shall forfeit two shillings and sixpence.

RULE XVIII   That if any member shall commit any theft, or fellony, or other crime, or offence, and be convicted, and be imprisoned for one calendar month or more, or be convicted of any dishonesty or offence, before a magistrate, and be fined in a penalty above one pound, or shall abscond from his place of abode on suspicion of any crime for the space of three calendar months, or shall leave his family unprovided for, such member shall be expelled and never more re-enter.

RULE XXIII   A Surgeon shall be chosen annually; he shall attend all members afflicted with sickness or disease or labouring under any external accident or infirmity, resident not more than four miles from the Doctor's residence, but in case any member's residence shall exceed four miles he shall pay the Doctor such additional mileage as shall be agreed on by him and the patient, beyond the distance of four miles, but in case any member's place of residence shall exceed eight miles from the Doctor's residence, he shall not be required to pay for the Doctor's services; nor be entitled to the benefit thereof, every member residing as above stated, shall pay one shilling per quarter for the Doctor's services, he is required to visit any sick member as soon as may be after application made to him and to sign a certificate (if required) stating the degree of the patient's illness; every sick member requiring the Doctor's services is to apply to the Secretary for an order for that purpose, and any sick member who may be able to walk to the Doctor's residence shall be required to do so, but the Doctor is not expected to attend any member for any complaint that will not entitle that member to the relief for which this Society is formed, but in case of the Doctor's absence when any serious complaint or accident happen, requiring immediate attention and any Surgeon should unavoidably be called in, it is expected that no charge will be brought either against that member or the Society generally, any such demand if made, must be paid by the Surgeon of the Society, but this refers only to such complaints or accidents as will entitle the suffering member to this Society's allowance, and not to any brought on by his own improper or disorderly conduct.

RULE XXIV   That there shall be an annual meeting of the members at Bradford Abbas on Trinity Tuesday, at such place as shall be agreed on at the monthly meeting preceding such annual meeting, where every member is expected to attend, by nine o'clock in the morning; members shall then go in procession to church, to hear divine service, on which occasion, the minister will be requested to preach a sermon and any member not behaving in a decent and becoming manner in going to or returning from church, or who shall leave the church during divine service (except on cases of urgent necessity) shall forfeit and pay the sum of two shillings for each offence. That a dinner shall be provided and each member that dines shall pay a sum as shall be agreed upon by the Society at the last monthly meeting preceding such annual dinner. No part of the expense of the annual dinner shall be paid out of funds of the Society.'

As far as possible all the rules of the society were rigidly enforced, but although it continued to thrive for a few years after the Second World War, the coming of the welfare state, sounded its death knell. Tommy Gill kept the society going up to 1964, albeit with a minimal number of members, and upon his retirement the final payout was made. The old banner does still survive, however, and at the present time it is in my possession. It is royal blue in colour with gold lettering and with two hands clasped in friendship. It may never be proudly paraded around the village again but it is nice to know some material evidence of the society still survives as well as the pleasant memories which I know many of the older inhabitants have, not only of the financial benefits to be gained in times of distress but also of the enjoyable social life which all took part in on club days and the fancy dress dances.

The idea of a *Friendship Club* for the elderly really sprang from the Women's Institute in 1972 when some members considered that it would be useful to have meetings in the Village Hall after the Playgroup's morning session, when the hall was still warm. With the co-operation of the Village Hall Committee it was agreed to run the club for a three-month experimental period, and it was fortunate that during this short period of time members were able to celebrate Mrs Kate Purchase's 90th birthday and Mr & Mrs Bill Gale's golden wedding. These events helped to get people together and since that time the club has never looked back. It now meets regularly on the first Tuesday afternoon in every month. There are also outings and a sumptuous Christmas dinner each year. Members pay a subscription but funds are also raised from a sales table, raffles, gifts etc., as well as coffee mornings and jumble sales. It has proved to be an extremely successful club and is still thriving.

It seems that the first detachment of the *Girl Guides* to be formed in Bradford Abbas was during the final months of the First World War. A meeting was called for 28th September 1918 in the Village Hall when a Mrs Mark Kerr, the Commissioner for Girl Guides in the London district gave an address to interested parents, fully explaining the objects of the movement. To add some interest to the proceedings a detachment of Girl Guides from Yeovil came to the meeting and gave a display of dancing and singing which was thoroughly enjoyed by all present.

As a result of this meeting sufficient interest was aroused in the village and a detachment was very soon formed under the captaincy of Mrs Gordon Wickham, the wife of the Vicar. The Bradford Abbas troop's first public engagement turned out to be the 'welcome home' celebrations held on 10th July 1919 when, prior to attending church, they were inspected by Bishop Joscelyn, and following the service they lined the church entrance to salute the guests as they left the church.

In the early years the Guides took part in most of the village activities and in the early 1920s (by now under Lady Anson's captaincy) they held their own socials in the Village Hall which were undoubtedly enjoyed by all who attended. However, like so many other organisations in Bradford

Abbas the Guides have not had an unbroken history and by the early 1930s, the detachment had been disbanded. In June 1936, however, several of the older girls at the school showed an interest in re-forming the troop and attended weekly meetings with this intention. And so, this time under the captaincy of Mrs Douglas (the Rev. Douglas's wife), with Miss Payne as her Lieutenant, a new troop was formed and on the 11th July 1936 the members were formally enrolled by Mrs Rose, the District Commissioner for Guides. At the enrolment she saw fit to compliment the girls on their smartness. Mrs Douglas left the village, however, when her husband resigned the incumbency and Miss Payne was promoted to Captain. In March 1939 Miss Payne resigned as leader, as she was leaving the parish, but her efforts on the girls' behalf did not go unrewarded, for quite apart from wishing her well, they presented her with a fruit knife and a cheese knife. Miss Payne was succeeded by Miss Scammell and the Guides continued to thrive, as a villager recorded:

'May 1939. The other occasion of the season was the parade of our little company of Girl Guides at church on Rogation Sunday, when they laid their colours at the altar of Christ's sacrifice. The conduct of the parade deserved the highest praise and I should like to commend the work of the Guides to the parents of all our girls. Miss Scammell is most ably carrying on for the guides the faithful work which Miss Payne was doing when she left us, and all who are interested in this useful work will feel grateful to these young women for so generously offering their time and skill.'

The coming of the Second World War caused the troop to close down, but very shortly after the end of hostilities, the detachment was revived and by 1955 the Bradford Abbas troop could boast of the only Guide in the district who had earned the First Class Guide Badge (Jacqueline Franke), to be followed a few years later when Caroline Robins became the troop's first Queen's Guide, in fact the first in the area.

At this time Mrs Meager was Captain and the Guides were particularly active:

'October 1955. Girl Guides of the 1st Bradford Abbas Company with members of the Brownie Pack went by coach to Sherborne and at the Methodist Church listened to a talk given by Mr George Cousdale of the National Children's Home. Mrs Meager, who had charge of the party, afterwards presented £8.0.10. to the

Children's Home on behalf of the local Guides and Brownies. A camp fire evening was held in the Village Hall recently. Guides' parents were invited, also friends of the Company and Guides and Guiders from the Sherborne and Yetminster Companies. During the evening, Jennifer Cox, a 'Golden Hand' Brownie 'flew up' to guides and Jacqueline Franke was presented with her first class badge by the District Commissioner, Miss Yeatman. Other badges presented were: Susan Durrant, Margaret Bridle, Susan Hurford. Athletics— Elizabeth Frank and Susan Durrant. Needlewoman, Susan Hurford. The Guides thanked Miss Lloyd for the use of the room for meetings, also Mr Underdown for the use of his orchard for summer meetings, and Mrs Loxton who gives so much time in testing them. The evening finished with camp fire singing.'

How successful the guides were at this time can be gauged from the fact that Bradford Abbas produced no less than three Queen's Guides.

When Mrs Meager left the village she was succeeded as leader by Mrs Eva Price. After the departure of Mrs Price, the Guides hit another sticky patch, but Mrs Chris Jones took over the task of leader and was responsible for reviving a very good village organisation.

It is a tradition in Bradford Abbas that the annual flower show is held on August Bank Holiday Monday—it is one of the 'big' days in the village calendar, when natives and newcomers, young and old flock to see the exhibits which are proudly displayed. The current flower shows are held under the auspices of the *Bradford Abbas, Clifton Maubank, Wyke & Silverlake Horticultural Society* which was founded in 1934.

The first show of which I have a record was held on 2nd October 1864 at the instigation of Professor Buckman, and a society was formed. The aims of this society were to encourage the growth of the best kind of vegetables; encourage well kept gardens and allotments, to stimulate a love of botany and finally to aid in the extinction of weeds. With regard to the latter a prize was awarded each year for the largest collection of thistles and docks. There were over 100 entries for the show and it was reported that the quantity of fruit and vegetables could not be excelled.

These shows continued year by year with just about every leading villager serving on the committee. However, it did not prosper and by 1901 the number of entries had fallen so drastically that the society ran into financial difficulties and it was necessary to hold a special concert to raise funds to balance the books. There does not appear to have been a show after 1901 and it was not until 1932 that there was another such venture.

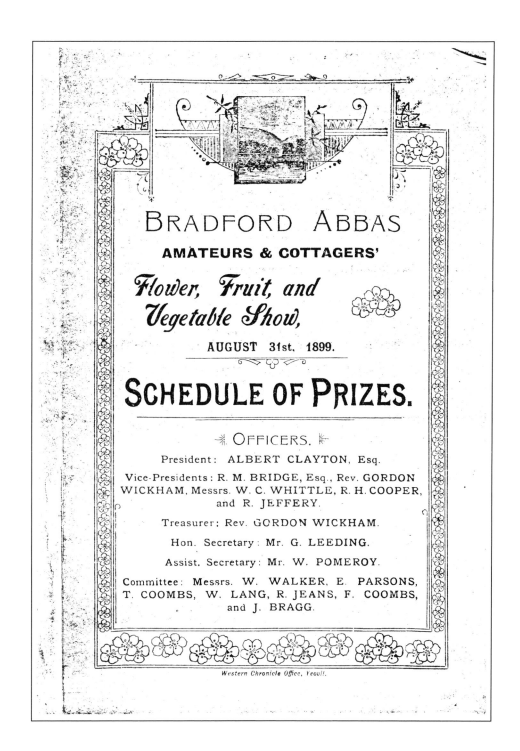

Horticultural Society Schedule, 1899.

YETMINSTER DISTRICT,

BEEKEEPERS' ASSOCIATION

will hold their

ANNUAL SHOW

On THURSDAY, August 13th, 1902,

In the Vicarage Grounds, BRADFORD ABBAS.

by kind invitation of Miss HATFIELD.

SCHEDULE OF PRIZES.

Class.		1st.	2nd.	3rd.	4th.
1.	For Bar Standard Size	5/-	4/-	4/-	2/-
2.	,, Shallow Bar Standard Size	4/-	3/-	2/-	1/-
3.	,, Six 1lb. Sections	5/-	4/-	3/-	2/-
4.	,, One Bell Glass over 10 lb.	5/-	4/-	3/-	2/-
5.	,, One Bell Glass under 10lb.	4/-	3/-	2/-	1/-
6.	,, Six 1lb. Bottles Dark Honey	5/-	4/-	3/-	2/-
7.	,, Six 1lb. Bottles Light Honey	5/-	4/-	3/-	2/-
8.	,, Bees' Wax, not less than 1lb. and not to exceed 1½ lb.	4/-	3/-	2/-	1/-
9.	,, **SPECIAL PRIZES** for the best collection of Honey and Bees' Wax. Space not to exceed 2ft. 6in. Prizes given as follows :—1st, Watch and Chain, given by Mr. TILLEY, of Dorchester ; 2nd, 4/6 ; 3rd, 2/6, given by the President, Col. GOODDEN.				
10.	**CHAMPION PRIZES** will be given for the Best Collection of Honey and Bees' Wax for those only who have taken First Prize in Collection Class 9 previous years. Space not to exceed 3ft. 6in. First Prize, 10/- ; 2nd, 7/- ; 3rd, 3/-. Given by Mrs. J. R. P. GOODDEN, Mrs. A. CLAYTON, and Mrs. GORDON WICKHAM.				

OPEN PRIZES.—Entrance Free.

11. For the Best 1lb. Bottle of Dark Honey :—1st, 10s ; 2nd, 6s ; 3rd, 4s.

12. For the best 1lb. Bottle of Light Honey :—1st, 10s ; 2nd, 6s ; 3rd, 4s. Exhibits in Classes 11 and 12 to become the property of the Association. Not less that 20 Entries or the Judges will be at liberty to withhold one prize at their discretion.

Exhibits in the Open Classes, *sent by post*, must reach the Secretary *one day* previous to the Show.

BOTTLES IN CLASSES 11 and 12 NOT TO EXCEED 6 INCHES IN HEIGHT.

13. Bee Flowers—For the Best Collection of Flowers sought after by Bees :—1st, 3s ; 2nd, 2s.

OPEN TO MEMBERS ONLY.

Prizes given by Mr. PETTER, Yeovil, for Competition in Bee Driving during the afternoon, under the instructions of Mr. TILLEY, of the Dorchester Bee Farm.

Exhibits must be Bee Proof.

All Entries to be sent not later than AUGUST 9th. to

G. LEEDING, Hon. Secretary, **Bradford Abbas, Sherborne**, Dorset.

NOTICE.

The Committee have pleasure in stating that they have bought an Extractor for the use of Members of the Association only, Free of Charge, and they hope the Members will make use of it. The only conditions are :—No Member must keep it more than *Three Days at a time*, and must return it **CLEAN** to Mr. J. ANDREWS, Thornford, who has kindly promised to take charge of it.

" Chronicle " Printing, Yeovil.—160—15-8-02

ENTRY FORM.

THIS FORM must be filled up by intending Exhibitors, and returned to the Hon. Sec. on or before **SATURDAY AUGUST 9th, 1902.**

Please insert the Schedule Number only of each Class in which you intend to exhibit. For Classes and Numbers see Schedule.

Class No...

I agree to be bound by the conditions set forth in the Schedule

Signature..Address.......................................

Date...

Beekeepers' Association, 1902.

This show was due largely to the efforts of six villagers—Messrs F. Whitehead, A. Smith, F. Gill, B. Garrett and A. Coombs, who was Secretary. Their efforts were well supported so two years later (June 1934) a general meeting was called and it was unanimously decided to form a Horticultural Society. Mr Bob Underdown was elected Chairman with the Schoolmaster, R.C. Day undertaking the arduous duties of Secretary and Treasurer. A decision was taken to hold a show that very year and such was the enthusiasm that the show was an outstanding success and the present society was safely launched. The pattern has remained basically the same but in more recent years, even though the village has grown considerably, it showed signs of decline. One year it was not possible to run the show but it is again thriving and regular monthly meetings are now held with visiting speakers in addition to the annual show.

It would not be proper to conclude this section without a special reference to Mr Bob Underdown who was the society's Chairman for 36 years until his death in 1970. He truly loved the society and his efforts have been fully recognised as a special Bob Underdown prize is presented each year.

Loners Lib is a small pressure group that was created by Miss Dainty in 1982 and regular monthly meetings are held throughout the year except during the winter months. For the inaugural meeting Miss Dainty held 'open house' and, as she obtained sufficient response, the organisation survives to this day. Its purpose is to speak for the five million lone householders it is estimated there are in Britain, a thing which Miss Dainty has done very well through the press and her demonstrations.

The earliest mention of a *Parent Teachers Association* associated with St Mary's V.C. School is as early as 1944 when the matter was considered by the School Managers, and again a year later. The parents had formed an association and the Chairman of the Managers expressed his appreciation of the interest shown in the school by the parents and hoped that the two bodies would work side by side in the interest of the pupils. Since those early days the Parent Teachers Association has grown in strength and regular fund-raising functions are held, the proceeds of which are used for the benefit of the school and the children.

The first meeting concerning the *Parish Council* was held in the schoolroom on 4th December 1894. It was an open meeting for the purpose of electing the first ever Parish Council, resulting from the Local

Government Act of 1894. The Chairman was the Schoolmaster, Mr Walter Walker and an election was held by a show of hands which resulted as follows:

William Lush	52 Votes
Albert Clayton	42 Votes
Wyatt Paul	29 Votes
James Bragg	28 Votes
Samuel Ring	23 Votes
Robert Jeanes	22 Votes
Edward Higgins	21 Votes

The first Chairman of the Council, was, not surprisingly, the Lord of the Manor, Mr Albert Clayton, who was to hold the office until he died in 1914. Meetings were held quarterly and one of the earliest motions to be considered was the provision of a recreation field. On the proposal of Mr Clayton, it was decided that 'there is at present no urgent demand for a playing field', and it was to be a further 75 years before such a facility was provided.

Another matter which caused concern to the councillors was the admission of the public to their meetings and a minute of 12th March 1895 makes interesting reading:

'Mr Clayton thought that the people who had elected the Councillors to conduct the business of the parish would have sufficient confidence in them that they would not desire to be present. He thought that the business should be confined to those who had to discharge it and showed that disorder might come through having irresponsible people present.'

It was, however, decided that although the public could not attend, they would be allowed to see the minute book if they so desired. The public are of course now allowed to be present and a ruling like the one of 1895 would obviously not be tolerated today.

It is true to say that the villagers took very little interest in the affairs of the council, for year after year only councillors (and not always all of them) attended the annual parish meeting. In 1924 the minute for the meeting read:

'Although notices convening the meeting had been published for the statutory period the only person present was the clerk. Consequently no business could be transacted.'

Street lighting was considered as early as 1911 and turned down on grounds of cost, and dangerous corners and the state of the roads etc., have been a continuing problem.

During its 93 years, the Parish Council has had only 11 Chairmen, the two longest serving being Mr Albert Clayton and Col Duff, who both occupied the position for 22 years. There have been only 7 Clerks, the longest serving being Mr Harry Warr with 33 years to his credit. There has never been a lady Clerk and for only one year has there been a lady chairperson—Mrs E. Burgess in 1985.

The *Playgroup* is one of the youngest organisations in the village having been formed as recently as April 1967 following an advertisement in the *Western Gazette* by a group of young mothers. It is also the first organisation in the village which has been formed by newcomers following the building boom of the early 1960s and it has been dominated by newcomers ever since. This was inevitable, of course, in view of the fact that the majority of children attending came from the new estates. There can be little doubt, however, that the Playgroup, which caters for children from three to five years, has been a useful innovation and gives the children a useful grounding for the day when they enter primary school.

The curriculum includes free play, sand and water play, painting, table work, building, music and movement, singing, stories and outside activities when weather permits. A fee is charged for each session and paid helpers are engaged by a committee of young mothers. This committee meets regularly and apart from considering the welfare of the children is also active in organising functions such as knit-ins and coffee mornings in order to boost their funds, their big event of the year being their annual Christmas Fayre.

Quoits is no longer played in Bradford Abbas and has not been for a number of years, but at one time many villagers gained much enjoyment from the sport. There has really been only one *Quoits Club* in its own right in the village for when the game was revived in 1923, it became very much the responsibility of the Men's Club.

The original Quoits Club was formed at a meeting held in the Parish Hall in March 1895, when the Rev. Gordon Wickham was elected President and Chairman, Mr G. Leeding Honorary Secretary, and Messrs J. Lang, G. Goodenough and S. Smith as committee. The Vicar made a piece of ground available on which the game could be played. Where this original quoits pitch was situated cannot be definitely located but I have reason to believe that it may well have been a small strip of a field adjoining Sherborne Road almost at the junction with Grant's Hill.

A copy of the rules of this early club still survive and read as follows:

'1   That this club be called the Bradford Abbas Quoits Club and its object shall be for social enjoyment.

2   That the club shall elect annually. President, Vice-President, Committee and Secretary who shall manage the above.

3   The first annual subscription should be one shilling and sixpence.

4   All subscriptons to be paid in advance, and shall become due on 25th March each year.

5   That only members will be allowed to play (but members having friends visiting them shall have the privilege of inviting them to play). This rule must be strictly adhered to.

6   The quoits will be kept at Mr Goodenough's and members wanting to use them must bring them back, unless other members wish to use them. Anyone breaking this rule shall be fined 6d.

7   That any member found throwing the quoits on the hard road taking them to and from the field shall be fined 6d.

8   Any member swearing or using abusive language shall be fined–for the first offence, 1d, for second, 2d, for the third, 3d and for any repetition of offences, 3d. All fines to be paid by the 25th of each month.'

How long the original club existed is not recorded but in 1923 it was revived as an off-shoot of the Men's Club. The pitch was where I suspect the original club played, and was laid out by Mr S. Ring, and four pairs of quoits were given by Mr W. Patch who also supplied the clay for making the pitch. Many games were played and enjoyed over the next few years but eventually interest waned and the pitch was no longer maintained, although should interest in such a club ever arise again, I understand that the quoits so generously given in 1923 are still in the possession of the Men's Club.

The Bradford Abbas branch of the *Royal British Legion* was formed in 1954 when its was felt it would be advantageous if the village had its own independent branch, as previously it was necessary to enrol at Thornford. Within a year of its foundation the branch had 47 fully paid-up members, a number which was steadily to increase over the next few years.

The objectives of the Royal British Legion are well known and the Bradford Abbas branch has not only contributed liberally to central funds but has assisted many members in the village itself, through their fund-raising efforts, such as dances, whist drives and the biggest money-spinner of all, bingo.

In co-operation with the Men's Club and the Women's Section of the legion, the branch organises a fortnightly bingo evening in the village Hall, which has always been extremely well supported and has become very much part of the village scene. The Branch has always worked very closely with the Men's Club, who a few years ago allowed the Legion members to use the club room on Friday evenings, with the result that the Legion were able to organise individual billiard and snooker competitions which created a great deal of interest. The village branch also continued its close relationship with the Thornford branch for a number of years and combined annual dinners were held alternately at Thornford and Bradford Abbas.

I suppose the most significant event in the history of the Legion in Bradford Abbas was the dedication of its standard on 7th June 1964. The standard was given by the then branch President Mr Fred Mear, a First World War prisoner and the village licensee for 28 years, and had been offically handed over to the Chairman, Wing Commander R.V. Moxey at a social evening in the Rose & Crown Inn earlier in the year.

After the standard had been dedicated in St Mary's Church by the Rev. G.R. Buchanan, there was a march-past of 20 standards, including the County Standard, and over 100 Legion members, when Mr Mear took the salute at the War Memorial. On the saluting base with Mr Mear that day were Mr J.N. Grange-Bennett (Dorset County Chairman), Mr John Shoobridge (County Life Vice-President), Brigadier A.F.S. Napier (County Vice-President), Mr T.W. Jesty (County Vice-Chairman), Mrs Napier (President South Western Area, Women's Section), Mrs K.G. Telfer (Chairman, County Women's Section), Lt Col G.N. Clark (Secretary, Sherborne Group), Mr R.H. White (President Sherborne Branch) and Mr J.R. Gammell (Chairman, Thornford Branch). Following the parade the village Women's Section provided tea in the Village Hall thus ending a day of which the members and Mr Mear were extremely proud.

In 1969 the branch were successful in winning the Group Knock-Out Skittle competition under the captaincy of Mr Fred Lucas and the members have, for the last few years, undertaken to distribute and pay for parcels for those less fortunate than themselves each Christmas.

Finally, mention must be made of 'Mr Legion', Ben Allcott. Ben was branch Secretary for almost twenty years during which period he served the Legion and its members faithfully and well. He was always instrumental in getting the branch to take its full part in village activities as well as continually searching for new members. When Ben Allcott died in 1973 the Legion—and the village—lost a loyal and trustworthy friend.

The death of Ben Allcott caused the branch to decline. It was not obvious at first but accelerated as the years advanced even though some attempts were made from time to time to revive it. Another attempt is now being made and hopefully it will succeed—if it does not it will not be due to any lack of effort on behalf of the present officers and committee.

The *Women's Section* of Bradford Abbas branch Royal British Legion was formed at a meeting held in the Village Hall on 7th September 1954. Since that date the ladies have probably met much more regularly than their male counterparts, although, throughout the section's history, the membership has been considerably smaller than that of the men. The membership reached its peak during 1965–6 when there were 32 members. In fact, the Women's Section has probably been one of the smallest-ever village organisations, and in 1958, they were the smallest Royal British Legion branch in Dorset. But whatever the branch may lack in numbers it does not lack in enthusiasm.

In 1961, for example, they came second in the Berkshire Cup, which is a competition amongst the smaller branches for the raising of funds. The ladies, many of whom are founder members, now meet once a month when after dealing with routine business they invariably settle down to listen to a guest speaker, followed by refreshments. Their fund-raising activities have included jumble sales, dances, skittles, whist drives and carol singing and they have been called upon to assist with other village activities. Until a few years ago the members took a very prominent part in the village's annual flower show every August Bank Holiday Monday. Like the men's section, the most important event in their history was when their own branch standard was dedicated on 22nd October 1966, and when, apart from their own, a further 21 standards were paraded through the village. But even on this, their day of days, they still found time to organise a collection for the Aberfan Disaster Fund which raised over £5.

The branch continues to flourish and I believe has a record as one of the most enterprising in the county. It still, with regularity, continues to win cups in county competitions.

On 2nd December 1886, the Rev. Gordon Wickham opened the dining room of the vicarage (now the Old Rectory) for use as a *Men's Club* and 13 men saw fit to attend, whilst only two evenings later, interest had been aroused to such an extent that the number wishing to join had increased to 25. It was decided that the club would be open on Mondays and Thursdays for men and on Wednesday and Saturdays for ladies. Throughout the whole of the winter of 1886–7 the vicarage dining room was the members' meeting place but by the time the club reopened for the winter session on the 24th October 1887, the new Parish Hall had been built in the vicarage grounds and it was resolved that the members would meet from 7.00 pm to 10.00 pm in the new hall on Mondays, Wednesdays and Thursdays. It was also decided that it would be necessary for the members to pay 1½d each week and as membership had swelled to such an extent it was also agreed that the age of admission would be sixteen.

It was obviously not a satisfactory arrangement for the Men's Club to be in control of the new Parish Hall for three nights of the week and during the summer of 1888 a moveable screen was erected so as to form a very comfortable room for the club whilst the remainder of the hall could then be used by other organisations at all times. It also had its advantages from the club's point of view as it meant that they could now meet every night of the week without inconveniencing anyone else. Membership was also increasing steadily and it was found possible to reduce the admission fees to 1d per week.

The club continued to meet in the Parish Hall until, in 1911, it moved its headquarters to the newly erected Village Hall. Billiards had by now become the members' main activity and their energetic secretary, Mr Harry Warr, introduced lantern lectures on such varying subjects as Tasmania and the popular artists of today, which proved to be very successful. Another innovation was the provision of daily newspapers for all to read—a service which was greatly used, as many could not afford to buy them. Many went to the clubroom every day to 'keep up with the news'.

Social evenings were regularly organised by the club committee which were open to all in the village and these socials, which were held in the Village Hall, proved to be very acceptable and were well supported and thoroughly enjoyed. The club was now in its heyday and was 'fulfilling its purpose and affording pleasant intercourse and social reunion, and friendly competition in various games'.

The main sporting competition, as I have said, was billiards and the club's individual knock-out tournament was keenly contested. The final always created considerable interest and discussion, as it still does today, particularly in 1919 when the finalists were father and son—W. Lang and R. Lang—'the latter having to acknowledge defeat by his father, who was cordially congratulated on his prowess'.

With the burning down of the Village Hall in December 1919 the club was temporarily forced to suspend its activities but within six months, coinciding with the opening of the new Village Hall, the club was safely installed in the room which was to be specifically set aside for its use. Throughout the 1920s, the club continued to provide a service for the village and I think that it is true to say that at the time nearly all the men in the village were members. By 1931, however, ominous clouds were gathering for, according to a minute of 6th October of that year, 'due to poor attendance there was talk of closing down the club'. With the help of the club chairman, Rev. Vassall, Secretary, D. Jones, Treasurer, W. Jeffrey, and members of the committee, the difficulties were overcome and within three years Mr D. Jones, who was now Treasurer as well as Secretary was able to report that the balance in hand was the best for many years. With the coming of the Second World War the club had no alternative but to close, as the Village Hall (including the club room) was being used by the school and the Public Assistance Officer. The possibility of reopening was considered in October 1942 but it was reluctantly felt that there was 'no possibility for the time being of the use of the club room by the Men's Club'. In fact, it was not until 1946 that the club was revived.

'Now that it has become possible to clear and redecorate the clubroom the Men's Club has come to life again and a welcome to its membership has been given to the younger generation. From these younger people the club's officers have been chosen. Edwin Mear becomes Secretary and the younger John Gillham,

Treasurer, working with a committee of which Mr Dunster is chairman. An excellent start has been made, and we are all looking forward to the benefit to the life of the village which shall come from this revival.'

Mr C. Johnny Gillham became Secretary of the club in 1948 and continues to be so today and it is during these 41 years, and more so in the last ten, that the club has really blossomed. When talk of building a new Village Hall began it soon became obvious that the Men's Club, as it still was, would have to find their own premises and originally an unsuccessful attempt was made to obtain what was the old Co-op shop in Westbury. From this failure, however came success for one of the older members, Mr. William Gale, mooted the idea of building a clubhouse if the ground could be obtained from the local landowner. He was approached and found to be agreeable to the idea and so talks were opened with the Football and Cricket Clubs with a view to amalgamation. After a general meeting the three clubs united, to become the Bradford Abbas Sports and Recreational Club.

Planning permission was applied for, and refused, which caused a great deal of disappointment but a second application was successful and so

Bradford Abbas Sports & Recreational Club—the player is Mr C.J. Gillham, club secretary for 40 years.

*Bradford Abbas
Sports &
Recreational Club,
opened 1979.*

work could now commence. With the aid of the grants and their own funds the building was well advanced by the summer of 1979, due largely to the hard work of many villagers who gave their time and expertise entirely free. And so, one week before Christmas 1979, the club was opened, the first man to receive a drink over the bar being none other than the club Secretary, Johnny Gillham. An official opening was held the following summer, at a spectacular fete, by Mr Mike Davis, the England rugby coach. A second room has been added and a skittle alley and more recently hard tennis courts, the latter being opened by the local M.P., Mr Jim Spicer.

The club is now highly successful and is undoubtedly one of the best, if not the best, in Dorset for quite apart from the clubhouse and tennis courts there are a further 9 acres upon which are football pitches and a cricket square. Finally a word about the club Secretary, Mr Johnny Gillham, who has worked so hard for the club over the years. When he became Secretary the club was almost broke but he has carefully nurtured it through both bad and good times. Not even he, however (and he would be the first to admit it), ever expected to see such a grand club as the village has today out of what started at the vicarage.

I have not been able to trace when the first Bradford Abbas *Skittles* team was formed. The earliest record I have is from 1932, but there must have been a skittles team long before that as the annual skittles supper was by that date a well-established function. These annual suppers were usually held at the Rose & Crown Inn with certain leading villagers such as the Vicar and the Headmaster being invited. Supper was usually followed by an entertainment by a local concert party. Suppers such as these have now faded from the scene but many do attend annual league dinners. Another event which sprang from the skittles teams was the annual men's outing. It started originally as an outing for skittles players only but it soon included any villager who wished to attend. It was usually held in early June when at an early hour, and invariably after a quick drink, the men would depart from the Rose & Crown Inn to undertake a trip to a destination of their own choice and after a day of merrymaking would usually return to the village in the early hours of the following day.

There are now several teams, including ladies' skittles teams in the village and games are now played at the Sports Club as well as the Rose & Crown Inn.

A *Temperance Society*, together with its junior section, the Band of Hope, was quite strong in Bradford Abbas at the end of the nineteenth century but it has, as far as I can tell, been extinct for seventy years or more. Undoubtedly, at the time, there was a need for such a society and the support it received fully justified its existence, and the cause it battled for.

The Society met regularly each month in the Parish Hall, the meetings consisting of an entertainment interspersed with speeches.

'24th January 1888. The monthly entertainment was held in the Parish Hall and attracted a good audience. The Rev. Abel Philips gave an interesting and practical address earnestly advocating courage, enthusiasm, trust, self-denial and sympathy in connection with temperance. Several of those present answered the Vicar's invitation to take the pledge.
'17th January 1889. Free tea given to members of the Band of Hope in the Parish Hall. About sixty-nine partook and each child received an orange from Mr Clayton and Miss Violet Clayton. At 6.30 pm a public tea was provided when over fifty sat down. The hall was decorated with flags and banners belonging to the society. At 8 o'clock a public meeting was held, when a large number attended for the purpose of hearing Mr R. Lewis on the evils of drink.'

As one would expect, the leading light in the society at this time was the Vicar, Rev. Gordon Wickham, who being a man of progressive ideas wished to further the cause of temperance amongst the men of all religions.

'18th November 1890. A pleasing and striking illustration of the possibility of churchmen and non-conformists uniting in Temperance work has just been witnessed in this parish. The genial and respected Vicar, Rev. Gordon Wickham, conceived the idea of establishing a Temperance organisation which would unite together irrespective of sect or creed, all the parishioners in the promotion of temperance. The Rev. Gentleman laid his ideas before the parishioners who received them with much cordiality, the result being that it was decided to form a society to be called the Bradford Abbas cum Clifton Maubank Temperance Prayer Union. The rules, three in number provided:

1.   For the use of a simple yet comprehensive form of prayer on Tuesday in each week.

2.   To attend the meeting for prayer and intercession on the second Sunday of each month.

3.   To further, to the best of my power, God helping me, the temperance cause.

The inaugural meeting of the newly formed society was held in the Parish Hall under the Presidency of the Rector. There was a large attendance of the parishioners.

The Rector opened the proceedings with prayer, after which a hymn was sung. The meeting then took a social turn, tea, buns, etc. being handed through the kindness of the Rector and Mrs Wickham. The Chairman then issued a brief address explanatory of the origin and rules of the society. He had long been impressed with the necessity of united temperance work in that parish, and he had been very pleased with the ready response which those who could not see with him in religious matters had given to his proposals.

'He might have formed a branch of the C.E.T.S.[1] in the parish, but he thought an organisation which would unite Churchmen and Non-Conformists, and which all interested in temperance work, whether abstainers or not could join, would be more likely to be successful. He believed that the idea had been put into his head by Almighty God, and that it would have his blessing (Cheers). Having apologised for the unavoidable absence of Mrs Clayton and stated that Mr Clayton thoroughly approved of the formation of the Society, the Rev. Gentleman concluded by paying a generous tribute to the temperance work carried on far many years past by the leaders of the Bradford Abbas Temperance Society. He then introduced the Rev. A. Phillips (Vicar of Hendford, Yeovil) who expressed the pleasure it gave him to take part in the inauguration of that society, with the objects of which he cordially sympathised. The Rev. Gentleman then proceeded to give an able address on several phases of the Temperance question and also referred with approval to the religious character of the newly

---

1 Church of England Temperance Society

formed society. He urged them to pray in order that God's blessing might rest upon their efforts, and strongly enforced the necessity of enthusiasm in temperance work.

'Mr G. Rives of Yeovil was the next speaker. He said he strongly approved of the distinctly Christian basis of the society, because he believed that those who were animated by the spirit of Christ were most qualified to carry on Temperance work. He than showed that whilst they had their differences, political and religious, yet they could all unite in the work of that society without any sacrifice of principle. The speaker then quoted some striking facts and figures showing the wide and far-reaching effects of intemperance, and urged that as a reason why they should be united in their work, and concluded with some earnest remarks on prayer and intercession in relation to temperance work. Mr R. Jeanes followed with a brief address in the course of which he expressed his hearty sympathy with the new society, enforced the need for prayer and unity, and gave some interesting reminiscences of his twenty-five years as a total abstainer. Mr J.J. Ring, in proposing a vote of thanks to the gentleman who had come over from Yeovil to address them, bore testimony to the great good which had been effected by the temperance reformation, and expressed his intention of joining the society. Mr Leeding seconded the motion stating that it was the best temperance meeting he had ever attended in the village. The motion was carried and suitably acknowledged by Rev. A. Phillips. The Chairman, in a few concluding remarks with reference to future meetings, said he had been much touched with the tone of the meeting.

Singing and prayer concluded a deeply interesting and successful meeting. Hymns were sung between the speeches, Mrs Wickham presiding at the piano. At the close a goodly number joined the society.'

It appears that monthly meetings of the United Temperance Society, as it was now called, together with an annual fête, continued until 1896, since which time no further record of the society exists. It is interesting to note, however, that although the Rev. Wickham had the idea 'put into his head' by Almighty God, it appeared that the society received little additional help from that source – the annual fêtes were invariably plagued with wet weather, whereas the Friendly Society, which was anything but temperate, continued on its merry way with the weather warm and bright on their club days. Nevertheless, with the amount of drinking there was in the village (some of the drinkers incidentally, being members of the Temperance Society), the society was of use in combating an evil, but one wonders why it did not survive longer than it did.

The Tug of War Team who proved to be so successful in the county championships.

A once-popular sport in Bradford Abbas was the *Tug-of-war*, and it was a sport at which, in the late 1920s the village excelled. At the time there was a healthy Agricultural Labourers' Union, admirably managed by their secretary, Mr Bill Gale, and it was through the union that a team from the village competed in the County Championships, each year. They were champions three years in succession. The team was A. Smith (Capt), B. Cook, E. Smith, W. Fowler, W. Gale, W. Turner, G. Cox, C. Smith and G. Wood.

In the September 1917 issue of the Parish Magazine, the Rev. Wickham recorded:

'A branch of the *Women's Institute* has been started in the parish and already numbers fifty-three members. Monthly meetings will be held for recreation and education and members are privileged to buy coal from October onwards at cost price.

President	Mrs C.E. Duff
Vice-President	Mrs Gordon Wickham
Secretary	Miss Anthea Firth
Treasurer	Miss W. Jeffrey

Committee	Mrs Wyatt Paul, Mrs Cooper, Mrs Down, Mrs W. Lang, Mrs F. Garrett, Mrs Hutchings, Mrs Lombard, Mrs Denslow.'

and the following month he advised his readers:

'The first meeting of the village branch was held in the hall. The President, Mrs Charles Duff, introduced Mr Turton of Sherborne Castle Gardens, who gave an interesting and practical address on 'Fruits and vegetables; picking and storing'. The following programme was rendered by the schoolchildren and teachers:

Song	Sgt Daddy V.C.	Schoolchildren
Recitation	Grandpapa's Spectacles	Infants
Song	Roses of Picardy	Miss Hodges
Recitation	My Ships	Ena Coombs
Song	Little Dutch Doll	Infants
Recitation	Bill's Dream	Infants
Song	Home, Lads, Home	Mr Warr
Pianoforte solo	Echoes from the Alps	Miss Hodges
Song	Mary Jane	Schoolchildren

GOD SAVE THE KING

Miss A. Firth, the Secretary was present. The attendance of members as regards numbers was disappointing.'

Bradford Abbas Women's Institute, 1917.

With few exceptions, meetings have been held monthly since the branch's formation, and the pattern of the meetings themselves has changed very little, if at all – business, followed by a speaker, following by an entertainment or games.

I would think that the three outstanding events of the institute year are the annual garden party at Wyke, the outing, and the Christmas party. I have chosen the accounts of these three events in 1926 to show that some 47 years later, things have changed very little and that what was enjoyed all those years ago continues to give pleasure today.

The first W.I. outing was to Sherborne Castle.

'Thursday July 24th 1919. The members of the W.I. spent an enjoyable afternoon in the Castle grounds, Sherborne, by permission of Major F. J. Wingfield Digby. The party was conveyed in a brake and various private carriages. The Abbey was reached at 3.15 pm and duly inspected before driving to the Castle where tea was provided. Aunt Sally etc. whiled away the time until the return journey much to the members' regret. Mrs Wickham (the President) was unable to go through illness but Mrs Cooper (Vice-President) was indefatigable. The Vicar met the party at the Abbey and spent some time in the Castle grounds.

Four new members were admitted, Mrs Dennett, Mrs E. Denman, Mrs White, Miss Pomeroy.

'July. The annual garden party of the local Women's Institute was held on Thursday at Wyke House, by the kind permission of Mrs Cooper, President. The weather was beautifully fine, and a large gathering assembled. Everything was done by Mr & Mrs Cooper and their daughters, Mrs Kent and Miss Cooper, to give the guests a thoroughly enjoyable time. A delightful tea was served on the lawn, and afterwards an interesting address was given by Mrs Ramsden of Beaminster, who spoke first of folk lore and Dorset superstitions, and later on "Ghosts and Toasts", Various games and competitions were afterwards enjoyed. Before the visitors dispersed, Mr H. Warr, on their behalf expressed the warmest thanks to Mr & Mrs Cooper for their kindness, and said how much Bradford owed to them for their kindly interest in the social life and parochial affairs generally. Both Mr & Mrs Cooper replied and said what a pleasure it was to them to entertain the members of the Institute. Before leaving, the gathering sang the Institute ode.'

'December 1926. Christmas Party: This annual event took place in the hall on Thursday evening, and was an unqualified success. The building which had been tastefully decorated by the members of the Committee, presented a very festive appearance. A large assembly of members and friends attended and spent a

*Women's Institute
outing, c.1950.*

*Women's Institute
Choir, 1955.*

thoroughly enjoyable time. An appreciated act of the committee was the issue of invitations to the old age pensioners of the parish, which met with an excellent response. The first half of the evening was devoted to a concert, the vocalists being Miss Ouvry and Mr Creech, of Dorchester. The latter, who was paying his first visit to the parish, is a humorist of a high standard and his items were enthusiastically received by the delighted audience. Miss Ouvry is the possessor of a voice of much charm and her songs were deservedly encored. Special mention must be made of a sketch entitled "Our Betty" the parts being sustained by Miss Woolacott, the Misses M. and K. Cooper, M. Coward, P. Jeanes amd M. Lang. Miss May Cooper as the parish old maid, Miss Katheen Cooper as the boisterous widow, and Miss Phylis Jeanes as the incomparable Betty proved themselves good exponents of the histrionic art. The other members of the cast also acquitted themselves well. Mr Warr cordially thanked all the performers and the audience vociferously concurred. Mrs Cooper, the President, ably voiced the general regret at the enforced absence of the Vicar, through illness. The concert concluded with the singing of the Institute ode. Justice was then done to the bountiful supply of refreshment provided, and the remainder of the evening was spent in dancing and games, Mrs Woolacott presiding at the piano. The ladies of the Committee, ably led by their enthusiastic Secretary, Mrs Hammill, are to be congratulated on adding another to their long list of successful achievements.'

In July 1967, the branch celebrated its golden jubilee with a party at Wyke when past Presidents and members of the County Executive Committee were invited to attend the festivities. Presentations were made to seven ladies, all of whom had joined shortly after the branch was formed. The two longest-serving members Mrs Gill and Mrs A. Smith were presented with pot plants and Wedgewood dishes, whilst the other five, Mrs E. Underdown, Mrs E. Fowler, Mrs W. Gale, Mrs F. Smith and Mrs Cook received the Wedgewood dishes only.

On Shrove Tuesday, 1969, the members accepted a challenge to a pancake race from Nether Compton, and the first race of what is now an annual event, was held in that village. The Bradford Abbas team that day were Angela Haigh (President), Sue Ward, Bella Abbot, Alma Anthony, Florrie Milsom and Evelyn Dainty and although dropped pancakes and lost shoes quickly put the Compton team in difficulties they managed to make up for lost time and their last runner just got ahead of the Bradford Abbas runner.

The Women's Institute continues to thrive and has only recently celebrated its 70th anniversary in the Village Hall, with a party, with members dressed in costumes covering the whole period of the institute's existence.

There is one major achievement for which the ladies can claim credit, and that is a magnificent scrapbook of the village which they compiled for a national competition in 1965. It has an embroidered cover and contains many photographs and articles written by members and friends of the Institute, and it was so good that it attained third place. Another such scrapbook, but on a more modest scale, was compiled in more recent years for a county competition.

Youth Clubs have come and gone in Bradford Abbas and have a very chequered history in the village. The first club was formed as long ago as 1893 and meetings were held in the Parish Hall once a week. There they played dominoes, ludo, solitaire and had boxing matches. The leader was Mr E Eliot and members paid $^1/_2$ d per week subscriptions. It appears that the club was well supported. It existed for some 5 years or so before it was forced to close through lack of funds. Another attempt was made to form a club in 1917 but it went the same way as its predecessor.

There is now once again a successful Youth Club which has survived for longer than most, largely due to the efforts of Mr Doug Holden who led it for several years, putting it on a firm foundation. Although he resigned the leadership, he is maintaining his interest by acting as Chairman of the committee.

The *Camera Club* is one of the newest organisations in the village and was created largely through the efforts of Mr and Mrs Graham Overton. Meetings are held regularly in the Village Hall and outside visits are arranged. It has proved to be a useful innovation to the village.

The *Historical Society* was formed in 1978 at a meeting in a private house. Although its membership is small it is enthusiastic and meetings, combined with various outings, are held 10 times a year.

The *Variety Club* is now a well-known village organisation and their shows, usually in February each year, are much-anticipated events. The first idea of a variety show emanated from a fund-raising activity in aid of Village Hall funds which proved to be so successful that those who took part decided to form a separate Variety Club as an organisation in its own right. It has proved eminently successful year by year. Some shows have been better than others, but there has been no lack of enthusiasm by the performers. It has done many shows for charity and it has recently celebrated its 10th anniversary. Some characters are becoming recognised more and more year by year and some of the performers' versatility is quite amazing. It is now a well-established village organisation and hopefully we shall benefit from the witticisms of Terry Scannell and the reverential awe of Peter Trickey (a founder member) for many years to come.

The *Scouts and Cubs* have never been very strong in Bradford Abbas but although the numbers may have been small they have never lacked enthusiasm. The Scouts and Cubs are also one of the younger organisations, the first Bradford Abbas Troop being created in February 1935, when, surprisingly, there was a reluctance by the lads to enrol. However, the Headmaster at that time Mr R.C. Day, who was a scoutmaster before he came to Bradford Abbas, undertook the work again and was shortly able to report that he had six scouts and four wolf cubs 'who had entered on their duties with great zeal'. The lads were encouraged in their efforts by the Lord of the Manor, Mr Wyatt Paul, who presented them with a silver challenge cup for the best scout at the end of each year. Within three months the scouts appeared in their uniforms for the first time at the King George V and Queen Mary Silver Jubilee celebrations in the village and were heartily congratulated on their turnout. Shortly after, Captain Charles Duff and the Vicar, Rev. E.C. Douglas, presented colours to the troop which were dedicated at evensong on 13th October 1935 and Mr & Mrs W. Gale presented the troop with a bugle.

The early efforts of both the Scouts and the Cubs were directed almost entirely towards raising funds for a camp to be held at Weymouth and it is to their great credit, and to the leadership of Mr Day and the support of parents, that after having only been in existence for six months, their ambitions and efforts were rewarded.

'August 1935. The First Bradford Abbas Troop of Boy Scouts and Wolf Cubs spent a week under canvas at Preston, near Weymouth. The first night was not spent too peaceably – that does not imply the Scouts or their Scoutmaster snored! – the excitement and the fact that some regiments nearby decided to leave at 3.30 am made the boys think that it might be their own bugler rousing them. Every morning the "Rouse" was sounded by P.L. Gale at 7.00 am. The camp turned out to wash, and prepare breakfast. At 8 o'clock we had Assembly and Prayers in one of the Patrol Tents and then followed breakfast; after breakfast there was a camp and kit inspection, followed by scouting exercises until noon. After dinner there was one hour's compulsory rest, and then to the sea for a bathe. After tea we had games or a tramp which was followed by "teeth drill" and "turn in" at 9.30 pm. "Lights out" was sounded by A.P.L. Dennis Puckett at 10.00 pm and silence reigned until 7.00 am. Each day a list of duties was posted at the Scoutmaster's tent, and every boy carried out his duty in true scout fashion. We were visited twice and each time our visitors were entertained to a scout meal. On the following Saturday it rained as though it had been overlooked for twelve months and we had to strike camp in a torrential downpour, but even that did not dampen the scout spirit. The scouts were truly grateful to all those who made such an enjoyable week possible. The District Commissioner for South Dorset paid us a visit of inspection and reported "a thoroughly good and orderly camp".

Jumble sales, concerts, open air whist drives were regularly held to augment funds and at the end of their first year the troop was financially sound, and strong in numbers—seventeen Scouts and a slightly smaller number of Cubs.

The second year's camp was held at Bude in August 1936 and the following month the troop was able to hold their first church parade led by their own band. Following morning service they proudly marched around the village, the band in particular putting up a very creditable performance. The troop continued to thrive and prosper but with the coming of the Second World War activities ceased and it was not until 1955, when it was thought there would be adequate support, that it was decided to re-form the troop with Mr D.Mundy as Scoutmaster and Mr B. Allcott as Assistant Scoutmaster, whilst the Cub pack was placed under the leadership of Mr F. Meade of Sherborne. The Cubs were the stronger with sixteen members against the Scouts' ten, but everyone concerned seemed satisfied with the progress being made, although there were insufficient funds to purchase more equipment which was urgently required to enable 'progressive training to be given'. However, as with the earlier troop various fund-raising functions were organised, resulting in a much improved financial situation. However, by 1969 and despite additional assistance from Mr O. Bowles, the Scouts and Cubs were going through a bad patch, which had been brought about very largely by the fact that Mr Mundy's business prevented him from giving the time to the troop which he had when it was re-formed. To add to the difficulties, Miss Susan Hurford, the 'Cubmaster', was no longer resident in the village, and along with Mr Mundy she felt obliged to resign. It was therefore decided that a meeting would be held to try and resolve the difficulties which had been encountered through no fault of any one person, but which had caused a complete shutdown of activities.

Mr W. Lucas volunteered to get the Cub pack going again and his offer was kindly accepted for a trial period of six months, but it was decided that the Scout troop should be dissolved and that the Cubs who reached the scout age of eleven should be encouraged to join the flourishing Scout troop at Yetminster. It was felt that if after a length of time that troop contained enough Bradford Abbas boys, the question of 'hiving off' from Yetminster and restarting in Bradford Abbas should be decided by the boys themselves. In more recent years the Scouts have not been completely independent as they are now part of the High Stoy Scout Group.

CHAPTER IX
Bits and Pieces

In my studies of local history and conversations with people who have lived in the village all of their life it has come to my attention that many events remain vivid in their memories. Although in fact they may contribute very little or nothing to the onward march of history, they are nevertheless of interest because many individuals can recall such events. Some of these happenings are amusing, some tragic and some are of only general interest but nevertheless they do contribute to the history of Bradford Abbas. In the following extracts from the village records and from conversations from time to time, I give a few 'bits and pieces'.

'5th March 1635 DORCHESTER ASSIZES
Order in the dispute between the parishes of Bradford Abbas and Lillington in Dorset and Henstridge, Somerset, about the settlement of Dorothy Browne and her unborn child. Richard King, counsel for Bradford Abbas and Lillington has informed the court that Browne was born at Henstridge where she lived for more than 21 years before entering service in Lillington. She lived there for two years in which time she became pregnant, and on the expiration of her term at Michaelmas last began a year's service with William Gapper of Bradford Abbas. After a month her pregnancy was discovered, whereupon she left Gapper's service by consent and returned to Henstridge. She was returned to Bradford Abbas, where she remains, by warrant of two Somerset J.P.s on the ground that she was on covenant service there. Upon counsel's plea for a court order, examination of the matter is referred to one or more of the J.P.s living nearest to Bradford Abbas and Lillington who are to certify their findings at the next Somerset Assizes, it shall not be to the prejudice of Bradford Abbas.'

There were several settlement disputes in which Bradford Abbas was involved during the next 200 years. These disputes were of great importance because if it was finally decided that a person should be 'settled' in a particular village that village was honour bound to support the person concerned.

'16th October 1643. HELES CHARITY

Sir John Hele, Knt, by will, dated 16th October 1643, gives to the poor of the parish of Bradford and the parish of Clifton Maubank, a yearly rent charge of 52s to be distributed among the poor of the said parishes, every Sunday in the year in white bread, and he gave the like sum, yearly to the poor of the parish of Winbury, Devon; and the like sum, yearly, to the poor of the parish of Yetminster. The said sums not to ease the inhabitants of their rates but for the better maintenance of the poor.

'The sum of £2. 12s per annum is received by the churchwardens from William Castleman Esq., of Wimborne Minster, as agent for the Marquis of Anglesea, and is distributed, in six penny loaves, every fourth Sunday, amongst the poor of Bradford Abbas not receiving parish relief. The poor of the parish of Clifton Maubank have not participated in the charity, the parish officers not being aware that they were entitled to do so; but this omission will in future be rectified.'

1657 'John Hobbe of ye towne of Yeovil binds himself to the Churchwardens and Overseers of the Parish of Bradford Abbas in the sum of fiftie pounds of lawful monie of England in respect of a child which Philip Collins doth keep.'

1719 Extract from an apprentice indenture dated 1719.

'During which term the said apprentice his master faithfully shall serve, his secrets keep, his lawful commands everywhere gladly do: he shall do no damage to his said master nor see to be done of others but to his power shall let or forthwith give warning to his said master of the same; he shall not waste the goods of the said master nor lend them unlawfully to any; he shall not commit fornication nor contract matrimony within the said term; he shall not play at cards, dice tables or any other unlawful games thereby his said master may have any loss with his own goods during the said term, without licence of his said master he shall neither buy nor sell; he shall not haunt taverns or playhouses, not absent himself from his master's service day or night unlawfully but in all things as a faithful apprentice he shall behave himself to his said master and all this during the said term.'

'25th March 1820.

An agreement made this 25th day of March 1820 between the Churchwardens and Overseers of the poor of Bradford Abbas and William Thorn of East Coker in the Countie of Somerset. viz:

'The said William Thorn on his part, his executors and administrations do hereby agree to catch the moles in the said parish to the satisfaction of the principal inhabitants of the said parish at the yearly wages of eight pounds for the term of fourteen years from the above date.'

'24th April 1845.
Resolved that the Surveyor shall impound or cause to be impounded all the stock found straying on the highway.

Vestry Minute.'

'11th March 1846.
It was resolved that the Overseer be direct to obtain summonses against Virtue Garrett, Eliza Parsons and Ann King for leaving their children chargeable to the parish.

Vestry Minute.'

'26th April 1848.
Mr G. Master agreed to take the scrapings of the roads from Lady Day 1848 to Lady Day 1849.

Vestry Minute.'

'20th September 1848.
A warrant was obtained against John Bere for leaving his wife and children, but it was not served upon him, the Tything man having gone to Portland in search of him but he had left.'

'21st June 1850.
At a vestry held this day to consider providing William Cabell with a wooden leg and by consulting the ratepayers, the Guardian was recommended to wish Mr Williams, Medical gentleman to get one from London, and also that the poor rate of his be revised and corrected before another is collected.

Vestry Minute.'

'9th September 1857.
It was resolved that the Churchwardens and Waywardens and Mr P. Rideout be a committee to go around the parish and inspect the state of the drains and privies, and have all heaps of filth etc. removed and lime thrown where necessary.

Vestry Minute.'

'7th March 1861.
The Waywardens were also authorised to withhold all money which is at the present time due, or shall hereafter be due to James King until the said James King shall have put the roads and drains in such a state as shall be satisfactory to the Waywardens.

Vestry Minute.'

'12th April 1862. FATAL ACCIDENT

A melancholy accident occurred on the South Western line of railway at Bradford Abbas. About the middle of the village there is a footway over the line which is not provided with a signal. About four o'clock in the afternoon a man named Richard Ridout, 74 years of age, was crossing this footpath when the express train came up and struck the poor old man before he was able to get off the line. He was carried on about 30 yards. His head was smashed and one of his legs cut off at the ankle. The engine driver stopped as soon as practicable and sent for a surgeon. Death, however, must have been instantaneous, as his brains were scattered over the line.

'The deceased was a tailor, and being a steady Christian man, was much respected in the parish. We understand the parish authorities remonstrated with the railway company, when constructing the line, on the "inadvisibility of a level crossing when a passage under might have been made at a small expense".'

'2nd July 1863.

It was stated by the Vestry that because Josiah Braggs's corpse was brought to his sister's house the day before the funeral the usual expense of tolling the bell and digging his grave were not to be allowed. The Vestry considered this to be unjust and the Overseer was directed to communicate their sentiments to the relieving officer.

Vestry Minute.'

'9th March 1865. SHERBORNE PETTY SESSIONS

Solomon Rendall summoned John Collins for stealing a duck belonging to him. Mr Fear appeared for the defendant. The plaintiff deposed that he lost the duck on 11th January last. He gave information to the police and about a month afterwards Supt Lewis brought him a duck, which he identified as his property. Supt Lewis proved that he found the duck in the garden of the prisoner. Mr Fear for the defence, said the duck was found by prisoner and another man who were working together in a field but till Supt Lewis came to him he could not find the owner for it. The case was dismissed for want of sufficient evidence.'

'23rd July 1865. FATALITY

An inquest was held in the village by J. Y. Melmoth, Esq., Coroner, on the body of George Gill. It appears from the evidence that the deceased, with several others, had been in the employ of Mr James Vincent of Clifton Farm and that on Saturday night they went to Stoford to divide their earnings. After having something to drink the other men went home to Bradford Abbas leaving the deceased at the inn drinking. The latter left the inn alone and it is supposed on going home to Bradford Abbas he must have slipped into the water as the path runs close to the river where the body was found. The jury returned a verdict of "found drowned in the River Yeo". The deceased is only 25 years of age.'

'18th August 1866.
On 18th August 1866 there was another accident at the crossing of the railway line when Susannah Ridout was killed, "the body being shockingly mangled".'

As a result of this accident and of the accident to Richard Ridout in 1862 the Railway Company built the culvert under the railway line between Higher Westbury and Churchwell Street.

'4th July 1867. SHERBORNE PETTY SESSIONS
John Bartlett and Robert Stevens, both of Bradford Abbas—for trespass in pursuit of game were fined 10s and 7s 6d. each or 14 days' imprisonment with hard labour.'

There were many similar cases such as this throughout the latter years of the nineteenth century.

'24th March 1882.
Messrs Sutton, seedsmen of Reading, have very liberally sent to Professor Buckman 400 packets of vegetable and flower seeds to be distributed amongst the villagers of Bradford Abbas.'

'31st December 1885. SHERBORNE PETTY SESSIONS
A case that excited considerable interest was a charge of assault brought by Charles Stephen Rawlings, a saddler, against John Dodge, a mason, both of Bradford Abbas, the alleged assault, apparently the outcome of political differences, being committed on 8th December, the polling day for North Dorset. Mr Sidney Watts of Yeovil appeared for the complainant and Mr Brennand of Blandford was for the defendant. Complainant's case as stated by Mr Watts represented he was a member of the Conservative Committee on the day of the election. About 5 o'clock he went to the Rose & Crown and as he entered the passage, wearing a primrose and blue ribbons he was hustled by a lot of boys. They also called him names and nearly pushed him down. Defendant then came forward and dealt him a violent blow in the eye, which caused him to fall to the ground and whilst there defendant kicked him. Complainant afterwards struck Dodge with his stick, feeling that he was perfectly justified in doing so in self

defence. Complainant bore out this statement in his evidence but in cross examination, while denying he had too much liquor on the day in question, admitted the landlord of the Rose & Crown persuaded him to go home. For the defence several witnesses were called who were of the opinion that complainant was drunk at the time the alleged assault was committed, one of these witnesses being P.C. Baverstock who said in consequence of his (complainant's) condition he advised him to go home. The Bench decided to dismiss the summons together with a cross summons which had been issued at the instance of Dodge.'

Also at the same sessions:

'Edward Parsons of Bradford Abbas was then charged with an assault upon Rawlings on the eve of the Polling Day. Complainant said having called at the Rose & Crown for a glass of beer he saw defendant. As he (complainant) was going out of the passage defendant tried to trip him up over the steps. He did not succeed, however, but up the road, near the well, defendant tripped him up, threw him into the brook and ran away. Three or four customers were called to provide an alibi—that defendant remained in the house after complainant had had his beer and left, and the Bench, without hearing all the witnesses for the defence dismissed the case.'

'29th September 1890. REMARKABLE OCCURRENCE
An apple tree in an orchard belonging to Mrs Mark Ridout is now in full bloom for the second time this year, and although so late in the season the bloom is very strong. Some of the fruit is beginning to form. There was only a small gathering of fruit from the first crop. This would seem to be a remarkable occurrence considering the season of the year.'

'22nd February 1894. DISTURBING A WEDDING
At Sherborne Petty Sessions Robert Symes, a lad of Bradford Abbas, was summoned by the Rev. Gordon Wickham of Bradford Abbas for disturbing him while performing the rite of matrimony in the Parish Church on February 6th. The defendant pleaded guilty but said "that other boys were as bad as he was". The Rev. Gordon Wickham said that he was performing a marriage service at the Parish Church when an arm was put through an open window over the altar holding a dog. Witness had to stop the service to shut the window. One of the doors was then opened and two dogs sent in. Services of all kinds had been interrupted by boys and the summons was taken out to stop the practice in future and to have God's house revered. George Higgins, an engine cleaner of Yeovil said he saw defendant open the church door and send in two dogs. Defendant was

bound over in his own recognisance in the sum of £5 to come up for judgement if called upon and the boy's father was also to be bound over, the boy to be kept in custody until he could come.'

'28th February 1901.
At a meeting of Sherborne Rural District Council the Rev. G.B. Wickham complained that some men, employed by the council to work on the roads, had been working for a gentleman at Bradford Abbas. He thought this kind of thing ought to be put an end to at once as the Bradford Abbas road was in a disgraceful state.

'The Chairman read a letter on this matter from Mr A. Clayton of Bradford Abbas also complaining of the state of the road. On it being discovered that he was the very person who had been employing the Council's workmen it was decided to leave the matter in the chairman's hands and he promised to reply to the letter.'

'20th May 1901. FLOWER CLASS
The highest number of specimens brought in was 107. Members will bear in mind that many flowers will be out of bloom before June is over, and that to obtain any prize they must overtop the number, which was about 300 last year.'
281 was the highest number collected in 1900 by Minnie Higgins.

'January 1902. FLOWER CLASS
The Bishop of Salisbury has sent prizes to the first three of this class.

Hilda Leeming	Age 11	337 specimens
Bertha Higgins	Age 14	299 specimens
Minnie Higgins	Age 18	298 specimens'

'October 1902. FLOWER CLASS
Hilda Leeming again holds the first place with 370 specimens.'

'20th July 1904. DEATH—GERTRUDE LAVINIA PARKHOUSE
Caught unaware by the one o'clock up express, near Yeovil Junction, her death was instantaneous. Married about two years ago she came to reside here with her husband. This sad accident brings home to us the dangers of the walk to the Junction, and the need of a safe path, which so far the railway authorities have not been able to supply. The Vicar presented some months ago a plan for connecting the village with the station to the SWR Company but this, which was his second attempt met with the answer, no funds.'

'30th March 1905. SHERBORNE PETTY SESSIONS—GROSS CRUELTY
Frederick Moody, a lad in the employ of Mr Tom Whittle of Bradford Abbas was summoned for cruelty to a horse by working it in an unfit state. Inspector Dale prosecuted for the Royal Society for the Prevention of Cruelty to Animals. Evidence was given in support of the charge by P.C. Ford and P.C. Light, and this was to the effect that although the horse, a very old animal, was suffering from a very painful wound on the back, Moody was seen belabouring it with a big stick every time it slackened its speed. Mr Whittle denied all knowledge of the condition of the horse, and the Bench dismissed the charge against him, but the lad was sent to prison for a fortnight.'

'1st December 1909.
Miss Violet Clapton has given and planted an oak tree in the open space adjoining to school.'

'27th March 1911. ELECTIONS
The school was closed at noon, and used as a polling station for the District Council Elections. The Vicar, Rev. Gordon Wickham, had retired as District Councillor to avoid a poll and Col. Charles Duff was nominated by A. Clayton Esq. and Mr W. Pomeroy. A poll was nevertheless forced upon the parish, Mr James Higgins, an ex-railwayman, was nominated.
Result: Col Duff 56 votes.   James Higgins 15.'

James Higgins has the distinction of receiving the lowest number of votes cast in Bradford Abbas at a local election whilst on the other hand Col Duff obtained his seat on the Sherborne Rural District Council with the lowest number of votes cast for a victorious candidate in the village. James Higgins was, however, to gain more lasting fame by being one of the 'lads of the village' in 1934.

'December 1912. BLACKMORE VALE FOX HOUNDS
Considerable excitement was caused in the village when the foxhounds which met at Compton came full cry through the village. "Master Reynard", closely followed by the hounds ran through the churchyard and was killed in Mr Tom King's field adjoining the Vicarage.'

'8th January 1921. TO THE EDITOR OF COUNTRY LIFE
'Sir
'One of my scholars at the school who lives near the River Yeo brought a heron to school yesterday which had been killed in attempting to swallow a water-vole.

The children were deeply interested in this riverside tragedy. I took a photograph of it which you may care to see.

H. Warr

Bradford Abbas, Dorset.'

'14th March 1926.

Mothering Sunday was observed for the first time for many years. Over 30 mothers came to Church with the children at 3.00 pm and a special service was held. Collections for the Mothers' Union banner in Westminster Abbey amounted to 6s. 3d.

'5th September 1928. INQUEST

Mr A.F. Grimley held an inquest on the bodies of Pearl Winifred Cox aged 5 years 3 months and Cecil Fred Cox, aged 3 years and 9 months, the son and daughter of Mr and Mrs Frederick Cox of The Cross, Bradford Abbas. The father is a platelayer in the employ of the Southern Railway. The children, with others went to the river at Mill Farm to play. The boy fell into the water and his sister, who went to his assistance was soon in difficulties. Another little girl, Marian Gillham, aged 8, went to the rescue of the two children and was carried away, but to the side of the river where she was pulled out by her 9 year old brother John. Fred Foot, a labourer at the farm got the two children from the water. Artificial respiration was tried by villagers and by Dr Colmer of Yeovil but their efforts failed to restore life and the bodies were taken home. The Coroner recorded a verdict of accidental drowning and he expressed the hope that this most unfortunate occurrence would be a warning to other children, and that parents in the village would take due precautions to see that their children did not go near that place. He was sure the tenant of Mill Farm could take some steps either by putting up a notice board or some stronger fence other than wire, because one could often get under barbed wire. Some action ought to be taken to prevent people from wandering from the public footpath and getting into private property, especially in a case where children could get into water which was dangerous.'

'21st August 1930.

The meeting was called primarily to discuss the situation caused by the refusal of the District Council to defray the cost of the collection of household refuse. It was felt that this great convenience to the parish should in some way be continued.

'Mr Underdown offered to do the work for the sum of £3 per annum and Col Duff generously offered to defray the cost himself, the collections to be on or near 1st September, 1st January and 1st May each year.

Parish Council Minute.'

'2nd July 1932.
Villagers had a magnificent view of the great airship Graf Zeppelin as it flew over Yeovil and Sherborne.'

'1935. A PARISH BIER
A general meeting of parishioners was held to discuss suggestions for the disposal of the balance remaining from the Jubilee Supper. Mr E.R. Underdown presided. The suggestion that a bier should be purchased was finally adopted by a large majority. It was regarded as a long felt necessity.'

'February 1947.
The winter has tried the patience and strength of many people. It has subjected workers to long hours and bitter conditions; it has made the business of getting about very hard; it has added to the common handicap of running our homes. I would like to say a word of appreciation to the drivers of our school buses, and I should wish to record the sympathy which we all feel for Mr Wyatt Paul and Mr Mellish in their serious losses and the baffling disturbance of their farm work. They are the sufferers in the parish among many throughout a widely spread district where the ravages of Foot & Mouth disease have been felt.'

'8th December 1959. SHARK FOUND IN RIVER
Stewart Wright, 15-year-old son of the Bradford Abbas postmistress found a three foot dead shark while fishing in the River Yeo at Smears Bridge.'

I have in my possession an advertisement of Messrs Eldridge Pope & Co Ltd., Brewers, of Dorchester which proclaims 'For long life and happiness—drink—Huntsman Ales and Stout.' Above the wording is a 'remarkable photograph of five of the "lads" of the village'. These 'lads' are George Chainey (aged 84) James Higgins (84) Samuel Ring (87) Thomas Coombs (86) and the 'baby' Sidney Parsons, a mere 78 years. Throughout the early 1930s they were to become well known not only in local circles but nationally when in 1935 British Movietown News made a film of the village with the 'lads' as the stars—which led them to claim that they were the oldest film stars in the world. They were photographed and fêted wherever they went and when the film was shown at the Gaumont Theatre, Yeovil, they, together with two old ladies of the parish, were introduced from the stage, and posed for flashlight photographs as they left the cinema. But it was at the cinema that a chance remark led a *Western Gazette* reporter to investigate whether or not it was true that they had

Lads of the Village. 1934.   Bradford Abbas. Dorset.

ELDRIDGE.POPE&Cᵒ
Are first in the field.

GEORGE CHAINEY. 87.   JAMES HIGGINS. 87.   SAMUEL RING. 90.   THOMAS COOMBS. 89.   SIDNEY PARSONS. 81
TOTAL   434 YEARS.

Lads of the Village, 1934

rivals in their own parish, a remark which as it turned out proved to be true, for living in Bradford Abbas were Mrs Edward Parsons (91), Mrs Mary Jane Munckton (87) Mrs E.H. Patch and Mrs G. Good (84), and Mrs Florence Wills (82)—combined ages of 428 years.

Mrs Parsons was born at Wyke and had lived in the village since she was a child. She felt that she knew as much about country life as anyone except possibly Sam Ring, who at the time was two years older than herself. She was well acquainted with hard times, having brought up ten children on her husband's wage of 9/- or 10/- per week. She could recall doing gloving work with Mrs Parsons to help the family budget and having to stitch for an hour to make a penny and then walking to Yeovil with the finished work. Mrs Patch was also a native of Bradford Abbas, and with her husband carried on business as bakers and confectioners for over 50 years. Mrs Wills, also a native of the village, was born in the house which previously stood on the site of the present Post Office, and she was in fact the village Postmistress for nearly 50 years. Mrs Good was the only one of the five who could not claim to be a native of the parish but she had lived the greater part of her life at North Farm, Bradford Abbas, where her husband was the tenant farmer.

Nevertheless it was the 'lads' who continued to hog the spotlight but in February 1936 Thomas Coombs died at the age of 91. He had been born at Winsham, near Chard in 1844 and at the age of 10 came to Bradford Abbas where he spent the last 69 years of his life in the same house. He spent his working life on the land and also served as a Parish Councillor, bell ringer, and as an officer of the Sick Benefit Club.

On 29th March 1937 George Chainey died and it was recorded at the time of his death that 'he will be missed in the village and in the church which he had loved so well and where he worshipped with such wonderful regularity'.

James Higgins died in 1940 in Kent, having been burnt out of his home in Bradford Abbas some eighteen months earlier. He had led a most interesting life and at one stage he emigrated to America, but returned to spend all of the remainder of his working life as a platelayer on the Great Western Railway.

He celebrated his 60th wedding anniversary in 1930 and at one time was Secretary of the Bradford Abbas Sick Benefit Club. He also holds the rather unhappy distinction of polling the lowest number of votes (15) in a District Council election. At the time of his death his old friend Sam Ring was in his terminal illness and he finally went to his Valhalla on 14th March 1940. Sam Ring was a well-known personality not only in Bradford Abbas but also in the surrounding villages. For many years he carried the Sick Benefit Club banner on club days and at the club day held in 1931 he claimed that in the 76 years that he worked he never missed a day. He was, at the time of his death, the oldest person living in the village, a feat, ironically enough, which was to be emulated by his daughter (Mrs Kate Purchase) some 30 years later.

The last of the legendary 'lads', the 'baby', died in November 1940 and with him went a small and interesting part of the history of Bradford Abbas.

The 'lads' are still very much a part of the village heritage and in 1971 a re-enaction of the 'lads' was held, the stars on this occasion being Henry

Lads of the Village, 1971.

Warry (83), Bill Gale (70), Charlie Smith (72), Harry Gillham (70), Tom Gosney (76), James Ferrett (77), Fred Cox (79) and George Bascombe (83). These grand old lads played a game of skittles against a team of local personalities and like their famous predecessors also saw themselves on film. It was not necessary for them to travel to Yeovil, however, as they could watch themselves from the comfort of their own houses on television.

In 1985 *The Times* decided that it was going to write an article on British public houses and although the village inn was not mentioned the picture

above the article showed five of the lads of Bradford Abbas. These 'lads' were not as old as their famous predecessors, but nevertheless Ian Davis, Mark Hopkins, Bradden Mear, Steve Gardner and Chris Fisher are now on the wall of the Rose & Crown alongside the photograph of their famous predecessors.

It is not surprising to learn that at the time of the original 'lads' the villagers were claiming that they were living in the healthiest village in Dorset.

Lads of the Village, 1985.

CHAPTER X
Recent Years

In the middle and late nineteenth century the village was more or less a self-contained unit. Although the vast majority of the male population were employed on the land there were butchers, tailors, millers, bakers, saddlers, carpenters, masons, dressmakers, cordwainers etc., several of whom had their own shops. In twentieth-century Bradford Abbas, the situation is very different and there is only one shop and that is combined with the Post Office. This means that most of the villagers do their weekly shopping elsewhere, whereas in the last century it would not be necessary to go outside the confines of the village to get any provisions that were required.

Of course there are craftsmen in the modern village but they are of an entirely different nature to those in the last century due to the movement away from agriculture. The number of farm workers can almost be counted on the fingers of one hand but there are engineers, draughtsmen, architects, solicitors, bank managers, clerks, accountants, book-keepers, company directors etc. In fact there is a considerable amount of talent in the village.

The two main reasons for the considerable change are not, of course, peculiar to Bradford Abbas. The mechanisation of farming and the building of houses in the countryside, the latter combined with a general rise in the standard of living, are what has brought it about. As indicated earlier there were five new residential estates built within the boundaries of Bradford Abbas within an overall period of about 6 years which was to more than double the population of the village. The new estates brought with them in the main young married couples and their children which resulted in a new school becoming necessary. It was opened in 1966. It took a little longer to realise what the social impact of the vast increase in the population would be but before too long it was becoming apparent that all was not well. There were many who came into the parish who very readily absorbed themselves into the village life but there were also many

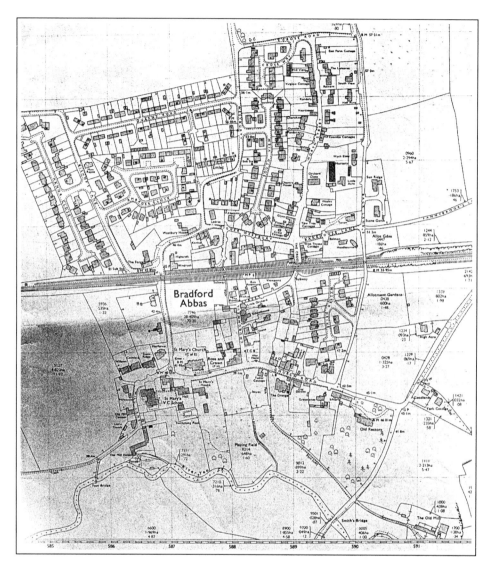

A contemporary map of Bradford Abbas.

who had no idea of village life and expected to find the same facilities in a small Dorset village that they had been used to in the towns and cities from whence they came. The main bones of contention appeared to arise over three issues: a recreation field for the children, street lights and a new Village Hall. The first two items were resolved very quickly as for many years the Parish Council had been negotiating to obtain a recreation field and these negotiations came to a successful conclusion in 1970 when the present playing field in Westbury was obtained. The question of street lighting was the subject of a parish meeting and was heavily defeated and has not been seriously considered since.

The main problems arose from the Village Hall, which was now approaching 50 years of age and which in the first instance had only been a second-hand building. It had been repaired very effectively several times but time and weather had now made serious inroads into the strength of the structure. It all really started when it was claimed that there were insufficient facilities for a youth club to be held in the hall and a newly formed organisation claimed that it was being victimised by having to pay a higher rent pro rata than other organisations in the village. I think it is fair to say that everyone realised that a new Village Hall had to be erected

An aerial view of Bradford Abbas, 1967.

and the members of the Village Hall Committee were aware of this as much as anyone else. The Committee at this time consisted mainly of the older inhabitants of the village who had served on the committee for many years. They had carried out their responsibilities exceedingly well, and were certainly not averse to the building of a new hall. There were quite insufficient funds to seriously consider putting in hand the provision of a new building but largely due to external pressure which manifested itself at the Annual General Meeting each year a fund-raising sub-committee was set up. But progress was not fast enough for many people and committees were set up, one calling itself the Bradford Abbas Youth Council, and another one aimed specifically at raising money. These committees were in direct opposition to the Village Hall Committee and although meetings were held in which the 'rivals' met there was much disagreement. The opposition committees tried very hard to get official recognition with the county authorities but in this they were unsuccessful and they were eventually dissolved. Pressure however, continued and at committee meetings tempers got very frayed with some of the new inhabitants claiming that they were being shut out of everything. It was rapidly developing into an 'old versus new' situation. One newcomer to the village, who has now left, and who was one of the leaders of the newcomers pressurising the Village Hall Committee said 'But with all due respect to the people of the village it does not matter whether you have lived here a few years or 100 years you are always a stranger if you are not born in the village', whilst an old inhabitant said, 'In my early days we were all farm workers and that was something we all had in common.'

In 1972 a local newspaper featured Bradford Abbas in an article entitled 'The divided village makes a new start' and in an editorial alongside it said: 'It is natural that a community faced with such a complete change of character and future would go through a testing period of readjustment.' However, the newspaper's article was a little premature and it was a few more years, and a few more disputes later, that there was any definite sign of any form of unity.

Eventually the principle of a new Village Hall was accepted by just about all concerned and fund-raising had commenced in earnest when a major new dispute broke out. Where was the new Village Hall to be sited? After much argument a planning application was submitted showing that the hall was required in the playing field which had been obtained a few years earlier. This in effect meant that many people wished the Village Hall to be moved from its present site which is freehold, having been given to the village in 1938 by Mr Wyatt Paul, to a new site which is leasehold. The Parish Council lease the property from the West Dorset District Council. This application raised a lot of anger, particularly amongst the older inhabitants, but also amongst many of the newcomers. The planning authority, however, decided to hold a public site meeting and one very experienced councillor later told me that it was the worst site meeting he had ever attended and that the whole meeting consisted of various people being rude to their opponents and vice-versa. The planning application however was refused and it was therefore later resolved that the new hall should remain on the original site.

From this time onwards the fund-raising really got motivated and the people did begin to unite and work together as should be the case in any community. One of the most spectacular and successful events was the Petticoat Lane which raised over £1000 and which was probably the biggest event in Bradford Abbas since the celebrations for Queen Victoria's Diamond Jubilee in 1897.

There have been no other major differences since the matter of the Village Hall was settled but there are still conflicting opinions as to whether the newer inhabitants have been beneficial to the village. Several village traditions have disappeared; and will never return, but no real new traditions have come to take their places. Generally speaking the committees in the village are now run by people in the village who have not lived here for any length of time and do not have much idea of the feelings of those who have worked so hard for the village in the past and still care very much about what decisions are made. Amongst certain newcomers there seems to be a view, probably sub-conscious, that because they have bought a house here they have bought the village and should have a say in everything that happens whether or not it materially affects them. This becomes quite apparent when planning applications are submitted from time to time.

Since the building of the new residential estates in the village the only new building that has taken place has been in the nature of infilling and virtually every vacant plot in the village has now been built upon. This in itself has brought problems which are not peculiar to Bradford Abbas, as the houses that are now being built are far too expensive for the local lads, who have lived here in the village all their lives, and the houses and bungalows on the new estates are invariably sold to retired couples. This is a situation which has been building up over a number of years and will, I believe, continue but many of these new people are opposed to any further development whatsoever. This is not to say that there should be development for the sake of it but hard and fast lines should not be drawn and persons who are already comfortably housed should consider more carefully the situation in which many of our youngsters find themselves today. It cannot be right that many who wish to marry in the next few years will not be able to and will in fact find themselves strangers in their own village. This has been exemplified on more than one occasion when functions have been advertised but tickets have only been available to a chosen group in order that others may be kept out. On more than one occasion I have heard it said that 'we're not wanted over there tonight'. These situations are now fading away but they should never arise in a village where community life was so important. The old community spirit has gone and has not yet been fully replaced. I do believe however that there is a pride in the village and that this pride is growing. There have been many excellent people coming into the village who have done extremely good work and will, I am sure, continue to do so, and there are others who have simply been destructive, trying to impose standards which are quite unsuitable for a village.

I can only write of the village I know but what I have learned in my travels around Dorset is that the spirit is much better in Bradford Abbas than in most other villages. Difficulties there have been and difficulties there will be, but in my opinion the future of the village looks healthy enough. If I did not believe that any problems that may arise could be overcome I would not have written this book about a village that has been home to my family for over 400 years—a village of which I am still very proud.

Appendix A

PROTESTATION RETURN FOR BRADFORD ABBAS 1641

Edward Buckler, Clerk
George Sterr, Vicar
Robert Master, Sen.
Charles Warren
John Sterr
Alexander Somers
Joseph Ring
John Traske
Thomas Master
Jasp. Master
George Master
Ellice Haggard
Richard Haggard
William Beere
George Hobbs
William Somers
William Barnes
Henry Byshop
Obediah Master
William Michell
Henry Valice
Richard Sutton
William Bartlett
William Master
George Garret
Robert Arnold Jnr.
John Master
William Bigwood
Richard Haggard
Robert Tolofield

Henry Byde
John Reade
Henry Punfold
Anthony Lane
Thomas Mitchell
Nicholas Byde Jnr.
Gyles Tolofield
William Arnold
Nicholas Frances
George King
Matthew Gyrdler
Robert Lane
John Ring
John Walters
James Tolofield
George Tolofield
Gyles Byshop
William Haggard
William Palmer
Thomas Arnold
Richard Moore
Edward Master
Isaac Collins
Nicholas Master
Richard Master
Thomas Collins
Humphry Ham
Cutber Moone
Raufe Hart
Thomas Hough

Gyles Michell
John Parker
William White
John Lane
Samuell Master
Anthony Master
William Collins
William Bawe
John Master
William Gapp
Gyles Gyrdler
George Gyrdler
Henry Lane
John Barnes
Honell Reade
Nicholas Byde
William Burd
Robert Ring
William Michell
Jonathan Penny
John Garret
Walter Dawson
Richard Barnes
Thomas Harrison
Nicholas Haggard
George Master
Ambrose Ridout
Symon Jennings
John Collins
Thomas Harrison

Edward Turke
Henry Bewsey
Robert Arnold
Thomas Goffe
George Hannam
Robert Ashe
John Newman
John Master
Robert Dibsdale
Richard Harrison
John Barber
Ellice Haggard
John Hannam
John Sparke
John Michell
Nicholas Master
George Read
William Ash
Leonard Puller
Regend Michell
Robert Pitman
Edward Penney
John Sterr, Jnr.
George Sterr being
p'sent when the
p'testation was tendred
here take it although
his habitaco be in
Somerset

The Protestation hath been taken by ye aforenamed in ye presence of:
John Penney, Curate
Robert Master)
John Steer) Overseers
William Girdler)
Thomas Punfold) Churchwardens

Appendix B

VICARS OF BRADFORD ABBAS

APPOINTED

1310	Richard Alewy
1316	Henry de Brandeston
1331	Roger de Fernham
1337	William de Pennell
?	Roger ......
1348	Richard de Killatrum
1349	John de Mulleborn
1361	William Play
1399	Edmund Kymerich
1420	William Haselgrove
1438	Richard Engeland
1439	Thomas Wotton
1449	Richard Lymyn
1450	William Larder
1463	Nicholas Kennel
1477	Thomas Taylour
1479	Richard Wygynton
1487	Thomas Laurence
1494	Andrew Kerver
?	Nicholas Ponfold
1526	Gilbert Style
1529	John Babearn
1538	Thomas Maister
1585	George Punfold
1643	George Stirr
1648	...... Pullham

1648	William Lovelidge
1660	Robert Butt died 1669
?	Charles White, died 1733
1733	William Preston
1742	Thomas Paget
1751	Narcissus Whittaker
1767	Conyers Place
?	Edward Matthew West, died 1812
1812	Edward Smedley
1825	Davis Williams
1828	Robert Grant
1886	Gordon Bolles Wickham
1921	John Godfrey Vassall
1934	Eric Campbell Douglas
1938	George Vincent Kendrick
1952	John Norman Dare Perkins
1955	Charles George Kerslake
1956	Donald Blackburn
1961	Laurence James Chesterman (Priest in charge)
1963	George Rowland Buchanan
1967	Gerald Squarey
1974	Richard John Mentern (Priest in charge)
1984	David Greene (Priest in charge)

Appendix C

POPULATION

1801	480
1811	516
1821	533
1831	595
1841	652
1851	621
1861	585
1871	578
1881	510
1891	523
1901	391
1911	428
1921	407
1931	348
1941	380
1951	424
1961	632
1971	943
1981	1050

Selected Bibliography

Fagerston, Anton	*Place Names of Dorset*, Upsala University, 1933.
Finn, Welldon R.	*An Introduction to Domesday Book*, Longman, Green & Co., 1963.
Fowler, Joseph	(1) *Mediaeval Sherborne*, Longmans, 1951.
	(2) *Sherborne Behind the Seen*, Sawtell, 1936.
	(3) *Description of Sherborne*, Sawtell, 1938.
Goodchild, John	*The Borough of Yeovil and its History and Government through the Ages*. Published by the Mayor, Aldermen and Burgesses of Yeovil, 1954.
Gourlay, A.B.	*History of Sherborne School*, Wykeham Press, 1951.
Hoskins, W.G.	*Local History in England*, Longman, Green & Co., 1959.
Hutchings, Monica	*Romany Cottage, Silverlake*, Hodder & Stoughton, 1946.
Hutchins, John	*History and Antiquities of the County of Dorset*, 4 vols, 3rd. Ed, Bourger Nichols, 1863-70.
Pitman, G	*Exploring Sherborne*, The Abbey Press, 1966.
Royal Commission On Historical Monuments	*An Inventory of the Historical Monuments in Dorset*, Vol 1, West Dorset, 1952.
Tate, W.G.	*The Parish Chest*, Oxford University Press, 1946.

Index